JOHN MARSHALL

Major Opinions and Other Writings

THE AMERICAN HERITAGE SERIES

THE

American Heritage

Series

UNDER THE GENERAL EDITORSHIP OF
LEONARD W. LEVY AND ALFRED YOUNG

JOHN MARSHALL

Major Opinions and Other Writings

EDITED WITH AN INTRODUCTION

AND COMMENTARY BY

JOHN P. ROCHE

Brandeis University

WITH STANLEY B. BERNSTEIN

THE BOBBS - MERRILL COMPANY, INC.

A Subsidiary of Howard W. Sams & Co., Inc.

INDIANAPOLIS • NEW YORK

Foreword

Had the signatories of the Constitution been free agents, they probably would have proposed a national government that was dominant over the states, one that had a formidable array of powers breathtaking in scope. John Marshall bequeathed to the people of the United States what it was not in the political power of the framers to give. He was the supreme framer, emancipated from a local constituency, boldly using his exalted judicial post as a stump from which to educate the country to the true meaning of the Constitution. He wrote as if words of grandeur and power and union could make dreams come true. By the force of his convictions he seemed to will a nation into being.

He remade the Constitution, giving voice to silences, clarification to ambiguities, content to omissions. Vitalizing the inert, still malleable parchment, he thrust it onto a course for "ages to come" that would make the government of the United States the supreme government in the federal system. Marshall was the only judge in our history whose distinction as a great nationalist statesman derived almost wholly from his judicial career. As Justice Holmes once said, "If American law were to be represented by a single figure, skeptic and worshipper alike would agree without dispute that the figure could be one alone, and that one, John Marshall." Yet Marshall was and remains controversial, not the least because of his repellent views of democracy and his contrived doctrines of vested rights.

This volume, edited by one of the nation's foremost experts in the realm of public law and politics, is the first compilation of Marshall's principal constitutional opinions in more than six decades. In the Introduction, which John P. Roche laces with his

v

engaging insights, is stressed both Marshall's nationalism and canny political acumen. Roche analyzes the reasons for Marshall's extraordinary success as Chief Justice, and demonstrates how his great opinions were influenced by his political posture. The extensive headnotes to the cases that helped shape our history contain some matchless commentary and deserve the thoughtful scrutiny of all students of constitutional law. Those headnotes buttress the editor's thesis that Marshall could be audacious almost beyond belief in matters of generalization and overall strategy, yet be narrow in actual grounds and tactics. The result is unusually instructive.

This book is one of a series created to provide the essential primary sources of the American experience, especially of American thought. The series, when completed, will constitute a documentary library of American history, filling a need long felt among scholars, students, libraries, and general readers for authoritative collections of original materials. Some volumes will illuminate the thought of significant individuals, such as James Madison or Louis Brandeis; some will deal with movements, such as the Antifederalists or the Populists; others will be organized around special themes, such as Puritan political thought, or American Catholic thought on social questions. Many volumes will take up the large number of subjects traditionally studied in American history for which surprisingly there are no documentary anthologies; others will pioneer in introducing new subjects of increasing importance to scholars and to the contemporary world. The series aspires to maintain the high standards demanded of contemporary editing, providing authentic texts, intelligently and unobtrusively edited. It will also have the distinction of presenting pieces of substantial length which give the full character and flavor of the original. The series will be the most comprehensive and authoritative of its kind.

Leonard W. Levy
Alfred Young

Contents

13. Tax Exemptions in Contracts, I:
    New Jersey v. Wilson   144
14. Natural Law and Contracts: *Ogden v. Saunders*   147
15. Tax Exemptions in Contracts, II:
    Providence Bank v. Billings   161

PART FOUR

The Protection of Federal Finance

16. The Union as Preferred Creditor:
    United States v. Fisher   165
17. Implied Powers: The Bank of the United States:
    McCulloch v. Maryland   168
18. Taxing Fiscal Instruments: *Weston v. Charleston*   187
19. State Currency: *Craig v. Missouri*   191

PART FIVE

Commerce and State Authority

20. Navigation as Commerce, I:
    Brig Wilson v. United States   197
21. Navigation as Commerce, II: *Gibbons v. Ogden*   206
22. Commerce in Original Packages:
    Brown v. Maryland   225
23. Commerce on Small Streams:
    Willson v. Blackbird Creek Marsh Co.   234

PART SIX

Treaties and Territories

24. Legislative Courts in the Territories:
    American Insurance Co. v. Canter   237
25. Land Claims under Treaties: *Foster v. Neilson*   244
26. The Constitutional Status of Indian Nations:
    Cherokee Nation v. Georgia   254

PART SEVEN
Civil Rights

Introduction

John Marshall's public career began in May 1775, when at age twenty he was appointed a lieutenant in the Virginia Militia. It ended sixty years later on July 6, 1835, when the Chief Justice of the United States slipped off peacefully to rejoin his generation. Between these dates there stretched a life of service unmatched, even in the remarkable elite which dominated the political destiny of the early Republic. Indeed, with the exception of John Quincy Adams of the next generation, it is difficult to find any American who has ever approximated Marshall's incredibly long and versatile performance as a public figure.

It is obviously impossible in a short introduction to attempt more than the necessary minimum of biography. This is particularly true since Albert J. Beveridge published, with loving and monumental detail, his immense *Life of John Marshall*— a work which, despite its filiopietistic compulsions, remains a landmark in American biography.[1] Moreover, we have judged that the specific details about Marshall's opinions and other writings should be explicated in the headnotes to the various documents rather than in an introductory narrative. The reader thus has at the relevant point the minutiae which might easily be lost in a broad historical treatment. Finally, we have not thought it necessary to intrude into Marshall's private life, though in some respects his tenderness towards his clearly disturbed (if not psychotic) wife gives him greater stature as a man than his contributions to his country.

---

[1] Albert J. Beveridge, *The Life of John Marshall,* 4 vols. (Boston and New York: Houghton Mifflin, 1916–1920). The detail in this essay, unless otherwise cited, is drawn from Beveridge.

Indeed, reading his deeply moving letter to Justice Joseph Story describing the death of a child, and his efforts to shield his wife from the terrible shock, one suddenly realizes the depth and intensity of his private burdens. The letter also deserves extensive quotation for the light it throws on the anguish involved in raising children in the early years of the Republic.

"You ask me," he wrote Story[2]—who had just lost his ten year old daughter, "if Mrs. Marshall and myself have ever lost a child. We have lost four, three of them bidding fairer for health and life than any that have survived them. One, a daughter about six or seven, was brought fresh to our minds by what you say of yours. She was one of the most fascinating children I ever saw. She was followed within a fortnight by a brother whose death was attended by a circumstance we can never forget. When the child was supposed to be dying I tore the distracted mother from the bedside. We soon afterwards heard a voice in the room which we considered as indicating the death of the infant [but he was] still breathing. . . . I concealed his being alive and prevailed upon [his mother] to take refuge with her mother. . . . The child lived two days, during which I was agonized with its condition and with the occasional hope . . . that I might enrapture his mother with the intelligence of his restoration to us."

When Mrs. Marshall refused to return to the house, Marshall wrote her a letter "in verse" with "a pressing invitation to return to me and her children." He tried to find a copy for Story, but it was "lost." His deep concern for his wife's precarious sanity was expressed time and again in his letters from France in 1798–99 to his relatives in Richmond who were looking out for "Polly." John Marshall—to borrow Walton Hamilton's fine phrase—clearly deserves promotion from immortality to mortality.

---

[2] See Marshall to Story, June 26, 1831, in Charles Warren, "The Story-Marshall Correspondence (1819–1831)," *William and Mary Quarterly,* Second Series, vol. 21 (1941), pp. 21–22.

The Formative Years

John Marshall was born into Virginia politics. His father Thomas Marshall was a leading political figure in western Virginia, a member of the House of Burgesses from Fauquier County, sheriff of the county, principal vestryman of Leeds Parish, clerk of Dunmore County, and captain of the militia. In a word, he was a magnate—a paradigm of the self-made frontier leader who rose to eminence on the implicit or explicit support of his neighbors, a member of the homemade elite which dominated the American countryside from Massachusetts to Georgia. Like his friends George Washington and Patrick Henry, Thomas Marshall responded automatically to British efforts to assert sovereignty over the colonies as usurpations of prescriptive rights; like Washington and Henry, it never entered his head that this was a "radical" response. He simply defined the "rights of Englishmen" as the status quo in Virginia—and drilled his militia company.

John Marshall, born on September 24, 1755, was the oldest of a family of fifteen children. Even the diligent Beveridge could discover little to say about his first twenty years except that he had a happy childhood and no significant formal education. Then the American Revolution began and Lieutenant Marshall went off to war with the Culpeper Minute Men—a march which for him was not to end until four years and many battles later. For when, in 1776, the Culpeper Minute Men were disbanded, John Marshall joined his father in the Third Virginia Regiment of the Continental Line. During the next three years he was with Washington's army, not—as in the state lines—on a temporary, come and go basis, but on a permanent footing. He spent the winter of 1777–78 at Valley Forge starving and freezing rather than retiring to his home for the winter, as did the state soldiers.

It is interesting to speculate on the impact of Continental service on Marshall, and on others who shared the fearful deprivations of Washington's standing army. Indeed, a fascinating study for statistical analysis would be the differences in political attitudes of Revolutionary veterans in terms of the forms their service took. It would be worthwhile, in particular, to see if there was any correlation in the 1780's between strong nationalism and service in the Continental Line. These soldiers bore the brunt of a war managed by ineffectual committees of an impotent Congress, and it would hardly be surprising if they had become, in every state, the carriers of a strong nationalist virus. In any case, this was clearly a strong formative influence on Captain John Marshall.

Discharged from the army, Marshall immediately determined upon a legal career and entered the College of William and Mary. He was to stay there only six weeks—long enough to get elected to the parent chapter of Phi Beta Kappa (presumably for academic potential!), do a little debating, and a great deal of reflecting on the merits of marriage. With that talent for direct action which was to characterize his work on the bench, he went to Richmond and was granted a license to practice law, signed by his cousin Thomas Jefferson, the governor. On August 28, 1780 he was admitted to the Richmond bar.

Then, as now, law was the supreme access route to politics. Marshall apparently did not spend much time on his briefs, but he made up for it by winning election to the Virginia House of Delegates in the fall of 1782. The following January he married seventeen–year–old Mary Ambler, a marriage which, as Beveridge said, "was inspired exclusively by an all-absorbing love,"[3] but which had the adventitious benefit of an alliance with one of Virginia's wealthiest families. By 1785 Marshall had accumulated a substantial practice and, moving up the magnate's ladder, accumulated his second public office: City Recorder of Richmond. His status was reinforced in 1786 when Edmund Randolph, upon election as governor, eliminated any

---

[3] Beveridge, *John Marshall*, vol. 1, p. 170.

conflict-of-interest problems by conveying his legal practice to the rising young attorney.[4]

From this point on, until he joined the Supreme Court, Marshall was a permanent fixture in Virginia politics. By all accounts he was a handsome, personable man with enormous charm. In addition, he had an invaluable political capacity (sorely lacking, for example, in Thomas Jefferson, John Adams, and Alexander Hamilton): he was a magnificent listener. He rarely clashed head-on with opponents (his correspondence on political matters is notable for his tendency to agree in ambiguous terms with his correspondents, whatever their positions) and always moved to blur lines of clear confrontation. An efficient vote-getter on his own (particularly among veterans), he had also inherited his father's accumulated political capital when the latter moved to Kentucky, and in addition, he picked up some from his father-in-law, the state treasurer. This was a formidable aggregation and it was not surprising that eleven days after he entered the Virginia legislature, he was elected by joint ballot of the Senate and House to the Executive Council—a body with extensive executive powers, particularly over appointments to office. However, in accepting this position he seems to have overextended his political lines by moving too far too fast; he shortly was attacked by some of the old magnates (notably Edmund Pendleton) for his lack of experience, and he resigned. He immediately was reelected to his seat in the House, even though he no longer lived in the county, and he settled in as a legislator.

The Marshall who emerged from the 1780's was a figure who would have been easily recognizable to the late Sir Lewis Namier, or to any who have read Namier's great studies of the structure of British politics in the eighteenth century.[5] In 1785,

---

[4] *Ibid.*, p. 190.

[5] See Sir Lewis Namier, *The Structure of Politics at the Accession of George III*, 2nd ed. (London: Macmillan Company, 1957); and *England in the Age of the American Revolution*, 2nd ed. (London: Macmillan Company, 1961).

for example, Marshall decided not to run for the legislature; in 1786 he chose to reenter the General Assembly and was elected from a different county. In the legislature, he was a firm nationalist who fought consistently against Virginia laws contravening the Treaty of Paris—notably those which, in effect, made it impossible for private British creditors to collect their pre-Revolutionary debts. He was, of course, a strong supporter of all efforts to invigorate the central government, that infirm, impotent creation of the Articles of Confederation.

Because he was not addicted to political metaphysics, Marshall never prepared for posterity a precise justification of his variety of nationalism. It has been suggested that he was basically a spokesman for the mercantile interests—the Richmond "capitalists" and land speculators to whom he was related both by family connections and economic interest. This, however, is of little analytical value: if the Richmond "capitalists" wanted a strong national market and credit structure, they had no economic interest in the enforcement of that part of the Treaty of Paris which validated their pre-Revolutionary debts to British merchants. Marshall was squarely for both.

Normally in politics—as William of Ockham suggested centuries ago—the simplest explanation of behavior is the most likely to be correct. In this spirit, it would appear that the decisive basis of Marshall's nationalism was his military experience and his worship of Washington. Like the General (whose life he would later write in the best "lives of the saints" tradition), Marshall felt that American international impotence was a standing invitation to aggression and perhaps division. Only a strong central government could assert and defend America's sovereignty in the Hobbesian international forum.

Marshall was a vigorous nationalist, but he had that singular political talent which makes it possible for a man to be strong-willed without being provocative. A case in point was his role in passing the resolution by which the Virginia legislature in the fall of 1787 summoned a state convention to deal with the newly written Constitution of the United States. Virginia was a key state and at the Constitutional Convention the Virginia delegation had ended up in total disarray: George Mason had flatly refused to sign alleging that to do so would be an act of treason; James Madison, who had wanted a stronger frame of government, signed and organized support; the influential governor, Edmund Randolph, also refused to put his name on the document and explained his action in Delphic terms. Back in Virginia, Patrick Henry, who had "smelt a rat" and refused to attend the convention in the first place (he appears to have believed that his archenemy Thomas Jefferson was behind the project!), was organizing his forces to defeat ratification. Before the decision was finally made one way or the other, there was obviously to be some rough play in Virginia.

The legislative resolution creating the state ratifying convention was the first stage, and the legislators immediately began to polarize in terms of their substantive views on the new Constitution. The pro-constitutionalists introduced a resolution calling on the ratifying convention to say either "yes" or "no" without qualifications. Henry and his allies, who were trying to stall, hoped to have the state convention equivocate, offer amendments as a prerequisite for endorsement, perhaps call for a second Constitutional Convention. After the debate had waxed hot and heavy, Marshall rose and performed a masterpiece of political magic: he agreed with everybody who had spoken—to some extent—and disagreed somewhat with the opinions on both sides—to some extent. He then proposed a compromise resolution of his own, "that a Convention should be called and that the new Constitution should be laid before them for their free and ample discussion."[6] There was a great sigh of relief (neither side seems to have felt confident of clear victory) and Marshall's resolution passed "unanimously."

The battlefield was now shifted from the legislature to the

---

[6] Beveridge, *ibid.*, pp. 246–247.

ratifying convention itself, and the pro-constitutional forces organized energetically and effectively. The delegates to this convention were elected by the people, but one should not assume that the electorate polarized on the same basis as the magnates. Indeed, each side picked as candidates its leading figures, whom the people were accustomed to designating as their political surrogates; and each side used its most distinguished prospects in districts that were doubtful. As Beveridge said, "the people simply would not vote against such men as Pendleton, Wythe, and Carrington."[7] Marshall was handed the particularly difficult task of contesting Henrico County (Richmond) where anti-constitutional opinion was allegedly very strong. The people voted him in, along with Governor Randolph (still believed to be opposed to the Constitution) and the militantly anti-constitutional George Mason! The populace seems to have operated on a quite sensible, division-of-labor principle: send the best men to the Convention and let them fight it out among themselves.

The proceedings of the Virginia Convention remain today a fascinating document. Except for Washington and Jefferson, all the notables were there, operating in an intimate political universe. Each had a political history, a few running back twenty-five years, and the others were fully aware of all of the details and quite prepared to point out inconsistencies in behavior. Patrick Henry completed a sonorous discourse on the evils of arbitrary government, for example, and was promptly asked to explain his dictatorial behavior in the case of Josiah Philips, an alleged Tory bandit whom Governor Henry, in 1778, had moved against by a bill of attainder. (The bill of attainder itself was drafted by a member of the legislature named Thomas Jefferson!)[8]

---

[7] Beveridge, *ibid.*, p. 359.

[8] See Leonard W. Levy, *Jefferson and Civil Liberties: The Darker Side,* p. 33 (Cambridge: Harvard University Press, 1963).

This is hardly the place for an extensive analysis of the Virginia Convention; suffice it to say that the constitutionalists clearly out-maneuvered their opponents, forced them into impossible political positions, and won narrowly.[9] The Virginia Convention could serve as a classic study in effective floor management: Patrick Henry had to be contained, and a reading of the debates discloses a standard two–stage technique. Henry would give a four– or five hour speech denouncing some section of the Constitution on every conceivable ground (the federal district, he averred at one point, would become a haven for convicts escaping from state authority!). When Henry had subsided, "Mr. Lee of Westmoreland" would rise and literally poleaxe him with sardonic invective. When Henry complained about the militia power, "Lighthorse Harry" really punched below the belt, observing that while the former governor had been sitting in Richmond during the Revolution, *he* had been out in the trenches with the troops and thus felt better qualified to discuss military affairs. "It was my fortune to be a soldier of my country. . . . I saw what the honorable gentleman did not see—our men fighting. . . ."[10] Then the gentlemanly Constitutionalists (Madison, Pendleton and Marshall) would pick up the matters at issue and examine them in the light of reason.

Marshall had performed nobly in the convention and, once the new national government was established, President Washington moved to reward him for his labors. He was offered the post of United States Attorney for Virginia immediately after the Judiciary Act, creating the structure of federal law enforce-

---

[9] The discussion of the Virginia Ratifying Convention here is adopted from "The Founding Fathers: A Reform Caucus in Action," in John P. Roche, *Shadow and Substance: Studies in the Theory and Structure of Politics* (New York: Macmillan Company, 1964).

[10] See Jonathan Elliot, *The Debates in the Several State Conventions on the Adoption of the Federal Constitution*, vol. 3, p. 178 (Washington, 1836).

ment, was passed. Inexplicably Marshall rejected the office and, after another year's absence, chose to run again for the Virginia legislature. Without detailing his record, it is clear that any time Marshall ran for anything in Henrico County, he was safely elected. If he chose not to run—perhaps in the interest of building his private practice—the Richmond electorate kept the spot warm for his next appearance.

This personal political stature was quite remarkable, particularly as Virginia politics became riven by ferocious factionalism with the anti-nationalists clearly in command. Part of it arose simply from his personality which made it possible for George Mason to refer to Marshall as "an intimate friend of mine" at a time when he was bitterly fighting Marshall's views on the constitutionality of Hamilton's assumption of state debts.[11] But part of it also derived from Marshall's astute political posture, comparable in our time to that of New York Republicans such as Jacob Javits and John Lindsay. While holding his strategic position firmly, Marshall's political tactic was always to roll with the punches: he never became an isolated nationalist ideologue.

When the Virginia legislature, led by Henry, took up a resolution denouncing the assumption of state debts, for example, Marshall did not enter an unconditional defense of assumption. Denying Henry's contention that assumption was unconstitutional, Marshall and his nationalist colleagues introduced an amendment decrying assumption as unjust to Virginia and inexpedient for the nation. (He was to employ this same tactic later on with respect to the Sedition Act of 1798.) This might not have been music to the ears of Alexander Hamilton in New York, but Marshall's constituency was in Virginia. A letter from Jefferson to Madison in 1792 suggests that Hamilton understood the realities of Virginia politics and provides an insight into Jefferson's *modus operandi*. Noting

---

[11] Beveridge, *John Marshall*, vol. 2, p. 78.

that Hamilton hoped Marshall would run for Congress in Richmond, Jefferson wrote: "I am told that Marshall has expressed half a mind to come. Hence I conclude that Hamilton has played him well with flattery and solicitation, and I think that nothing better could be done than to make him a judge."[12] Although Jefferson was referring to a state judgeship, there is —in the light of later events—a certain historical irony in the proposal.

By 1796 "General" Marshall (of the Virginia militia) was clearly the leading pro-administration spokesman in Virginia. American politics was dominated by the struggle between the emergent Jeffersonians and Federalists which had been precipitated, though not caused, by the arguments over foreign relations centering on the Jay Treaty. Washington had unsuccessfully tried to bring Marshall into the Cabinet as Attorney General in 1795, and in 1796 he offered him the ticklish post of Minister to France. But Marshall showed great reluctance about leaving Richmond and his most successful legal career. He did, however, carry the burden of defending Washington and his policies in the hostile environment of the Virginia legislature, though—in the best tradition of the legal profession—he did not permit his public position on the treaty power to deter him from acting as counsel for a group of debtors who challenged the supremacy of the Treaty of Paris over Virginia legislation which had relieved them of their private obligations to British merchants. Marshall lost in the Supreme Court— *Ware v. Hylton,* 1796[13]—and, unfortunately, we do not know whether he rejoiced in his public capacity or grieved in his professional role.

Marshall's long-delayed entrance to national political life occurred in 1797 when President Adams named him one of the three envoys to negotiate a detente with the French Republic.

---

[12] Beveridge, *ibid.,* p. 80.
[13] 3 Dallas 199.

French leaders had been infuriated by the Jay Treaty and had retaliated by authorizing privateers to prey on American shipping and by insulting the new American Minister, Charles Cotesworth Pinckney. With Marshall in the delegation were Pinckney and the unpredictable Elbridge Gerry of Massachusetts (inventor of the "Gerrymander"), a Jeffersonian by persuasion but a personal friend of Adams who had cast his electoral vote for the latter.

The negotiations, which lasted into the spring of 1798, were a shambles with overtones of *opera bouffe*. The French Directory, whose general Napoleon Bonaparte was unrivalled in the field of battle, was itself unrivalled in political corruption. The Americans found themselves in a Kafkaesque environment: in and out of their lodgings flitted the three incredible agents of Talleyrand the French Foreign Minister, who have lived on in history as "X, Y, and Z." It was suggested that France could be bribed to end its depredations on American commerce; but before the Americans could get the opportunity to consent to this bribe, they had to pay antecedent bribes to get the French in the right mood. Marshall and Pinckney carried the burden of these non-negotiations, and the former patiently recorded their travail in dispatches to President Adams. They flatly refused to pay the antecedent bribes and told the French that they had no authority to make a "loan" (the form of the major bribe was the purchase by the United States of worthless Dutch securities at par value—a fraudulent "loan"). After interminable discussions with X, Y, and Z and utterly inconclusive, brief talks with Talleyrand, capped by threats of further French hostility, Marshall and Pinckney decided to terminate the farce. The French cooperated by ordering them out of the country, keeping the more pliable Gerry around in the hope of dividing the mission. Pinckney's daughter was ill, and he was permitted to take her to southern France for recuperation. On April 24, 1798 Marshall sailed home alone.

On June 18, 1798 he arrived in Philadelphia a national hero.

The background for this was the greatest political miscalculation of Thomas Jefferson's career. Convinced that Adams was pro-British and that the negotiations in Paris were a masquerade, aimed in no way at reaching an understanding with the French, the Jeffersonians denounced the President as a warmonger. They drummed up pro-French and anti-British feeling. In March, Adams, having received Marshall's first dispatches, suddenly informed Congress that the nation should prepare for war with France, and his opponents went into a frenzy: Vice President Jefferson referred to his chief's message as "insane."[14] Amazingly sure of their ground, the Jeffersonians demanded the full publication of the dispatches; after some delay, Adams transmitted them in full to Congress (disguising the French agents as X, Y, and Z).

As the stunned Jeffersonians—caught in a paradigmatic self-gambit—took cover, public opinion rose in a tidal wave of anti-French sentiment. James Morton Smith has given us a superb description of this period and of Alexander Hamilton's program for using the surge of chauvinism to dispose of the Jeffersonian party and fortify the Federalists in power.[15] Marshall's tumultuous welcome was from a political viewpoint completely justified: he had provided the instrument with which it seemed the growing Republican movement could be annihilated. President Adams promptly offered him a position on the Supreme Court vacated by the death of James Wilson, but Marshall, who was in financial difficulties arising from his land speculation, felt he could not afford to leave his practice.

He could, however, run for the House of Representatives without what we today would call conflict-of-interest problems, and the Virginia Federalists implored him to make the race in Richmond. A Marshall victory in the Jeffersonian heart-

---

[14] Beveridge, *ibid.*, p. 336.

[15] See his *Freedoms' Fetters: The Alien and Sedition Laws and American Civil Liberties* (Ithaca: Cornell University Press, 1956).

land would be a real Federalist accomplishment—and no one else could possibly achieve it. Marshall agreed and promptly had the alien and sedition laws (passed in the summer of 1798) as a political albatross draped around his neck. Madison, with Jefferson's urging, returned from Congress to the Virginia legislature to lead the struggle against the Federalist repressive statutes. The outcome was, of course, the Virginia Resolutions declaring the federal laws unconstitutional (and the similar Kentucky Resolutions secretly penned by Jefferson).

Marshall, as was his custom, avoided a total confrontation with Jeffersonian power. Much to the chagrin of New England Federalist ideologues, the Federalist candidate in Richmond engaged in some intricate broken-field running. In the Virginia legislature (apparently aided by his close friend and ally General Henry Lee) he drafted the "Address of the Minority" which—at tedious length—dealt with the Virginia Resolutions;[16] in his congressional fight he answered a series of questions put to him by "Freeholder."[17] The gist of his views was that while the alien and sedition laws were constitutional, they were unnecessary—a strategic affirmation of federal power, yet it enabled him to avoid defending the specific, and in Virginia highly unpopular, statutes. Fisher Ames fumed and called Marshall "the meanest of cowards";[18] Theodore Sedgwick said he had "degraded himself by a mean and paltry electioneering trick"[19]—but they were writing in Massachusetts. The important consideration in Virginia was that in April 1799, when the congressional election was held in Richmond, John Marshall won by 108 votes. This was a bad year for the Jeffersonians in Virginia—they won only eleven of the nineteen seats in the House of Representatives. Anticipating trouble in the presi-

---

[16] See Document 4, *infra.*
[17] See Document 3, *infra.*
[18] Beveridge, *ibid.*, p. 391.
[19] *Ibid.*

dential election of 1800, Madison hastily pushed through the Virginia legislature a statute shifting from the "district" to the "at-large" system of choosing presidential electors.

The Sixth Congress met on December 2, 1799, and Marshall was soon launched on his abbreviated congressional career; it was to last barely six months. Marshall followed the habits of a lifetime in politics: strategically a good Federalist, he reserved the right to tactical independence. He refused to endorse the Sedition Act and played a vital role in destroying the prize creation of the high Federalists: the Disputed Elections Bill. This was a measure, passed by the Senate, establishing a Grand Committee to determine all contests in presidential elections (it resembled the commission established after the election of 1876 and doubtless would have fulfilled the same partisan function). It was particularly designed with an eye to the tight Pennsylvania situation, where a legislature in which each party held one house would have the task of choosing the electors. Marshall proposed a substitute which converted the commission, in essence, into an investigating committee without final jurisdiction, and his views were endorsed by the House. When Senate and House could not reach agreement, the measure vanished into limbo. The disgusted Speaker of the House, Sedgwick (who had never trusted Marshall's ideological credentials) accused Marshall of "dissipating our majority" which "never could again be compacted."[20]

The Federalists, temporarily triumphant, were in fact sitting on a time bomb, John Adams by name; by profession, President of the United States. In the spring of 1800, Adams discovered that Alexander Hamilton had been quietly running his administration, caucusing privately with his Cabinet, and playing *deus ex machina* for the Federalist leadership in Congress. The bomb went off in May: Adams summarily fired Secretary of War James McHenry and Secretary of State Timothy Pickering

---

[20] Beveridge, *ibid.*, p. 457.

and offered Marshall first the War Department (which he refused) and then the State Department. After some meditation, Marshall accepted in June the Secretaryship of State and entered Adams' Cabinet. Marshall had always been interested in foreign policy; his most enduring speech in the House of Representatives had dealt with the Robins/Nash case and had been a masterful presentation of the role of the President in the conduct of foreign relations.[21]

The Federalist *gotterdämmerung*—which enlivened the election year 1800—has been analyzed in detail by Manning J. Dauer and we need not linger on the details.[22] Suffice it for our purposes to say that Marshall managed to retain simultaneously the confidence of John Adams and Alexander Hamilton; as Secretary of State he went his own way, performed his hardly burdensome functions admirably, and (as far as one can discover) avoided the savage civil war which was racking the Federalists. As a result, on January 20, 1801, when Adams nominated Marshall Chief Justice of the United States, there was no controversy among the Federalists: he formally took office on February 4, but agreed to stay on as Secretary of State for the remainder of Adams' term. While he accepted only the salary of the Chief Justice ($4,000), his work that last month was exclusively in the partisan, political sphere—he was industriously sealing the commissions of lame-duck Federalist appointees including, of course, the famous "midnight judges."

The Chief Justice

On March 4, 1801, the new Chief Justice performed his first official act in that capacity: he administered the oath of office to Thomas Jefferson as President of the United States. It was an ironic confrontation for in Henry Adams' words Marshall

---

[21] See Document 5, *infra*.

[22] See *The Adams Federalists* (Baltimore: The Johns Hopkins Press, 1953).

. . . "nourished one weakness. Pure in life; broad in mind, and the despair of bench and bar for the unswerving certainty of his legal method; almost idolized by those who stood nearest him, and loving warmly in return,—this excellent and amiable man clung to one rooted prejudice: he detested Thomas Jefferson. He regarded with quiet, unspoken, but immovable antipathy the character and doings of the philosopher standing before him, about to take the oath to preserve, protect, and defend the Constitution. No argument or entreaty affected his conviction that Jefferson was not an honest man."[23] It need hardly be added that Jefferson reciprocated these sentiments in full.

Given the extensive character of both the headnotes and the readings in this volume, it would be superfluous here to enlarge on Marshall's career as Chief Justice, at least in its legal dimensions. However, a few things might be highlighted to throw his accomplishments into sharper perspective. First of all, it should be noted how the strategy of his opinions was derived from his political posture: he invariably seized the high ground with unnerving aplomb, and then he became extremely wary and flexible in his tactics.

The case of *United States v. Judge Peters* (6 Cranch 114, 1809) is a good example of this technique and, since it is often cited as an early demolition of the states'-rights concept of "interposition" and is impossible to edit meaningfully, let us examine Marshall in action.

The Court was confronted by a particularly vitriolic clash between Pennsylvania and the federal judiciary which arose when Richard Peters, United States District Judge in Philadelphia, set aside a decision of the Pennsylvania admiralty court. The State tribunal had in 1778 awarded a prize to one

---

[23] Henry Adams, *History of the United States of America During the Administration of Thomas Jefferson*, vol. 1, p. 194 (New York: Scribners, 1889).

set of litigants, but its decision then was overruled in favor of Gideon Olmstead by the Court of Commissioners of Appeals in Prize Cases—the only national court established under the Articles of Confederation.

Pennsylvania simply ignored the appellate decision asserting that the Court of Commissioners had exceeded its statutory *vires* when it overturned a jury determination in the Pennsylvania Court. The problem vanished into limbo for the next fifteen years.

The circumstances under which this litigation again surfaced between 1803 and 1809 defy brief analysis. They are fully described in the introduction to the Supreme Court decision and by Charles Warren.[24] The net outcome was that in 1803 Judge Peters reaffirmed the validity of the earlier appellate holding, favoring Olmstead, which brought the federal court into a head-on collision with the militantly Jeffersonian state authorities.

Governor McKean of Pennsylvania immediately mobilized state power to frustrate Peters' judgment, with the state legislature passing a law (designed to inject the Eleventh Amendment as a barrier to federal jurisdiction) vesting the funds at issue in the state treasurer, David Rittenhouse. Olmstead then went to the Supreme Court for a mandamus requiring Peters to execute his judgment—that cautious jurist had been stalling with the obvious hope that a compromise could be effected—and in 1808 the writ was granted. Peters then informed the high court that "an act of the legislature of Pennsylvania had commanded the governor . . . to call out an armed force to prevent the execution of any process."

In 1809, the Supreme Court had to meet the issue squarely. Marshall drew upon his resources and wrote an opinion which, first, asserted the supremacy of national law; second, held that

---

[24] Charles Warren, *The Supreme Court in United States History*, rev. ed., vol. I, pp. 374–387 (Boston: Little, Brown, 1947).

—properly understood—there was no conflict between the federal government and Pennsylvania because; third, David Rittenhouse was holding the funds in dispute in his *private*, not public, capacity.

Despite the actual ground of the holding, Marshall's opinion has been cited ever since for one majestic (and decisionally irrelevant) paragraph:

> If the legislatures of the several states may, at will, annul the judgments of the Courts of the United States, and destroy the rights acquired under those judgments, the Constitution itself becomes a solemn mockery, and the nation is deprived of the means of enforcing its laws. . . .

The *Cohens* case[25] is another model of this technique, and *Marbury v. Madison*[26] ranks close to it. (Chief Justice Earl Warren has been criticized for the ambiguity of some of his constitutional holdings, but compared to Marshall, Warren is a model of precision.) It must be remembered that Marshall spent the years 1801–1835 on the Court with no hope of reinforcement from the ranks of the Federalists—and he dissented in only nine decisions![27]

Which is not to say that he always concurred with his brethren; in 1827 he noted in one of his rare dissents (*Bank of United States v. Dandridge*)[28] that it was his normal policy when in disagreement to "acquiesce silently" in the Court's opinion. Concerned as he was with the Court's role and status in American life, he was apparently convinced that unanimity helped to maintain the standing of the Justices among the people. Moreover, as one might suspect, he was characterologically disinclined to lead quixotic charges on a lost battlefield. He saved his energy and logic for more favorable occasions,

---

[25] See Document 7, *infra*.

[26] See Document 6, *infra*.

[27] Warren, *Supreme Court*, vol. 1, p. 813, fn. 2.

[28] 12 Wheaton 64, 90.

and—in personal terms—he banked a certain amount of credit with fellow Justices who appreciated his silence.

The secret of Marshall's success was his remarkable talent as a committee chairman, a small-group manager. One new Justice after another was appointed to the Court by the Virginia dynasty, and each seemed to vanish into Marshall's sector of influence. In 1822, Thomas Jefferson irately pointed this out to his first appointee, Justice William Johnson, denouncing the practice of unanimous opinions as "convenient for the lazy, the modest and the incompetent."[29] To a Virginia friend, the ex-President wrote on the same theme: "An opinion is huddled up in conclave, perhaps by a majority of one, delivered as if unanimous, and with the silent acquiescence of lazy or timid associates, by a crafty chief judge, who sophisticates the law to his mind, by the turn of his own reasoning."[30] Johnson, in reply, gave a very frank explanation of Marshall's influence. Explaining that he had not found the Court a "bed of roses," Johnson recounted his experience when he joined the bench in 1804:

> Some case soon occurred in which I differed from my brethren, and I thought it a thing of course to deliver my opinion. But, during the rest of the session I heard nothing but lectures on the indecency of judges cutting at each other, and the loss of reputation which the Virginia appellate court had sustained by pursuing such a course. At length I found that I must either submit to circumstances or become such a cypher in our consultations as to effect no good at all. I therefore bent to the current. . . .[31]

In a small room with his six (five until 1807) colleagues, Marshall's personal charm was most effective. Moreover, in that era—with Washington still a primitive administration

---

[29] Jefferson to Johnson, October 27, 1822, cited in Donald G. Morgan, *Justice William Johnson*, p. 169 (Columbia: University of South Carolina Press, 1954).

[30] Jefferson to Thomas Ritchie, December 25, 1820, cited by Morgan, *ibid.*, p. 172.

[31] Johnson to Jefferson, December 10, 1882, cited by Morgan, *ibid.*, p. 181.

capital—the Justices of the Supreme Court tended to live an almost monastic existence, sharing rooms in a boarding house, eating together, attending the same social functions. Moreover, in this close and familiar context, Marshall moved as the dominant figure for that greatest of all reasons, the timeless foundation of committee leadership, he was willing to do most of the work. Various studies have yielded slightly different figures, but Charles Warren's computation was that "between 1801 and 1835, there were 62 decisions involving constitutional questions in 36 of which Marshall wrote the opinion; . . . Of a total of 1215 cases during that period, in 94, no opinions were filed; in 15 the decision was by the court; and in the remaining 1106 Marshall delivered the opinion in 519, . . . In the same period there were 195 cases involving questions of international law or in some way affecting international relations. In 80 of these, the opinion was delivered by Marshall. . . ."[32] In short, the Chief Justice was a prodigious worker whose personal virtues and willingness to carry the burden of writing opinions probably played a greater role in his dominance than the logic of his views.

In any event, he found a Supreme Court which in 1801 existed on the margin of American political consciousness. One Chief Justice had used the position as a launching pad in his candidacy for Governor of New York—John Jay ran and lost in 1792; in 1795, he was successful and resigned from the Court. Jay's successor, John Rutledge, was refused confirmation by the Senate, apparently on the ground that he was mentally deranged; and Washington's next two nominees, Patrick Henry and William Cushing (the latter an Associate Justice), refused the honor. Marshall's immediate predecessor, Oliver Ellsworth, followed another of Jay's precedents in accepting a concurrent diplomatic assignment abroad, and while in France as Minister resigned both positions on grounds of health.[33] President

---

[32] Warren, *Supreme Court*, p. 813, *n*. 2.

[33] Warren, *Supreme Court*, pp. 124–172.

Adams then offered Jay his old post—and the latter was in fact approved by the Senate—but Jay rejected it because, as he put it, "I left the Bench perfectly convinced that under a system so defective, it would not obtain the energy, weight, and dignity which are essential to its affording due support to the National Government, nor acquire the public confidence and respect which, as the last resort of the justice of the nation, it should possess."[34]

Marshall thus moved into a judicial vacuum and in thirty-five years converted the Supreme Court from an object of derision, even contempt, to a major coordinate agency of the national government. He did not—as both admirers and critics have maintained—run the country, and he was quite capable of cutting his losses and liquidating his liabilities when the political pressure became too heavy. Indeed, one has the distinct impression that the Chief Justice put a considerable amount of energy and ingenuity into skirting the most explosive constitutional issue of the era: the status of the slave and the legal position of slavery in American law. He had no reluctance to assault the states' rights doctrine, and in his *Cohens* opinion (written against a background of the congressional debates over slavery in the territories) Marshall deprecated "sections." But on slavery itself, the root of so much constitutional controversy, the Chief Justice refused to be drawn:

> It appears that he regretted the existence of slavery, feared the result of it, saw no way of getting rid of it, but hoped to lessen the evil by colonizing in Africa such free black people as were willing to go there. . . . He was far more concerned that the Union should be strengthened, and dissension in Virginia quieted, than he was over the problem of human bondage, of which he saw no solution.[35]

---

[34] *Ibid.*, p. 173.
[35] Beveridge, *John Marshall*, Vol. 4, pp. 478–479.

In this connection, Marshall's circumspect handling of the Virginia law barring free Negroes from entering the state (*Brig Wilson v. U.S.*, 1820)[36] should be compared with Justice Johnson's head-on collision with the South Carolina authorities over a similar statute, which the Justice (also on Circuit) declared to be an unconstitutional intrusion on interstate and foreign commerce (*Elkison v. Deliesseline*, 1823).[37]

As the years went by, the Supreme Court became more and more established as a principal instrument of the national government. Partly this arose from the singular stability of Court membership. During Marshall's tenure as Chief Justice, four other members of the bench served for more than twenty years: Todd, Duval, Story, and Washington. And a fifth, Livingston, served for seventeen years. In the fifteen-year period 1811–1826, only *one* vacancy occurred, and that in 1823. After 1827 this pattern of continuity was disrupted, but the Court had taken full advantage of its homogeneity and had become a "traditional" entity in its own right.

So had the Chief Justice, who was in his person something of a historical monument. As we have seen, Marshall was always a political "loner," and once elevated to the Court he largely disengaged himself from Virginia politics and from the fortunes of the dispirited and declining Federalists. His closest friends were, however, drawn from the ranks of hard-core Federalism, and it appears that in the period 1807–1812—when the Embargo and related enforcement measures brought sections of New England into open insurrection against federal authority—these friends cherished the hope that Marshall would run against Madison for President.[38] The Chief Justice was strongly opposed to the foreign policy of the Virginia dynasty and doubtless considered himself adequately equipped

---

[36] See Document 20, *infra*.

[37] 8 Fed. Cas. 493, No. 4366.

[38] Beveridge, *ibid.*, pp. 30–35.

for the presidency, but his characteristic caution led him to express his critical views only in correspondence. In fact, Marshall was so closed-mouthed that his long-time friend James Monroe, Secretary of State when war was declared in 1812, communicated with him on the apparent assumption that the Chief Justice was a supporter of administration policy vis-à-vis Great Britain![39] The presidential boomlet that Pickering and others were promoting never gained any headway.

In terms of judicial politics—and Marshall was incapable of thinking in other than political terms—this policy of non-intervention was soundly conceived. The ambitious dabbling of early Chief Justices had undoubtedly contributed to the low opinion of the Court which prevailed throughout the first decade. A Supreme Court that was prepared to confront state power in Virginia, Pennsylvania, Maryland, Ohio and Kentucky on basic substantive issues had to imitate Caesar's wife. Any partisan political activities on the part of the Justices would merely arm the enemies of their doctrines. In fact, Marshall—like an old-fashioned, regular army officer—did not vote in presidential elections after 1804 (with the possible exception of 1828).[40] He apparently regretted his one venture into public controversy: a series of three articles in the Philadelphia *Union* in April 1819 (by "A Friend of the Union") defending his *McCulloch* holding against the savage attack of Chief Justice Spencer Roane of Virginia.[41] (At least he refused to send a copy of the series—it was "mangled" by the editor, he said—to Justice Story and refused the latter's request that it be republished in Boston.)[42]

While not playing any active political role in Virginia, Marshall did on occasion undertake various assignments: in 1812,

---

[39] *Ibid.*, p. 41.

[40] *Ibid.*, pp. 462, 464.

[41] Beveridge, *ibid.*, pp. 318–320.

[42] *Ibid.*, p. 322.

for example, he vanished into the wilderness of western Virginia as the head of a body of commissioners to survey a route through the mountains (the Chesapeake and Ohio Railroad later followed roughly the path he surveyed).[43] In 1829, he participated (with former Presidents James Madison and James Monroe) in the Virginia Constitutional Convention, where—joined interestingly enough by Madison on most substantive issues!—he played an active and thoroughly conservative role.[44]

Towards the end of his career, with Jacksonian Justices driving him even to dissent, Marshall became somewhat despondent; but he never relaxed his efforts to assert the supremacy of the Constitution as he read it, whether over contumacious states or an arrogant President. There was poignant symbolism in the three dissents "from the grave" that his old friend and ideological twin, Joseph Story, registered in 1837 on behalf of his dead chief (*New York v. Miln*,[45] *Charles River Bridge v. Warren Bridge*,[46] *Briscoe v. Bank of Kentucky*[47]). John Marshall was no longer merely a judge; he was an incarnation of American constitutionalism, one whose views on public law should be enshrined (Story believed) despite his departure from the bench.

In the immediate sense, Story failed, but in the long view the shade of John Marshall has hovered over the growth of judicial power in the United States. Whatever his opinions on the merits of anti-New Deal decisions might have been, Marshall would surely have chuckled as that brilliant judicial politician, Charles Evans Hughes, demolished Franklin D. Roosevelt's "court packing" plan. American constitutional law,

---

[43] *Ibid.*, pp. 42–45.

[44] *Ibid.*, pp. 467–507.

[45] 11 Peters 102.

[46] 11 Peters 420.

[47] 11 Peters 257.

he recognized, was in some of its aspects more a body-contact sport than a jurisprudential exercise; and Hughes alone among subsequent Chief Justices has approximated Marshall's tactical skill.

Finally, what Justice would not agree with the ironic Virginian that the "acme of judicial distinction means the ability to look a lawyer straight in the eyes for two hours and not hear a damned word he says?"[48]

---

[48] Beveridge, *ibid.*, pp. 82–83.

Selected Bibliography

Documents

ELLIOTT, JONATHAN, ed. *Debates in the Several State Conventions on the Adoption of the Federal Constitution*, 5 vols. 2d ed. Philadelphia: J. B. Lippincott, 1901.

FARRAND, MAX, ed. *The Records of the Federal Convention of 1787*, 3 vols. New Haven: Yale University Press, 1911.

GALES, JOSEPH, comp. *The Debates and Proceedings in the Congress of the United States, 1789–1824*, 42 vols. Washington, D.C.: Gales and Seaton, 1834–56.

MASON, FRANCIS N., ed. *My Dearest Polly*. Richmond: Garrett and Massie, 1961.

ROBERTSON, DAVID, ed. *Reports of the Trials of Aaron Burr*, 2 vols. Philadelphia: Hopkins and Earle, 1808.

WARREN, CHARLES. "The Story-Marshall Correspondence (1819–1831)," *William and Mary Quarterly*, Second Series, Vol. 21 (1941), 1–26.

WHARTON, FRANCIS, ed. *State Trials of the United States During the Administrations of Washington and Adams*. (Philadelphia: Carey and Hart, 1849).

Judicial Biography

BEVERIDGE, ALBERT J. *The Life of John Marshall*, 4 vols. Boston: Houghton Mifflin, 1916–19.

COMMAGER, HENRY S. "Joseph Story," in *The Gaspar G. Bacon Lectures on the Constitution of the United States 1940–1950*. Boston: Boston University Press, 1953, 31–94.

CORWIN, EDWARD S. *John Marshall and the Constitution*. New Haven: Yale University Press, 1919.

MORGAN, DONALD G. *Justice William Johnson, the First Dissenter.* Columbia: University of South Carolina Press, 1954.

JONES, W. MELVILLE, ed. *Chief Justice John Marshall.* Ithaca: Cornell University Press, 1956.

The Federal Convention

ADAIR, DOUGLASS. "The Tenth Federalist Revisited," *William and Mary Quarterly,* Third Series, Vol. 8 (1951), 48–67.

BEARD, CHARLES. *An Economic Interpretation of the Constitution of the United States.* New York: Macmillan, 1913.

BROWN, ROBERT E. *Charles Beard and the American Constitution.* Princeton: Princeton University Press, 1956.

ELKINS, STANLEY, and McKITRICK, ERIC M. "The Founding Fathers —Young Men of the Revolution," *Political Science Quarterly,* Vol. 78 (1961), 181–218.

FARRAND, MAX. *The Framing of the Constitution of the United States.* New Haven: Yale University Press, 1913.

KENYON, CECILIA M. "Men of Little Faith: The Anti-Federalists on the Nature of Representative Government," *William and Mary Quarterly,* Third Series, Vol. 12 (1955), 3–43.

McDONALD, *E. Pluribus Unum.* Boston: Houghton Mifflin, 1965.

———— *We the People: The Economic Origins of the Constitution.* Chicago: University of Chicago Press, 1958.

ROCHE, JOHN P. "The Founding Fathers: A Reform Caucus in Action," in *Shadow and Substance, Essays on the Theory and Structure of Politics.* New York: Macmillan, 1964, 91–126.

WARREN, CHARLES. *The Making of the Constitution.* Boston: Little Brown, 1928.

Constitutional Interpretation

CORWIN, EDWARD S., ed. *The Constitution of the United States of America: Analysis and Interpretation.* Washington, D.C.: Government Printing Office, 1955.

———— *The Doctrine of Judicial Review.* Princeton: Princeton University Press, 1914.

_____ The "Higher Law" Background of American Constitutional Law. Ithaca: Cornell University Press, 1957.

CROSSKEY, WILLIAM W. *Politics and the Constitution in the History of the United States*, 2 vols. Chicago: University of Chicago Press, 1953.

FRANKFURTER, FELIX. *The Commerce Clause Under Marshall, Taney and Waite*. Chapel Hill: University of North Carolina, 1937.

HURST, WILLARD. "Treason in the United States," *Harvard Law Review*, Vol. 58 (1944–45), 226–72, 395–444, 806–57.

LEVY, LEONARD W. *The Legacy of Suppression: Freedom of Speech and Press in Early American History*. Cambridge: Belknap Press of Harvard University Press, 1960.

WRIGHT, BENJAMIN F. *The Contract Clause of the Constitution*. Cambridge: Harvard University Press, 1938.

Political History

ABERNATHY, THOMAS P. *The Burr Conspiracy*. New York: Oxford University Press, 1954.

ADAMS, HENRY. *History of the United States during the Administrations of Jefferson and Madison*, 9 vols. New York: C. Scribner's Sons, 1889–91.

CHARLES, JOSEPH. *The Origins of the American Party System*. New York: Harper Torchbacks, 1961.

FISCHER, DAVID H. *The Revolution of American Conservatism*. New York: Harper and Row, 1965.

HAMMOND, BRAY. *Banks and Politics in America*. Princeton: Princeton University Press, 1957.

LEVY, LEONARD W. *Jefferson and Civil Liberties: The Darker Side*. Cambridge: Belknap Press of Harvard University Press, 1963.

LIPSET, SEYMOUR MARTIN. *The First New Nation*. New York: Basic Books, 1963.

SMITH, JAMES M. *Freedom's Fetters, The Alien and Sedition Laws and American Civil Liberties*. Ithaca: Cornell University Press, 1956.

WARREN, CHARLES. *The Supreme Court in United States History, 1789–1835*. Boston: Little, Brown, 1947.

Editor's Preface

Anyone who has taught American constitutional history has known the sense of frustration that even the best casebook creates. Yet, at the same time, one must recognize that a book of readings designed to accompany the history of the Supreme Court must be kept in brief compass. The decisions of the Court now fill a wall-sized bookcase. Moreover, a casebook editor must of necessity concentrate on the modern period. The consequence is that the decisions of the Marshall Court tend to emerge as highly abbreviated snippets centering on the holdings, whereas the most fascinating aspect of Marshall's characteristic technique was the route he took to reach his predetermined conclusions.

Thus it was a great pleasure for us to be given an opportunity to provide John Marshall with the space he needs if the student of American constitutionalism is to get the real flavor of his creative genius.

J. P. R.
S. B. B.

Waltham, Massachusetts
December 5, 1966

JOHN MARSHALL

Major Opinions and Other Writings

Part One

PRE-JUDICIAL STATEMENTS

1. *At the Virginia Ratifying Convention* (*1788*)

Marshall's first major public address, ironically in the light of later events, was devoted to defending the Constitution against its Virginia detractors. He expounded particular advantages, powers, and controls which he ascribed to the federal government, stressing the primary values of peace and stability. Peace would come only through military preparedness, and Virginia's security was dependent upon adequate federal revenue derived from the power of the Union to tax its citizenry. Thus, from the outset, Marshall as spokesman for the Union emphasized the need for a powerful international image to be projected by an adequately provisioned government. This concern with America's international image marked the Founding Fathers significantly more, say, than any consensus among them on property and commerce. Indeed, they were prepared to argue that only a strong international image could guarantee the prerequisite conditions for a flourishing economy.

If the Founding Fathers were nationalists, they were also committed democrats. Thus, Marshall stressed that electoral responsibility, the fundamental democratic institution, would insure popular political control over the governing class. He was surely no apologist for aristocracy, and his sensitivity to democratic control ought to be kept in mind when reading his purportedly elitist Supreme Court opinions. He may well have chaffed at the democratic bit and sought legal strategies for aiding property interests, but for all that, he was committed—in his own fashion perhaps—to a "well-regulated democracy." He may have stressed the need for social and political discipline, but order was only a necessary attribute of the substance, democracy.

Among the institutions for checking majority rule was an independent judiciary. As part of his assignment in defending specific constitutional provisions, Marshall had to refute various criticisms of the federal judiciary. Not surprisingly the criticisms centered upon the issue of jurisdiction, and we find Marshall here already entangled in the technicalities of diversity jurisdiction.

DEBATES

[June 10, 1788]

Mr. JOHN MARSHALL. Mr. Chairman, I conceive that the object of the discussion now before us is, whether democracy or despotism be most eligible. I am sure that those who framed the system submitted to our investigation, and those who now support it, intend the establishment and security of the former. The supporters of the Constitution claim the title of being firm friends of the liberty and the rights of mankind. They say that they consider it as the best means of protecting liberty. We, sir, idolize democracy. Those who oppose it have bestowed eulogiums on monarchy. We prefer this system to any monarchy, because we are convinced that it has a greater tendency to secure our liberty and promote our happiness. We admire it, because we think it a well-regulated democracy. It is recommended to the good people of this country: they are, through us, to declare whether it be such a plan of government as will establish and secure their freedom.

From Jonathan Elliot, ed. *The Debates* in the Several State Conventions on the Adoption of the Federal Constitution (Philadelphia, 1836, 5 vols.), III, 222–33, 410, 551–564.

Permit me to attend to what the honorable gentleman (Mr. Henry) has said. He has expatiated on the necessity of a due attention to certain maxims—to certain fundamental principles, from which a free people ought never to depart. I concur with him in the propriety of the observance of such maxims. They are necessary in any government, but more essential to a democracy than to any other. What are the favorite maxims of democracy? A strict observance of justice and public faith, and a steady adherence to virtue. These, sir, are the principles of a good government. No mischief, no misfortune, ought to deter us from a strict observance of justice and public faith. Would to Heaven that these principles had been observed under the present government! Had this been the case, the friends of liberty would not be so willing now to part with it. Can we boast that our government is founded on these maxims? Can we pretend to the enjoyment of political freedom or security, when we are told that a man has been, by an act of Assembly, struck out of existence without a trial by jury, without examination, without being confronted with his accusers and witnesses, without the benefits of the law of the land? Where is our safety, when we are told that this act was justifiable because the person was not a Socrates? What has become of the worthy member's maxims? Is this one of them? Shall it be a maxim that a man shall be deprived of his life without the benefit of law? Shall such a deprivation of life be justified by answering, that the man's life was not taken *secundum artem* because he was a bad man? Shall it be a maxim that government ought not to be empowered to protect virtue?

The honorable member, after attempting to vindicate that tyrannical legislative act to which I have been alluding, proceeded to take a view of the dangers to which this country is exposed. He told us that the principal danger arose from a government which, if adopted, would give away the Mississippi. . . . How shall we retain it? By retaining that weak government which has hitherto kept it from us? Is it thus that we shall secure that navigation? Give the government the power of retaining it, and then we may hope to derive actual advantages from it. Till we do this, we cannot expect that a government which hitherto has not been able to protect it, will have the power to do it hereafter. Have we attended too long to consider whether this government would be able to protect us? Shall we wait for further proofs of its inefficacy? . . .

He then stated the necessity and probability of obtaining amendments. . . . There are in this state, and in every state in the Union, many who are decided enemies of the Union. Reflect on the probable conduct of such men. What will they do? They will bring amendments which are local in their nature, and which they know will not be accepted. What security have we that other states will not do the same? We are told that many in the states were violently opposed to it. They are more mindful of local interests. They will never propose such amendments as they think would be obtained. Disunion will be their object. This will be attained by the proposal of unreasonable amendments. This, sir, though a strong cause, is not the only one that will militate against previous amendments. Look at the comparative temper of this country now, and when the late federal Convention met. We had no idea then of any particular system. The formation of the most perfect plan was our object and wish. It was imagined that the states would accede to, and be pleased with, the proposition that would be made them. Consider the violence of opinions, the prejudices and animosities which have been since imbibed. Will not these operate greatly against mutual concessions, or a friendly concurrence? This will, however, be taken up more properly at another time. He says, we wish to have a strong, energetic, powerful government. We contend for a well-regulated democracy. He insinuates that the power of the government has been enlarged by the Convention, and that we may apprehend it will be enlarged by others. The Convention did not, in fact, assume any power.

They have proposed to our consideration a scheme of government which they thought advisable. We are not bound to adopt it, if we disapprove of it. Had not every individual in this community a right to tender that scheme which he thought most conducive to the welfare of his country? Have not several gentlemen already demonstrated that the Convention did not exceed their powers? But the Congress have the power of making bad laws, it seems. The Senate, with the President, he informs us, may make a treaty which shall be disadvantageous to us; and that, if they be not good men, it will not be a good Constitution. I shall ask the worthy member only, if the people at large, and they alone, ought to make laws and treaties? Has any man this in contemplation? You cannot exercise the powers of government personally yourselves. You must trust to agents. If so, will you dispute giving them the power of acting for you, from an existing possibility that they may abuse it? As long as it is impossible for you to transact your business in person, if you repose no confidence in delegates, because there is a possibility of their abusing it, you can have no government; for the power of doing good is inseparable from that of doing some evil. . . . Can any thing be more dissimilar than the relation between the British government and the colonies, and the relation between Congress and the states? We *were not* represented in Parliament. Here we are represented. Arguments which prove the impropriety of being taxed by Britain, do not hold against the exercise of taxation by Congress.

Let me pay attention to the observation of the gentleman who was last up, that the power of taxation ought not to be given to Congress. This subject requires the undivided attention of this house. This power I think essentially necessary; for without it there will be no efficiency in the government. We have had a sufficient demonstration of the vanity of depending on requisitions. How, then, can the general government exist without this power? The possibility of its being abused is urged as an argument against its expediency. To very little purpose did Virginia discover the defects in the old system; to little purpose, indeed, did she propose improvements; and to no purpose is this plan constructed for the promotion of our happiness, if we refuse it now, because it is possible that it may be abused. The Confederation has nominal powers, but no means to carry them into effect. If a system of government were devised by more than human intelligence, it would not be effectual if the means were not adequate to the power. All delegated powers are liable to be abused. Arguments drawn from this source go in direct opposition to the government, and in recommendation of anarchy. The friends of the Constitution are as tenacious of liberty as its enemies. They wish to give no power that will endanger it. They wish to give the government powers to secure and protect it. Our inquiry here must be, whether the power of taxation be necessary to perform the objects of the Constitution, and whether it be safe, and as well guarded as human wisdom can do it. What are the objects of the national government? To protect the United States, and to promote the general welfare. Protection, in time of war, is one of its principal objects. Until mankind shall cease to have ambition and avarice, wars will arise.

The prosperity and happiness of the people depend on the performance of these great and important duties of the general government. Can these duties be performed by one state? Can one state protect us, and promote our happiness? The honorable gentleman who has gone before me (Governor Randolph) has shown that Virginia cannot do these things. How, then, can they be done? By the national government only. Shall we refuse to give it power to do them? We are answered, that the powers may be abused; that though the Congress may promote our happiness, yet they may prostitute their powers to destroy our liberties. This goes to the destruction of all confidence in agents. Would you believe that men who had merited your highest confidence would deceive you? Would you trust them again after one deception? Why then hesitate to trust the general government? The object of our inquiry is, *Is the power necessary, and is it guarded?* There must be men and money to protect us. How are armies to be raised? Must we not have money for that purpose? But the honorable gentleman says that we need not be afraid of war. Look at history, which has been so often quoted. Look at the great volume of human nature. They will foretell you that a defenceless country cannot be secure. The nature of man forbids us to conclude that we are in no danger from war. The passions of men stimulate them to avail themselves of the weakness of others. The powers of Europe are jealous of us. It is our interest to watch their conduct, and guard against them. They must be pleased with our disunion. If we invite them by our weakness to attack us, will they not do it? If we add debility to our present situation, a partition of America may take place.

It is, then, necessary to give the government that power, in time of peace, which the necessity of war will render indispensable, or else we shall be attacked unprepared. The experience of the world, a knowledge of human nature, and our own particular experience, will confirm this truth. When danger shall come upon us, may we not do what we were on the point of doing once already—that is, appoint a dictator? Were those who are now friends to this Constitution less active in the defence of liberty, on that trying occasion, than those who oppose it? When foreign dangers come, may not the fear of immediate destruction, by foreign enemies, impel us to take a most dangerous step? Where, then, will be our safety? We may now regulate and frame a plan that will enable us to repel attacks, and render a recurrence to dangerous expedients unnecessary. If we be prepared to defend ourselves, there will be little inducement to attack us. But if we defer giving the necessary power to the general government till the moment of danger arrives, we shall give it then, and with an *unsparing hand.* America, like other nations, may be exposed to war. The propriety of giving this power will be proved by the history of the world, and particularly of modern republics. I defy you to produce a single instance where requisitions on several individual states, composing a confederacy, have been honestly complied with. Did gentlemen expect to see such punctuality complied with in America? If they did, our own experience shows the contrary.

We are told that the Confederation carried us through the war. Had not the enthusiasm of liberty inspired us with unanimity, that system would never have carried us through it. It would have been much sooner terminated had that government been possessed of due energy. . . . A bare sense of duty, or a regard to propriety, is too feeble to induce men to comply with obligations. We deceive ourselves if we expect any efficacy from these. If requisitions will not avail, the government must have the sinews of war some other way. Requisitions cannot be effectual. They will be productive of delay, and will ultimately be inefficient. By direct taxation, the necessities of the government will be supplied in a peaceable manner, without irritating the minds of the people. But requisitions cannot be rendered efficient without a civil war—without great expense of money, and the blood of our citizens. . . .

It is objected, that Congress will not know how to lay taxes so as to be easy and convenient for the people at large. Let us pay strict attention to this objection. If it appears to be totally without foundation, the necessity of levying direct taxes will obviate what the gentleman says; nor will there be any color for refusing to grant the power.

The objects of direct taxes are well understood: they are but few: what are they? Lands, slaves, stock of all kinds, and a few other articles of domestic property. Can you believe that ten men selected from all parts of the state, chosen because they know the situation of the people, will be unable to determine so as to make the tax equal on, and convenient for, the people at large? Does any man believe that they would lay the tax without the aid of other information besides their own knowledge, when they know that the very object for which they are elected is to lay the taxes in a judicious and convenient manner? If they wish to retain the affections of the people at large, will they not inform themselves of every circumstance that can throw light on the subject? Have they but one source of information? Besides their own experience—their knowledge of what will suit their constituents—they will have the benefit of the knowledge and experience of the state legislature. They will see in what manner the legislature of Virginia collects its taxes. Will they be unable to follow their example? The gentlemen who shall be delegated to Congress will have every source of information that the legislatures of the states can have, and can lay the taxes as equally on the people, and with as little oppression, as they can. If, then, it be admitted that they can understand how to lay them equally and conveniently, are we to admit that they will not do it, but that, in violation of every principle that ought to govern men, they will lay them so as to oppress us? What benefit will they have by it? Will it be promotive of their reëlection? Will it be by wantonly imposing hardships and difficulties on the people at large, that they will promote their own interest, and secure their reëlection? To me it appears incontrovertible that they will settle them in such a manner as to be easy for the people. . . . If they are to be chosen for their wisdom, virtue, and integrity, what inducement have they to infringe on our freedom? We are told that they may abuse their power. Are there strong motives to prompt them to abuse it? Will not such abuse militate against their own interest? Will not they and their friends feel the effects of iniquitous measures? Does the representative remain in office for life? Does he transmit his title of representative to his son? Is he secured from the burden imposed on the community? To procure their reëlection, it will be necessary for them to confer with the people at large, and convince them that the taxes laid are for their good. If I am able to judge on the subject, the power of taxation now before us is wisely conceded, and the representatives are wisely elected. . . .

The extent of the country is urged as another objection, as

being too great for a republican government. This objection has been handed from author to author, and has been certainly misunderstood and misapplied. To what does it owe its source? To observations and criticisms on governments, where representation did not exist. As to the legislative power, was it ever supposed inadequate to any extent? Extent of country may render it difficult to execute the laws, but not to legislate. Extent of country does not extend the power. What will be sufficiently energetic and operative in a small territory, will be feeble when extended over a wide-extended country. The gentleman tells us there are no checks in this plan. What has become of his enthusiastic eulogium on the American spirit? We should find a check and control, when oppressed, from that source. In this country, there is no exclusive personal stock of interest. The interest of the community is blended and inseparably connected with that of the individual. When he promotes his own, he promotes that of the community. When we consult the common good, we consult our own. When he desires such checks as these, he will find them abundantly here. They are the best checks. . . .

The temple of liberty was complete, said he, when the people of England said to their king, that he was their servant. What are we to learn from this? Shall we embrace such a system as that? Is not liberty secure with us, where the people hold all powers in their own hands, and delegate them cautiously, for short periods, to their servants, who are accountable for the smallest mal-administration? Where is the nation that can boast greater security than we do? We want only a system like the paper before you, to strengthen and perpetuate this security.

The honorable gentleman has asked if there be any safety or freedom, when we give away the sword and the purse. Shall the people at large hold the sword and the purse without the interposition of their representatives? Can the whole aggregate community act personally? I apprehend that every gentleman will see the impossibility of this. Must they, then, not trust them to others? To whom are they to trust them but to their representatives, who are accountable for their conduct? He represents secrecy as unnecessary, and produces the British government as a proof of its inutility. Is there no secrecy there? When deliberating on the propriety of declaring war, or on military arrangements, do they deliberate in the open fields? No, sir. The British government affords secrecy when necessary, and so ought every government. In this plan, secrecy is only used when it would be fatal and pernicious to publish the schemes of government. We are threatened with the loss of our liberties by the possible abuse of power, notwithstanding the maxim, that those who give may take away. It is the people that give power, and can take it back. What shall restrain them? They are the masters who give it, and of whom their servants hold it. . . . The government is not supported by force, but depending on our free will. When experience shall show us any inconveniences, we can then correct it. But until we have experience on the subject, amendments, as well as the Constitution itself, are to try. Let us try it, and keep our hands free to change it when necessary. . . . There is such a diversity of sentiment in human minds, that it is impossible we shall ever concur in one system till we try it. . . .

[June 14, 1788]

Mr. JOHN MARSHALL asked if gentlemen were serious when they asserted that, if the state governments had power to interfere with the militia, it was by implication. If they were, he asked the committee whether the least attention would not show that they were mistaken. The state governments did not derive their powers from the general government; but each government derived its powers from the people, and each was to act according to the powers given it. Would any gentleman deny this? He demanded if powers not given were retained by implication. Could any man say so? Could any man say that this power was not retained by the states, as they had not given it away? For, says he, does not a power remain till it is given away? The state legislatures had power to command and govern their militia before, and have it still, undeniably, unless there be something in this Constitution that takes it away.

For Continental purposes Congress may call forth the militia,—as to suppress insurrections and repel invasions. But the power given to the states by the people is not taken away; for the Constitution does not say so. . . . The truth is, that when power is given to the general legislature, if it was in the state legislature before, both shall exercise it; unless there be an incompatibility in the exercise by one to that by the other, or negative words precluding the state governments from it. But there are no negative words here. It rests, therefore, with the states. To me it appears then, unquestionable that the state governments can call forth the militia, in case the Constitution should be adopted, in the same manner as they could have done before its adoption. . . .

[June 20, 1788]

Mr. JOHN MARSHALL. Mr. Chairman, this part of the plan before us [Article III, the Judiciary] is a great improvement on that system from which we are now departing. Here are tribunals appointed for *the decision of controversies* which were before either not at all, or improperly, provided for. That many benefits will result from this to the members of the collective society, every one confesses. Unless its organization be defective, and so constructed as to injure, instead of accommodating, the convenience of the people, it merits our approbation. After such a candid and fair discussion by those gentlemen who support it,—after the very able manner in which they have investigated and examined it,—I conceived it would be no longer considered as so very defective, and that those who opposed it would be convinced of the impropriety of some of their objections. But I perceive they still continue the same opposition. Gentlemen have gone on an idea that the federal courts will not determine the causes which may come before them with the same fairness and impartiality with which other courts decide. What are the reasons of this supposition? Do they draw them from the manner in which the judges are chosen, or the tenure of their office? What is it that makes us trust our judges? Their independence in office, and manner of appointment. Are not the judges of the federal court chosen with as much wisdom as the judges of the state governments? Are they not equally, if not more independent? If so, shall we not conclude that they will decide with equal impartiality and candor? If there be as much wisdom and knowledge in the United States as in a particular state, shall we conclude that the wisdom and knowledge will not be equally exercised in the selection of judges?

The principle on which they object to the federal jurisdiction seems, to me, to be founded on a belief that there will not be a fair trial had in those courts. If this committee will consider it fully, they will find it has no foundation, and that we are as secure there as any where else. What mischief results from some causes being tried there? Is there not the utmost reason to conclude that judges, wisely appointed, and independent in their office, will never countenance any unfair trial? What are the subjects of its jurisdiction? Let us examine them with an expectation that causes will be as candidly tried there as elsewhere, and then determine. The objection which was made by the honorable member who was first up yesterday (Mr. Mason) has been so fully refuted that it is not worth while to notice it. He objected to Congress having power to create a number of inferior courts, according to the necessity of public circumstances. I had an apprehension that those gentlemen who placed no confidence in Congress would object that there might be no inferior courts. I own that I thought those gentlemen would think there would be no inferior courts, as it depended on the will of Congress, but that we should be dragged to the centre of the Union. But I did not conceive that the power of increasing the number of courts could be objected to by any gentleman, as it would remove the inconvenience of being dragged to the centre of the United States. I own that the power of creating a number of courts is, in my estimation, so far from being a defect, that it seems necessary to the perfection of this system. After having objected to the number and mode, he objected to the subject matter of their cognizance. [Here Mr. Marshall read the 2d section.]

These, sir, are the points of *federal jurisdiction* to which he objects, with a few exceptions. Let us examine each of them with a supposition that the same impartiality will be observed there as in other courts, and then see if any mischief will result from them. With respect to its cognizance in all cases arising under the Constitution and the laws of the United States, he says that, the laws of the United States being paramount to the laws of the particular states, there is no case but what this will extend to. Has the government of the United States power to make laws on every subject? Does he understand it so? Can they make laws affecting the mode of transferring property, or contracts, or claims, between citizens of the same state? Can they go beyond the delegated powers? If they were to make a law not warranted by any of the powers enumerated, it would be considered by the judges as an infringement of the Constitution which they are to guard. They would not consider such a law as coming under their jursidiction. They would declare it void. . . .

Does the gentleman think that the state courts will have no cognizance of cases not mentioned here? Are there any words in this Constitution which exclude the courts of the states from those cases which they now possess? Does the gentleman imagine this to be the case? Will any gentleman believe it? Are not controversies respecting lands claimed under the grants of different states the only controversies between citizens of the same state which the federal judiciary can take cognizance of?

The case is so clear, that to prove it would be a useless waste of time. The state courts will not lose the jurisdiction of the causes they now decide. They have a concurrence of jurisdiction with the federal courts in those cases in which the latter have cognizance.

How disgraceful is it that the state courts cannot be trusted! says the honorable gentleman. What is the language of the Constitution? Does it take away their jurisdiction? Is it not necessary that the federal courts should have cognizance of cases arising under the Constitution, and the laws, of the United States? What is the service or purpose of a judiciary, but to execute the laws in a peaceable, orderly manner, without shedding blood, or creating a contest, or availing yourselves of force? If this be the case, where can its jurisdiction be more necessary than here?

To what quarter will you look for protection from an infringement on the Constitution, if you will not give the power to the judiciary? There is no other body that can afford such a protection. But the honorable member objects to it, because he says that the officers of the government will be screened from merited punishment by the federal judiciary. The federal sheriff, says he, will go into a poor man's house and beat him, or abuse his family, and the federal court will protect him. Does any gentleman believe this? Is it necessary that the officers will commit a trespass on the property or persons of those with whom they are to transact business? Will such great insults on the people of this country be allowable? Were a law made to authorize them, it would be void. The injured man would trust to a tribunal in his neighborhood. To such a tribunal he would apply for redress, and get it. There is no reason to fear that he would not meet that justice there which his country will be ever willing to maintain. But, *on appeal,* says the honorable gentleman, what chance is there to obtain justice? This is founded on an idea that [the federal courts] will not be impartial. There is no clause in the Constitution which bars the individual member injured from applying to the state courts to give him redress. . . .

But, sir, where is the necessity of discriminating between the three cases of chancery, admiralty, and common law? Why not leave [the details of federal jurisdiction] to Congress? Will it enlarge their powers? Is it necessary for them wantonly to infringe your rights? Have you any thing to apprehend, when they can in no case abuse their power without rendering themselves hateful to the people at large? When this is the case, something may be left to the legislature freely chosen by ourselves, from among ourselves, who are to share the burdens imposed upon the community, and who can be changed at our pleasure. Where power may be trusted, and there is no motive to abuse it, it seems to me to be as well to leave it undetermined as to fix it in the Constitution.

With respect to disputes between *a state and the citizens of another state,* its jurisdiction has been decried with unusual vehemence. I hope that no gentleman will think that a state will be called at the bar of the federal court. Is there no such case at present? Are there not many cases in which the legislature of Virginia is a party, and yet the state is not sued? It is not rational to suppose that the sovereign power should be dragged before a court. The intent is, to enable states to recover claims of individuals residing in other states. I contend this construction is warranted by the words. But, say they, there will be partiality in it if a state cannot be defendant—if an individual cannot proceed to obtain judgment against a state, though he may be sued by a state. It is necessary to be so, and cannot be avoided. I see a difficulty in making a state defendant, which does not prevent its being plaintiff. If this be only what cannot be avoided, why object to the system on that account? If an individual has a just claim against any particular state, is it to be presumed that, on application to its legislature, he will not obtain satisfaction? But how could a state recover any claim from a citizen of another state, without the establishment of these tribunals?

The honorable member objects to suits being instituted in the federal courts, by the citizens of one state, against the citizens of another state. Were I to contend that this was necessary in all cases, and that the government without it would be defective, I should not use my own judgment. But are not the objections to it carried too far? Though it may not in general be absolutely necessary, a case may happen, as has been observed, in which a citizen of one state ought to be able to recur to this tribunal, to recover a claim from the citizen of another state. What is the evil which this can produce? Will he get more than justice there? The independence of the judges forbids it. What has he to get? Justice. Shall we object to this, because the citizen of another state can obtain justice without applying to our state courts? It may be necessary with respect to the laws and regulations of commerce, which Congress may make. It may be necessary in cases of debt, and some other controversies. In claims for land, it is not necessary, but it is not dangerous. In the court of which state will it be instituted? said the honorable gentleman. It will be instituted in the court of the state where the defendant resides, where the law can come at him, and nowhere else. By the laws of which state will it be determined? said he. By the laws of the state where the contract was made. According to those laws, and those only, can it be decided. Is this a novelty? No; it is a principle in the jurisprudence of this commonwealth. If a man contracted a debt in the East Indies, and it was sued for here, the decision must be consonant to the laws of that country. Suppose a contract made in Maryland, where the annual interest is at six per centum, and a suit instituted for it in Virginia; what interest would be given now, without any federal aid? The interest of Maryland most certainly; and if the contract had been made in Virginia, and suit brought in Maryland, the interest of Virginia must be given, without doubt. It is now to be governed by the laws of that state where the contract was made. The laws which governed the contract at its formation govern it in its decision. To preserve the peace of the Union only, its jurisdiction in this case ought to be recurred to. Let us consider that, when citizens of one state carry on trade in another state, much must be due to the one from the other, as is the case between North Carolina and Virginia. Would not the refusal of justice to our citizens, from the courts of North Carolina, produce disputes between the states? Would the federal judiciary swerve from their duty in order to give partial and unjust decisions? . . .

He objects, in the next place, to its jurisdiction in controversies between a state and a foreign state. Suppose, says he, in such a suit, a foreign state is cast; will she be bound by the decision? If a foreign state brought a suit against the commonwealth of Virginia, would she not be barred from the claim if the federal judiciary thought it unjust? The previous consent of the parties is necessary; and, as the federal judiciary will decide, each party will acquiesce. It will be the means of preventing disputes with foreign nations. On an attentive consideration of these points, I trust every part will appear satisfactory to the committee. . . .

The honorable member [Patrick Henry] says that he derives no consolation from the wisdom and integrity of the legislature, because we call them to rectify defects which it is our duty to remove. We ought well to weigh the good and evil before we determine. We ought to be well convinced that the evil will be really produced before we decide against it. If we be convinced that the good greatly preponderates, though there be small defects in it, shall we give up that which is really good, when we can remove the little mischief it may contain, in the plain, easy method pointed out in the system itself? . . .

We have reason to believe the regulations with respect to juries will be such as shall be satisfactory. Because it does not contain all, [*i.e.*, a guarantee of jury trial in both civil *and* criminal suits] does it contain nothing? But I conceive that this committee will see there is safety in the case, and that there is no mischief to be apprehended.

He states a case, that a man may be carried from a federal to an anti-federal corner, (and *vice versa*) where men are ready to destroy him. Is this probable? Is it presumable that they will make a law to punish men who are of different opinions in politics from themselves? Is it presumable that they will do it in one single case, unless it be such a case as must satisfy the people at large? The good opinion of the people at large must be consulted by their representatives; otherwise, mischiefs would be produced which would shake the government to its foundation. . . . He says that the establishment of these tribunals, and more particularly in their jurisdiction of controversies between citizens of these states and foreign citizens and subjects, is like a retrospective law. Is there no difference between a tribunal which shall give justice and effect to an existing right, and creating a right that did not exist before? The debt or claim is created by the individual. He has bound himself to comply with it. Does the creation of a new court amount to a retrospective law?

We are satisfied with the provision made in this country on the subject of trial by jury. Does our [Virginia] Constitution direct trials to be by jury? It is required in our bill of rights, which is not a part of the Constitution. Does any security arise from hence? Have you a jury when a judgment is obtained on a replevin bond, or by default? Have you a jury when a motion is made for the commonwealth against an individual; or when a motion is made by one joint obligor against another, to recover sums paid as security? Our courts decide in all these cases, without the intervention of a jury;

yet they are all civil cases. The bill of rights is merely recommendatory. Were it otherwise, the consequence would be that many laws which are found convenient would be unconstitutional. What does the government before you say? Does it exclude the legislature from giving a trial by jury in civil cases? If it does not forbid its exclusion, it is on the same footing on which your state government stands now. The legislature of Virginia does not give a trial by jury where it is not necessary, but gives it wherever it is thought expedient. The federal legislature will do so too, as it is formed on the same principles.

The honorable gentleman says that unjust claims will be made, and the defendant had better pay them than go to the Supreme Court. Can you suppose such a disposition in one of your citizens, as that, to oppress another man, he will incur great expenses? What will he gain by an unjust demand? Does a claim establish a right? He must bring his witnesses to prove his claim. If he does not bring his witnesses, the expenses must fall upon him. Will he go on a calculation that the defendant will not defend it, or cannot produce a witness? Will he incur a great deal of expense, from a dependence on such a chance? Those who know human nature, black as it is, must know that mankind are too well attached to their interest to run such a risk. I conceive that this power is absolutely necessary, and not dangerous; that, should it be attended by little inconveniences, they will be altered, and that they can have no interest in not altering them. Is there any real danger? When I compare it to the exercise of the same power in the government of Virginia, I am persuaded there is not. The federal government has no other motive, and has every reason for doing right which the members of our state legislature have. Will a man on the eastern shore be sent to be tried in Kentucky, or a man from Kentucky be brought to the eastern shore to have his trial? A government, by doing this, would destroy itself. I am convinced the trial by jury will be regulated in the manner most advantageous to the community.

2. *Address to Richmond on Diplomacy (1798)*

The following selection marked Marshall's "triumphant" return as onetime emissary to the French Directory. His diplomatic accomplishment was almost wholly symbolic: he had asserted the unwillingness of America to suffer insults in the antechambers of international diplomacy. That is, he refused to meet the prerequisites for negotiations as relayed by Talleyrand's graft collectors, the notorious agents X, Y, and Z, who had demanded a pledge of a 12 million dollar loan, an apology for an impolite speech delivered by President Adams to Congress in May 1797, and payment in advance of Talleyrand's consultation fee of $250,000. Although the Duke of Tuscany and the Elector of Bavaria had both accepted the bishop's system of graduated fees, the plenipotentiaries of the young nation balked at such galling practices. Typical of the American reaction to the XYZ affair was President Adams' promise to Congress that he would not send another minister to France "without assurance that he will be received, respected and honored, as the representative of a great, free, powerful and independent nation."

Marshall's exposé of the XYZ affair brought him considerable popularity. And a benevolent Congress awarded him close to $20,000 for his year's service—enough to meet the debts from land speculation which motivated him to accept the mission in the first place. Perhaps Congress rewarded him so handsomely because his report provided the Federalists with a political windfall: a chance for party advantage as a righteous persecutor of war. But Marshall preferred a policy of peace, national independence, and neutrality. Fortunately, he could be neutral against France and did not hesitate to lecture his fellow Virginians on the true character of the new regime.

GENERAL MARSHALL'S ANSWER TO AN ADDRESS OF THE CITIZENS OF RICHMOND, VIRGINIA

I WILL not, Gentlemen, attempt to describe the emotions of joy which my return to my native country, and particularly to this city, has excited in my mind; nor can I paint the sentiments of affection and gratitude towards you which my heart has ever felt, and which the kind and partial reception now given me by my fellow citizens cannot fail to increase. He only who has been . . . absent from a much loved country, and from friends greatly and deservedly esteemed—whose return is welcomed with expressions, which, di[rec]ted by friendship, surpass his merits or his ho[pes,] will judge of feelings to which I cannot do justice.

The situation in which the late Envoys from [the] United States to the *French Republic* found themselves in *Paris* was, indeed, attended with the unpleasant circumstances which you have traced.—Removed far from the councils of their country, and receiving no intelligence concerning it, the scene before them could not fail to produce the most anxious and disquieting sensations. Neither the ambition, the power, nor the hostile temper of *France,* was concealed from them; nor could they be unacquainted with the earnest and unceasing solicitude felt by the government and people of the *United States* for peace. But midst these difficulties, they possessed, as guides, clear and explicit instructions, a conviction of the firmness and magnanimity, as well as of the justice and pacific temper of their government, and a strong reliance on that patriotism and love of liberty, which can never cease to glow in the American bosom. With these guides, however thorny the path of duty

---

From Columbian Centinel (Boston, Sept. 22, 1798).

might be, they could not mistake it. It was their duty, unmindful of personal considerations, to pursue peace with unabating zeal, through all the difficulties with which the pursuit was embarrassed by a haughty and victorious government, holding in perfect contempt the rights of others, but to repel, with unhesitating decision, any propositions, an acceptance of which would subvert the independence of the *United States.*—This they have endeavoured to do. I delight to believe that their endeavours have not dissatisfied their government or country, and it is most grateful to my mind to be assured that they receive the approbation of my fellow-citizens in *Richmond,* and its vicinity.

I rejoice that I was not mistaken in the opinion I had formed of my countrymen. I rejoice to find, though they know how to estimate, and therefore seek to avoid the horrors and dangers of war, yet they know also how to value the blessings of liberty and national independence:—They know that peace would be purchased at too high a price by bending beneath a foreign yoke, and that peace so purchased could be but of short duration. The nation thus submitting would be soon involved in the quarrels of its master, and would be compelled to exhaust its blood and its treasure, not for its own liberty, its own independence, or its own rights, but for the aggrandizement of its oppressor. The modern world unhappily exhibits but too plain a demonstration of this proposition. I pray heaven that *America* may never contribute its still further elucidation.

Terrible to her neighbors on the continent of *Europe,* as all must admit *France* to be, I believe that the *United States,* if indeed united, if awake to the impending danger, if capable of employing their whole, their undivided force—are so situated as to be able to preserve their independence. An immense ocean placed by a gracious Providence, which seems to watch over this rising empire, between us and the European world, opposes of itself such an obstacle to an invading ambition, must so diminish the force which can be brought to bear upon us, that our resources, if duly exerted, must be adequate to our protection, and we shall remain free if we do not deserve to be slaves.

You do me justice, gentlemen, when you suppose that consolation must be derived from a comparison of the Administration of the American Government, with that which I have lately witnessed. To a citizen of the *United States,* so familiarly habituated to the actual possession of liberty, that he almost considers it as the inseparable companion of man, a view of the despotism, which borrowing the garb and usurping the name of freedom, tyrannizes over so large and so fair a proportion of the earth, must teach the value which he ought to place on the solid safety and real security he enjoys at home. In support of these, all temporary difficulties, however great, ought to be encountered, and I agree with you that the loss of them would poison and embitter every other joy; and that deprived of them, men who aspire to the exalted character of freemen, would turn with loathing and disgust from every other comfort of life.

To me, gentlemen, the attachment you manifest to the government of your choice affords the most sincere satisfaction. Having no interests separate from or opposed to those of the people, being themselves subject in common with others, to the laws they make, being soon to return to that mass from which they are selected for a time in order to conduct the affairs of the nation, it is by no means probable that those who administer the government of the *United States* can be actuated by other motives than the sincere desire of promoting the real prosperity of those, whose destiny involves their own, and in whose ruin they must participate. Desirable as it is at all times, a due confidence in our government, it is peculiarly so in a moment of peril like the present, in a moment when the want of that confidence must impair the means of self defence, must increase a danger already but too great, and furnish, or at least give the appearance of furnishing, to a foreign real enemy, those weapons, which have so often been so successfully used.

Accept, gentlemen, my grateful acknowledgements for your kind expressions concerning myself, and do me the justice to believe, that your prosperity, and that of the city of *Richmond* and its vicinity, will ever be among the first wishes of my heart.

3. *Campaign Tract* (*1798*)

Marshall's effort to secure the Richmond Congressional seat produced the following item. Running more or less as a Federalist, Marshall had to avoid committing political suicide—the reward for orthodox Federalists—in a state hardly hospitable to the party of the alien and sedition laws. Marshall probably suggested or even designed the questions himself, and they nicely presented him with the opportunity to adopt the middle course. For example, the Jeffersonians insisted that the Alien and Sedition Acts were unconstitutional, but here Marshall was prudently silent on that contention and chose rather to satisfy his constituency by affirming his opposition to an extension of the acts. This was hardly the point of contention. His stance on neutrality met the accusation that he was pro-British; furthermore, he fudged the issue of foreign alliances by opposing permanent ones. Note that he rested his foreign policy upon an interest in commerce. Needless to say, the New England Federalists accused him of rank, unprincipled, political cowardice. For all this rhetoric and artful dodging, he won the election on the basis of his popularity, with help from a last-minute endorsement by Patrick Henry.

FREEHOLDER'S QUESTIONS TO
GENERAL MARSHALL

VIRGINIA. Fredericksburg, Oct. 2 [1798]

POLITICAL QUESTIONS

Addressed to General MARSHALL *with his Answer thereto*
To J. MARSHALL, ESQ.   RICHMOND, SEPT. 12.

DEAR SIR,

Under a conviction that it will be of utility, should the an-
swers to the following questions be such as I anticipate, I
state them with a confidence of your readiness to give replies.
They will, at all events, greatly satisfy my mind.

1st. Do you not in heart, and sentiment, profess yourself an
American—attached to the genuine principles of the Constitution, as sanctioned by the will of the people, for their general liberty, prosperity and happiness?

2nd. Do you conceive that the true interest and prosperity
of *America,* is materially, or at all, dependent upon an alliance
with any foreign nation? If you do, please state the causes,
and a preference, if any exists, with the reasons for that preference.

3d. Are you in favor of an alliance, offensive and defensive,
with *Great Britain?* In fine, are you disposed to advocate any
other, or a closer connection with that nation, than exists at
the ratification of the treaty of 1794? If so, please state your
reasons.

4th. By what general principles, in your view, have the
measures of our Administration and Government, in respect to
France, been consistent with true policy or necessity? And

From *Times and Virginia Advertiser* (Alexandria, Oct. 11, 1798).

could not the consequences have been avoided by a different line of conduct on our part?

5th. Are you an advocate for the Alien and Sedition Bills? Or, in the event of your election, will you use your influence to obtain a repeal of these laws?

A FREEHOLDER

MARSHALL'S ANSWERS TO FREEHOLDER'S QUESTIONS

RICHMOND, SEPT. 20, '98.

DEAR SIR:—

I have just received your letter of yesterday, [*sic*] and shall with equal candor and satisfaction, answer all your queries. Every citizen has a right to know the political sentiments of the man who is proposed as his representative; and mine have never been of a nature to shun examination. To those who think another gentleman more capable of serving the district than myself, it would be useless to explain my opinions because whatever my opinions may be, they will, and ought, to vote for that other; but I cannot help wishing that those who think differently, would know my real principles, and not attribute to me those I never possessed; and with which active calumny has been pleased to asperse me.

Answ. 1. In heart and sentiment, as well as by birth and interest, I am an American, attached to the genuine principles of the constitution, as sanctioned by the will of the people, for their general liberty, prosperity and happiness. I consider that constitution as the rock of our political salvation, which has preserved us from misery, division and civil wars; and which will yet preserve us if we value it rightly and support it firmly.

2. I do not think the interest and prosperity of America, at all dependent on the alliance with any foreign nation; nor does the man exist who would regret more than myself the forma-

tion of such an alliance. In truth, America has, in my opinion, no motive for forming such connection, and very powerful motives for avoiding them. Europe is eternally engaged in wars in which we have no interest; and with which the fondest policy forbids us to intermeddle.

We ought to avoid any compact which may endanger our being involved in them. My sentiments on this subject are detailed at large in the beginning of the memorial addressed by the late envoys from the United States to the minister of foreign affairs of the French Republic, where the neutrality of the United States is justified, and the reasons for that neutrality stated.

3rd. I am not in favor of an alliance offensive and defensive with Great Britain nor for closer connection with that nation than already exists. No man in existence is more decidedly opposed to such an alliance, or more fully convinced of the evils that would result from it. I never have, in thought, word, or deed, given the smallest reason to suspect I wished it; nor do I believe any man acquainted with me does suspect it. Those who originate and countenance such an idea, may (if they know me) design to impose on others, but they do not impose on themselves.

The whole of my politics respecting foreign nations are reducible to this single position. We ought to have commercial intercourse with all, but political ties with none. Let us buy cheap and sell as dear as possible. Let commerce go wherever individual, and consequently national interest, will carry it; but let us never connect ourselves politically with any nation whatever.

I have not a right to say, nor can I say positively, what are the opinions of those who administer the Government of the United States; but I believe firmly that neither the President, nor any one of those with whom he advises, would consent to form a close and permanent political connection with any nation upon earth.

Should France continue to wage an unprovoked war against us, while she is also at war with Britain, it would be madness and folly not to endeavor to make such temporary arrangements as would give us the aid of the British fleets to prevent our being invaded; but I would not, even to obtain so obvious a good, make such a sacrifice as I think we should make, by forming a permanent political connection with that, or any other nation on earth.

4th. The measures of the administration and government of the United States with respect to France have in my opinion been uniformly directed by a sincere and unequivocal desire to observe, faithfully, the treaties existing between the two nations and to preserve the neutrality and independence of our country. —Had it been possible to maintain peace with France without sacrificing those great objects, I am convinced that our government would have maintained it.

Unfortunately it has been impossible. I do not believe that any different line of conduct on our part, unless we would have relinquished the rights of self government, and have become the colonies of France, could have preserved peace with that nation.—But be assured that the primary object of France is and for a long time past has been, dominion over others. This is a truth only to be disbelieved by those who shut their eyes on the history and conduct of that nation.

The grand instruments by which they effect this end, to which all their measures tend, are immense armies on their part, and divisions, which a variety of circumstances have enabled them to create, among those whom they wish to subdue. Whenever France has exhibited a disposition to be just toward the United States, an accurate attention to facts now in possession of the public, will prove that this disposition was manifest in the hope of involving us in her wars, as a dependent and subordinate nation.

5th. I am not an advocate for the alien and sedition bills; had I been in Congress when they passed, I should, unless my judgment could have been changed, certainly have opposed them. Yet, I do not think them fraught with all those mischiefs which many gentlemen ascribe to them. I should have opposed them because I think them useless; and because they are calculated to create unnecessary discontents and jealousies at a time when our very existence, as a nation, may depend on our union—

I believe that these laws, had they been opposed on these principles by a man, not suspected of intending to destroy the government, or being hostile to it, would never have been enacted. With respect to their repeal, the effort will be made before I can become a member of Congress.

If it succeeds there will be an end of the business—if it fails, I shall on the question of renewing the effort, should I be chosen to represent the district, obey the voice of my constituents. My own private opinion is, that it will be unwise to renew it for this reason: the laws will expire of themselves, if I recollect rightly the time for which they are enacted, during the term of the ensuing Congress. I shall indisputably oppose their revival; and I believe that opposition will be more successful, if men's minds are not too much irritated by the struggle about a repeal of laws which will, at the time, be expiring of themselves.

J. Marshall.

4. *Upholding the Alien and Sedition Acts (1798)*

Marshall, for the Federalist minority in the Virginia legislature, wrote a full-dress reply to the Kentucky-Virginia Resolutions and Madison's accompanying report. (For all of Virginia's libertarian concerns, the legislature refused to subsidize the printing of such a Federalist tract at public expense.) The major points are reprinted below.

Generally, it may be said that the Jeffersonian case against the sedition law had a markedly states' rights tone: the states were the only proper authorities for suppressing sedition. Ironically, Marshall in *Barron v. Baltimore* (1833) later sustained this states' rights interpretation of the Bill of Rights: the states he held were not limited by the Fifth Amendment. But in 1798, Marshall was probably quite sound in maintaining that the Sedition Act did not abridge the First Amendment guarantee of freedom of speech and press as properly construed. Whatever merit Madison's report had as a libertarian position paper, there is compelling evidence that the Founders had only intended to incorporate in the First Amendment the common law doctrine of "no prior restraint." Thus, the Sedition Act, oddly enough, advanced in a libertarian direction by adding to standard libel procedures the further protections of jury trial and truth as a defense. (Madison had been singularly evasive in his handling of this aspect of the Sedition Act. The reason for his reticence was, of course, that the federal Sedition Act created much higher procedural standards than those existing in the states.)

Marshall was prepared to do more than refute the Jeffersonian points based on the intention of the First Amendment; his positive argument for the act was, at least, ingenious: Congress had the legislative power under the necessary and proper clause to penalize resistance to the execution of the law. (Here for the first time Marshall stamped his hallmark on constitutional interpretation.) Then Marshall proceeded to mull over the need of governments to protect law-abiding citizens from those who would undermine confidence in government.

The Jeffersonians argued cogently, however, that contesting for office could not be termed subversive activity and that Marshall's definition of the proper role of government would close down a democratic system based on party competition for public office. Thus, the Sedition Act threatened to rule out competition by calling it subversion, by eliminating the opposition's right to undermine confidence in government.

One senses that Marshall appreciated the Jeffersonian argument about the competitive conditions necessary for democratic government. For all of the logic of his constitutional points, Marshall—an old professional politician—must have realized that the Republican case was compelling in terms of the democratic political process, however opportunistic and unpatriotic (in his jaundiced view) the Jeffersonians had been in advancing and elaborating it. Marshall insisted upon the *de jure* constitutionality of the Sedition Act for that reason, but thought it a counter-productive, self-defeating measure when applied to the Republican Party to forestall the circulation of the Federalist elite.

THE ADDRESS OF THE MINORITY IN THE VIRGINIA LEGISLATURE TO THE PEOPLE OF THAT STATE, CONTAINING A VINDICATION OF THE CONSTITUTIONALITY OF THE ALIEN AND SEDITION LAWS [DEC. 1798]

. . . In the opinion of some, to deliberate on [the constitutionality of the Alien and Sedition Laws] is criminal, and to pause before we declare that the constituted authorities have knowingly and intentionally violated that sacred charter by which they hold their political existence, is to be inimical to that republican liberty, which constitutes the pride and happiness of our country, and which can only be preserved by preserving that government which is now so boldly arraigned. Had the measures which profess their origin from these laws, been confined to ordinary peaceable and constitutional efforts to

From *Journal*, Virginia House of Delegates (Dec. 1798).

effect their repeal; had a decent respect for the real majority of the American people been maintained, no opposition would have been made by those who now address you.—But when a partial irritation, in some degree produced by misconception, is sought to be excited into general hostility against the government of our country, is seized as affording a fair occasion for proceedings which may sap the foundation of our union, we must in obedience to that duty which gave birth to this reply, submit to our fellow citizens, some reflections on these laws.

The act concerning aliens, makes it lawful for the President of the United States, to order all such aliens as he shall judge dangerous to the peace and safety of the United States, or shall have reasonable grounds to suspect are concerned in any treasonable or secret machinations against the government thereof, to depart out of the territory of the United States within such time as shall be expressed in such order.

This law has been declared to be unconstitutional, because—first, it transcends the powers of Congress; 2nd, it violates that article which restrains the prohibition of migration till 1808; 3d, It unites legislative, executive and judicial powers in the chief magistrate. 4th, It deprives aliens of the constitutional right of the trial by jury.

Time will not allow a minute investigation of this subject, the several objections will be but briefly reviewed.

1st, It is alleged to be an exercise of a power not delegated. The constitution of the United States, is in its organization dissimilar to any scheme of government which has been heretofore devised.

It presents to us for many purposes an entire nation, and for other purposes several distinct and perfect sovereignties— Perpetual peace among ourselves; a complete participation of privileges through all the states, and above all safety from abroad, were perhaps the strong motives which induced America to unite under one government. All objects which are general in their nature, which interest all America, which are connected with the general safety; all external objects can only be obtained by the co-operation of the whole, and therefore the powers necessary for their attainment would be naturally vested in the government of the whole. The vast mass of local and interior regulation can be most beneficially attended to by the state sovereignties, and therefore the government of the union is, and ought to be excluded from participating in their formation.

When we examine the situation of the United States, and the objects for which its government must necessarily have been formed, the mind is irresistibly led to the demarcation of a plain line of partition between the general and particular sovereignties. Since the general and state governments equally represent the people, and are alike dependent on them for their origin and their continuance, and are alike accountable to them for their misconduct, those powers which are essential to our happiness and protection, may, with equal safety, as to their abuse, be trusted to the one or to the other. It is therefore rational to suppose, that they are placed where they can be exercised most beneficially, and that they are given to that government which is destined to effect the particular object for which those powers are calculated. This obvious principle seems to have actuated those who framed our constitutions; the powers of peace, war and commerce, of external intercourse in all its variety of forms, of calling out and directing the force and wealth of the nation, are placed in the general government: they are rightly placed, because to that government we look for protection from enemies of every denomination.

With respect to these objects, America is one nation, and therefore the state governments are restrained from interfering with these great acts of sovereignty: The power of protecting the nation from the intrigues and conspiracies of dangerous aliens who may have introduced themselves into the bosom of our country, seems to be of the class with those necessarily delegated to the general government: security to the union from their wicked machinations, cannot otherwise be ensured, and this security is essential to the common good. The means of obtaining intelligence of their plots are in possession only of the general government, nor can any one state do more than expel them from its territory; their right of residence is not unfrequently provided for in treaties, and treaties can only be formed or dissolved by the general government. If in the act of removing them unjustifiable injuries be committed, reparation is demandable by the sovereign of their nation.

This reparation is demandable not from the state, but from the United States government. All America is therefore interested in the manner in which this power shall be exercised, and would consequently choose to place it in hands which all America controls.

In conformity then with the general theory of our government, the power of protecting us from the conspiracies of aliens should be associated in the same hands with the force of the nation and the general power of protection from hostility of every kind. Yet it is admitted, that if in the formation of our constitution a different arrangement is made, that arrangement, however inconvenient, must be sacredly obeyed till constitutionally changed.

It behoves us, however, to satisfy ourselves completely on this interesting point.

The government of the United States is indubitably limited as to its objects, however it may be as to the means of obtaining those objects. It possesses only delegated powers, and it is proper to enquire whether the power now under consideration be delegated or not. It is necessary, in pursuing this enquiry, to bear in mind that we are investigating a constitution which must unavoidably be restricted in various points to general expressions, making the great outlines of a subject, and not a law which is capable of descending to every minute detail.

If we construe the former by rules strictly applicable to the latter, the power of fortifying our ports and harbours might well be questioned; nor could the utility of the clause authorising Congress to make all laws necessary and proper for carrying into execution all powers vested by the constitution in the government of the United States, or in any department or officer thereof, be readily pointed out. It would be difficult too to assign a reason for omitting, in the 12th amendment of our constitution which is evidently copied from the 2d article of the ancient confederation, the very material word *expressly*. That article of the ancient confederation, and the amendment of our constitution, were designed as a plain and explicit admission of the principle, that the powers not delegated are retained. In the confederation all powers not *expressly* delegated, are retained, but in the amendment this very operative word is wisely omitted.

In reviewing then our constitution, to decide on the powers vested for general purposes, in our general government, we must examine the whole paper, we must examine it fairly, but liberally.

Congress has power "to declare war, grant letters of marque and reprisal, and make rules concerning captures on land and water." To make reprisals is a power distinct from, and which not unfrequently precedes war; as a branch of this power, those members of Congress who are decided in their declarations against the alien law, united in 1794 in support of the bill for sequestering British *property*. But reprisals may be made on the *persons* as well as the *property* of aliens; and as sequestration is the exercise, in an inferior degree, of the general power of reprisal on property, so may the removal of aliens be power of reprisal on persons. If the whole power of reprisal be delegated, the particular degree or manner in which it shall be exercised, is a question of particular discretion, and not of constitutional authority.

Congress has power "to define and punish piracies and felonies, committed on the high seas, *and offences against the law of nations."*

By the law of nations, or by particular treaty, an alien acquires a right of residence in a country at peace with his own, and it is an offence against that law to become dangerous to the peace and safety or to be concerned in any treasonable or secret machinations against the government of the country in which he resides. These offences congress may both *define* and *punish.*

Congress may call forth the militia, "to suppress insurrections and repel invasions;" and further, "the United States shall guarantee to every state in the union, a republican form of government, and *shall protect each of them against invasions."*

By this latter clause, something further was intended than merely to *repel* invasion. Invasion actually made is to be *repelled,* and for that purpose the militia may be called out. But congress is to do more than merely to repel the actual invasion. This power having been granted by the 8th section of the first article, the constitution in the 4th section of the fourth article, gives the additional power, and makes it the duty of Congress to *protect* each state against invasion. To *protect* against an evil, includes the right of taking proper and necessary steps for its prevention. Of these proper and necessary steps, the government possessed of the power must judge. To cause to depart from our territory the individuals of a nation from whom invasion was apprehended, is most obviously a measure of precaution dictated by prudence and warranted by justice. It appears then to be fairly deducible, from the theory of the constitution, and from a correct view of its particular parts, that the power of protecting the American commonwealth against dangerous aliens, whether dispersed through the interior of our country, or embodied in arms against us, is an existing efficient power placed like all others necessary for the common safety, in the only hands which can bring it into complete and beneficial operation. . . .

3dly. This law is also objected to, because it unites legislative, executive and judiciary powers in the President of the United States.

Legislation is the act of making or giving laws, Congress therefore in making this law, performed the part of the legislature, nor is there any thing legislative in the execution of it. If indeed Congress by itself, or perhaps by commissioners appointed by itself, had executed the law, the charge would have worn some semblance of truth; but the commission of the execution of this law to the person charged by the constitution with the execution of all the laws of the union, is certainly in itself unexceptionable. Nor does this act transfer to the President powers belonging properly to the judiciary. It does not involve a decision that its object has committed a crime. It is a measure of general safety, in its nature political and not forensic, the execution of which is properly trusted to the department which represents the nation in all its interior relations—Every law, in its execution, requires some judgment, but the execution of the law is not on that account judicial.

4th. This act deprives the alien of his right of trial by jury. To this extraordinary allegation, it has again and again been answered, that this is a measure of preventive and not of punishing justice. Who would require that a jury should be impanelled, in order to decide whether a nation had or had not cause to suspect a particular alien of dangerous designs against its peace? who would require that the President should unfold to juries throughout the United States all the intelligence he may have received, perhaps from persons within the reach of those employing the aliens, and which establishes in his mind the reality of the danger to be apprehended. Certainly a vested right is to be taken from no individual without a solemn trial, but the right of remaining in our country is vested in no alien; he enters and remains by the courtesy of the sovereign power, and that courtesy may at pleasure be withdrawn. That Virginia considers the two last objections groundless, is demonstrated by her own act on the same subject. By the 2d section of the sixty-second chapter of our laws, it is enacted, that "it shall and may be lawful for the Governor, with the advice of the council of state, to apprehend and secure, or cause to be apprehended and secured, or compelled to depart this commonwealth, all suspicious persons, being the subjects of any foreign power or state who shall have made a declaration of war, or actually commenced hostilities against the said states, or from whom the President of the United States shall apprehend hostile designs against the said states; provided information thereof shall have been previously received by the executive from him. And in all such cases the Governor, with the advice of the council of state, shall, and he is hereby empowered to send for the person and papers of any foreigner within this state, in order to obtain such information as he may judge necessary."

If the alien law of the United States be an union of legislative, executive and judiciary powers, so is that of Virginia: if one is unconstitutional by depriving an alien of trial by jury, so is the other. This is a question entirely separated from the powers of the different governments; because the provisions of the one constitution, are in these respects as explicit as those of the other. This act of our legislature was not passed hastily or inconsiderately—It was originally enacted in 1785 under the auspices of some of the most zealous opposers of powers of the act of Congress—It was revised, corrected, and reported by the judges and others appointed to collate and digest all the laws of the state. It was then re-enacted in 1792.

Never, during this investigation and re-investigation, did it occur to a single individual, that to order an alien to depart the commonwealth, first under the suggestion of Congress under the old confederation, and afterwards on the suggestion of the President under our improved constitution, united legislative, executive and judicial powers, or deprived an alien of a trial to which he was entitled, viz. trial by jury.

That this measure should originally have been suggested as necessary for national safety, that it should have been preserved through a long course of reflection, that it should be deemed free from the objection of uniting the powers of different departments in the executive, as also of depriving an alien from his residence without a trial by jury, and yet that it should for the same causes produce a ferment in some states, as soon as the principle was adopted by Congress, might warrant reflections which we will not permit ourselves to express.

The act entitled "An act in addition to the act entitled an act for the punishment of certain crimes against the United States," and which is commonly called the Sedition Law, subjects to a fine not exceeding two thousand dollars, and to imprisonment not exceeding two years, any person who shall write, print, utter or publish, or cause or procure to be written, printed, uttered or published, any false, scandalous, malicious writing or writings against the government of the United States, or either house of Congress of the United States, or the President of the United States, with intent to defame the said government, or either house of Congress, or the said President, or to bring them, or either of them, into contempt or disrepute, or to excite against them, or either or any of them, the hatred of the good people of the United States, or to stir up sedition within the United States, or to excite any unlawful combinations therein for opposing or resisting any law of the United States, or any act of the President of the United States, done in pursuance of such a law, or of the powers in him vested by the constitution of the United States, or to resist, oppose or defeat any such law or act; or to aid, encourage or abet any hostile design of any foreign nation, against the United States, their people or government; the person accused is to be tried by jury, and may give in evidence the proof of the matter contained in the libel.

To constitute the crime, the writing must be false, scandalous and malicious, and the intent must be to effect some one of the ill purposes described in the act.

To contend that there does not exist a power to punish writings coming within the description of this law, would be to assert the inability of our nation to preserve its own peace, and to protect themselves from the attempt of wicked citizens, who incapable of quiet themselves, are incessantly employed in devising means to disturb the public repose.

Government is instituted and preserved for the general happiness and safety; the people therefore are interested in its preservation, and have a right to adopt measures for its security, as well against secret plots as open hostility. But government cannot be thus secured, if, by falsehood and malicious slander, it is to be deprived of the confidence and affection of the people. It is in vain to urge that truth will prevail, and that slander, when detected, recoils on the calumniator. The experience of the world, and our own experience prove that a continued course of defamation will at length sully the fairest reputation, and will throw suspicion on the purest conduct. Although the calumnies of the factious and discontented may not poison the minds of a majority of the citizens, yet they will infect a very considerable number, and prompt them to deeds destructive of the public peace, and dangerous to the general safety. This the people have a right to prevent: and therefore, in all the nations of the earth, where presses are known, some corrective of the licentiousness has been indispensable. But it is contended, that though this may be theoretically true, such is the peculiar structure of our government, that this power has either never been confided to, or has been withdrawn from the legislature of the union. We will examine these positions. The power of making all laws which shall be necessary and proper for carrying into execution all powers vested by the constitution in the government of the United States, or in any department or officer thereof, is by the concluding clause of the eighth section of the first article, expressly delegated to Congress. This clause is admitted to authorise Congress to pass any act for the punishment of those who would resist the execution of the law, because such an act would be incontestably necessary and proper for carrying into execution the power vested in the government. If it authorises the punishment of actual resistance, does it not also authorise punishment of those acts which are criminal in themselves, and which obviously lead to and prepare resistance? Would it not be strange, if, for the purpose of executing the legitimate powers of the government, a clause like that which has been cited should be so construed as to permit the passage of laws punishing acts which constitute the germ from which resistance springs? That the government must look on, and see preparation for resistance which it shall be unable to control, until they shall break out in open force? This would be an unreasonable and improvident construction of the article under consideration. That continued calumnies against the government have this tendency, is demonstrated by uninterrupted experience. They will, if unrestrained, produce in any society, convulsions which, if not totally destructive of, will yet be very injurious to its prosperity and welfare. . . .

To publish malicious calumnies against an individual, with an intent to defame him, is a wrong on the part of the calumniator, and an injury to the individual, for which the laws afford redress. To write or print these calumnies is such an aggravation of the crime, as to constitute an offence against the government, and the author of the libel is subject to the additional punishment which may be inflicted under an indictment. To publish malicious calumnies against government itself, is a wrong on the part of the calumniator, and an injury to all those who have an interest in the government.

Those who have this interest and have sustained the injury, have, the natural right to an adequate remedy. The people of the United States have a common interest in their government, and sustain in common the injury which affects that government. The people of the United States therefore have a right to the remedy for that injury, and are substantially the party seeking redress. By the 2d section of the third article of the constitution, the judicial power of the United States is extended to controversies to which the United States shall be a party; and by the same article it is extended to all cases of law and equity arising under the constitution, the laws of the United States and treaties made or which shall be made under their authority. What are cases arising under the constitution, as contradistinguished from those which arise under the laws made pursuant thereof? They must be cases triable by a rule which exists independent of any act of the legislature of the union. That rule is the common or unwritten law which pervades all America, and which declaring libels against government to be a punishable offence, applies itself impartially and protects any government which the will of the people may establish. The judicial power of the United States, then, being extended to the punishment of libels against the government, as a common law offence, arising under the constitution which creates the government, the general clause gives to the legislature of the union the right to make such laws as shall give that power effect.

That such was the contemporaneous construction of the constitution, is obvious from one of the amendments which have been made to it. [The First Amendment] which declares that Congress shall make no law abridging the property of the press, is a general construction made by all America on the original instrument, admitting its application to the subject: It would have been certainly unnecessary thus to have modified the legislative powers of Congress concerning the press, if the power itself does not exist.

But although the original constitution may be supposed to have enabled the government to defend itself against false and malicious libels, endangering the peace, and threatening the tranquility of the American people, yet it is contended the [First] amendment to that instrument, has deprived it of this power. The amendment is in these words. "Congress shall make no law respecting an establishment of religion, or prohibiting the free exercise thereof, or abridging the freedom of speech, or of the press."

In a solemn instrument, as is a constitution, words are well weighed and considered, before they are adopted. A remarkable diversity of expression is not used, unless it be designed to manifest a difference of intention. Congress is prohibited from making any law respecting a religious establishment, but not from making any law respecting the press. When the power of Congress relative to the press is to be limited, the word *respecting* is dropped, and Congress is only restrained from passing any law abridging its liberty. . . .

All abridgment of the freedom of the press is forbidden, but it is only an abridgment of that freedom which is forbidden. It becomes then necessary in order to determine whether the act in question be unconstitutional or not to inquire whether it does in fact *abridge* the freedom of the press.

The act is believed not to have that operation, for two reasons.

1st. A punishment of the licentiousness is not considered as a restriction of the freedom of the press.

2. The act complained of does not punish any writing not before punishable, nor does it inflict a more severe penalty than that to which the same writing was before liable.

1st. If by freedom of the press is meant a perfect exemption from all punishment for whatever may be published, that freedom never has, and most probably never will exist. It is known to all, that the person who writes or publishes a libel, may be both sued and indicted, and must bear the penalty which the judgment of his country inflicts upon him. It is also known to all that the person who shall libel the government of the state, is for that offence punishable in the like manner. Yet this liability to punishment for slanderous and malicious publications, has never been considered as detracting from the liberty of the press. In fact the liberty of the press is a term which has a definite and appropriate signification, completely understood. It signifies a liberty to publish, free from previous restraint, any thing and every thing at the discretion of the printer only, but not the liberty of spreading with impunity false and scandalous slanders, which may destroy the peace, and mangle the reputation, of an individual or of a community.

If this definition of the term be correct, and it is presumed that its correctness is not to be questioned, then a law punishing the authors and publishers of false, malicious and scandalous libels can be no attack on the liberty of the press.

But the act complained of is no abridgment of the liberty of the press, for another reason.

2d. It does not punish any writing not before punishable, nor does it inflict a heavier penalty than the same writing was before liable to.

No man will deny, that at common law, the author and publisher of a false, scandalous and malicious libel, against the government or an individual, were subject to fine and imprisonment, at the discretion of the judge. Nor will it be denied, that previous to our revolution, the common law was the law of the land throughout the United States.

We believe it to be a principle incontestibly true, that a change of government does not dissolve obligations previously created, does not annihilate existing laws, and dissolve the bonds of society; but that a people passing from one form of government to another, retain in full force all their municipal institutions, not necessarily changed by the change of government. If this be true, then the common law continued to be the law of the land after the revolution, and was of complete obligation even before the act of our assembly for its adoption. Whether similar acts have been passed by the legislatures of other states or not, it is certain that in every state the common law is admitted to be in full force, except as it may have been altered by the statute law. The only question is, whether the doctrines of the common law are applicable to libels against the government of the United States, as well as to libel against the governments of the particular states. For such a distinction there seems to be no sufficient reason. It is not to a magistrate of this or that description that the rules of the common law apply. That he is a magistrate chosen by the people, is a sufficient title to the protection of the common law. The government of the United States is for certain purposes as entirely the government of each state, chosen by the people thereof, and cloathed with their authority, as the government of each particular state is the government of every subdivision of that state; and no satisfactory reason has been heretofore assigned why a general rule common to all, and punishing generally the malicious calumniators of magistrates, should not be as applicable to magistrates chosen for the whole, as those chosen for its different parts.

If then it were even true that the punishment of the printer of malicious falsehoods affected the liberty of the press, yet the act does not *abridge* that liberty, since it does not substitute a harsher or severer rule of punishment than that which before existed.

On points so extremely interesting, a difference of opinion will be entertained. On such occasions all parties must be expected to maintain their real opinions, but to maintain them with moderation and with decency. The will of the majority must prevail, or the republican principle is abandoned, and the nation is destroyed. If upon every constitutional question which presents itself, or on every question we choose to term constitutional, the constructions of the majority shall be forcibly opposed, and hostility to the government excited throughout the nation, there is an end of our domestic peace, and we may for ever bid adieu to our representative government. . . .

5. *The Authority of the President (1800)*

In his one term in Congress, Marshall chanced to deliver a major speech on the dimensions of executive authority under the treaty power. A partisan Jeffersonian maneuver in the House challenged President Adams for acting under the authority of article 27 of the Jay Treaty. The article at issue required the President to extradite persons on American soil who had committed crimes under British jurisdiction; in this instance a certain Thomas Nash was ordered by the President to be delivered to the British authorities once the President was satisfied that Nash had committed murder on board the British vessel, Hermione. (Two years after the murder had been committed, Nash was spotted and identified by the British in Charleston.)

The Jeffersonians got their opening when Nash falsely claimed to have been an impressed American seaman, Jonathan Robins of Danbury, Connecticut, who had mutinied to regain his freedom. Thus, the Jeffersonians depicted Adams as a villain callously sending an aggrieved fellow citizen to death at the hands of the despicable British. When Nash's British citizenship was proven and the Danbury clerk found no evidence of any Jonathan Robins in the record books, the Jeffersonians modified their indictment against the President by protesting that even a British citizen should have been tried by a jury and that Adams had interfered with the judiciary beyond his constitutional powers. (Jefferson was soon afterwards to demonstrate his respect for the independent judiciary by instigating a purge of Federalist judges. see *Marbury v. Madison*, Document 6.)

In the House debate on the Jeffersonian resolution castigating Adams, Marshall masterfully refuted its spurious legal reasoning.

First he contended that the American courts had no jurisdiction to try a British criminal. Then, in the concluding section reprinted below, he refuted the charge that Adams had acted *ultra vires*. The district court, in hearing evidence on the identity of Nash, was not conducting a trial—it had no such jurisdiction—but merely an inquest to help the President make his decision on whether or not to extradite the accused. Marshall claimed the inquest was not a judicial proceeding and thus the President could not be accused of interfering with the autonomy of the federal courts.

Marshall also commented on the special sort of legal judgments involved in the process of executing treaties, asserting that in such matters the President's determination of points of law was final and not reviewable elsewhere. (Such determinations constitute the "political questions of law" and have been circularly defined as those which courts may not review.) Marshall indicated that in foreign affairs the President has great discretionary power, meaning that the Chief Executive operates outside of the normal arena of constitutional limitations.

Almost as an afterthought, Marshall referred to the hypothetical case of a request by the British authorities for the extradition of a bona fide impressed American who *had* committed homicide in order to regain his freedom. Marshall suggested that if one kept his definitions straight, he would realize that the President would never extradite such a party. But what of the hypothetical case of one who was mistakenly extradited on the basis of rigged evidence denying his American citizenship? Marshall knew better than to be led into that bog of legal quicksand; he was not going to canvass the possibility of unreviewable executive error just to supply his opponents with a parade of horrors. (The Jeffersonians had rumored that a lackey of the Secretary of State had purposefully destroyed Robins' birth record!) In any case, Marshall's speech was evidently so effective that Albert Gallatin, who had been scheduled to reply, simply conceded and the resolution was subsequently defeated. (Marshall left Congress a few months later to become Adams' Secretary of State.)

[March 7, 1800]

. . . it has been contended that, although Thomas Nash ought to have been delivered up to the British Minister, on the requisition made by him in the name of his Government, yet, the interference of the President was improper.

This, Mr. M. said, led to his second proposition, which was:

That the case was a case for Executive and not Judicial decision. He admitted implicitly the division of powers, stated by the gentleman from New York [Edward Livingston], and that it was the duty of each department to resist the encroachments of the others.

This being established, the inquiry was, to what department was the power in question allotted?

The gentleman from New York had relied on the second section of the third article of the Constitution, which enumerates the cases to which the Judicial power of the United States extends, as expressly including that now under consideration. Before he examined that section, it would not be improper to notice a very material misstatement of it made in the resolutions, offered by the gentleman from New York. By the Constitution, the Judicial power of the United States is extended to all cases in law and equity, arising under the Constitution, laws, and treaties of the United States; but the resolutions declare that Judicial power to extend to all questions arising under the Constitution, treaties, and laws of the United States. The difference between the Constitution and the resolutions was material and apparent. A case in law or equity was a term well understood, and of limited signification. It was a controversy between parties which had taken a shape for judicial decision. If the Judicial power extended to every question under the Constitution, it would involve almost every subject proper for Legislative discussion and decision; if, to every question under the laws and treaties of the United States, it

---

From *Annals of Congress*, 6th Congress, 2d Sessions, pp. 606–618.

would involve almost every subject on which the Executive could act. The division of power which the gentleman had stated, could exist no longer, and the other departments would be swallowed up by the Judiciary. But it was apparent that the resolutions had essentially misrepresented the Constitution. . . . By extending the Judicial power to all cases in law and equity, the Constitution had never been understood to confer on that department any political power whatever. To come within this description, a question must assume a legal form for forensic litigation and judicial decision. There must be parties to come into court, who can be reached by its process, and bound by its power; whose rights admit of ultimate decision by a tribunal to which they are bound to submit.

A case in law or equity proper for judicial decision may arise under a treaty, where the rights of individuals acquired or secured by a treaty are to be asserted or defended in court. . . . But the Judicial power cannot extend to political compacts; as the establishment of the boundary line between the American and British dominions; the case of the late guarantee in our Treaty with France, or the case of the delivery of a murderer under the twenty-seventh article of our present Treaty with Britain.

The gentleman from New York has asked, triumphantly asked, what power exists in our courts to deliver up an individual to a foreign Government? Permit me, said Mr. M., but not triumphantly, to retort the question. By what authority can any court render such a judgment? What power does a court possess to seize any individual and determine that he shall be adjudged by a foreign tribunal? Surely our courts possess no such power, yet they must possess it, if this article of the treaty is to be executed by the courts.

Gentlemen have cited and relied on that clause in the Constitution, which enables Congress to define and punish piracies and felonies committed on the high seas, and offences against the law of nations; together with an act of Congress, declaring the punishment of those offences; as transferring the whole subject to the courts. But that clause can never be construed to make to the Government a grant of power, which the people making it do not themselves possess. It has already been shown that the people of the United States have no jurisdiction over offences committed on board a foreign ship against a foreign nation. Of consequence, in framing a Government for themselves, they cannot have passed this jurisdiction to that Government. The law, therefore, cannot act upon the case. But this clause of the Constitution cannot be considered, and need not be considered, as affecting acts which are piracy under the law of nations. As the judicial power of the United States extends to all cases of admiralty and maritime jurisdiction, and piracy under the law of nations is of admiralty and maritime jurisdiction, punishable by every nation, the judicial power of the United States of course extends to it. On this principle the Courts of Admiralty under the Confederation took cognizance of piracy, although there was no express power in Congress to define and punish the offence.

But the extension of judicial power of the United States to all cases of admiralty and maritime jurisdiction must necessarily be understood with some limitation. All cases of admiralty and maritime jurisdiction which, from their nature, are triable in the United States, are submitted to the jurisdiction of the courts of the United States.

There are cases of piracy by the law of nations, and cases within the legislative jurisdiction of the nation; the people of America possessed no other power over the subject, and could consequently transfer no other to their courts: and it has already been proved that a murder committed on board a foreign ship-of-war is not comprehended within this description. . . .

The clause in the Constitution which declares that "the trial of all crimes, except in cases of impeachment, shall be by jury," has also been relied on as operating on the case, and transferring the decision on a demand for the delivery of an individual from the Executive to the Judicial department.

But certainly this clause in the Constitution of the United States cannot be thought obligatory on, and for the benefit of, the whole world. It is not designed to secure the rights of the people of Europe and Asia, or to direct and control proceedings against criminals throughout the universe. It can then be designed only to guide the proceedings of our own courts, and to prescribe the mode of punishing offences committed against the Government of the United States, and to which the jurisdiction of the nation may rightfully extend.

It has already been shown that the courts of the United States were incapable of trying the crime for which Thomas Nash was delivered up to justice. The question to be determined was, not how his crime should be tried and punished, but whether he should be delivered up to a foreign tribunal, which was alone capable of trying and punishing him. A provision for the trial of crimes in the courts of the United States is clearly not a provision for the performance of a national compact for the surrender to a foreign Government of an offender against that Government.

The clause of the Constitution declaring that the trial of all crimes shall be by jury, has never even been construed to extend to the trial of crimes committed in the land and naval forces of the United States. Had such a construction prevailed, it would most probably have prostrated the Constitution itself, with the liberties and the independence of the nation, before the first disciplined invader who should approach our shores. Necessity would have imperiously demanded the review and amendment of so unwise a provision. If, then, this clause does not extend to offences committed in the fleets and armies of the United States, how can it be construed to extend to offences committed in the fleets and armies of Britain or of France, or of the Ottoman or Russian Empires?

The same argument applies to the observations on the seventh article of the amendments to the Constitution. That article relates only to trials in the courts of the United States, and not to the performance of a contract for the delivery of a murderer not triable in those courts.

In this part of the argument, the gentleman from New York has presented a dilemma, of a very wonderful structure indeed. He says that the offence of Thomas Nash was either a crime or not a crime. If it was a crime, the Constitutional mode of punishment ought to have been observed; if it was not a crime, he ought not to have been delivered up to a foreign Government, where his punishment was inevitable.

It had escaped the observation of that gentleman, that if the murder committed by Thomas Nash was a crime, yet it was not a crime provided for by the Constitution, or triable in the courts of the United States; and that if it was not a crime, yet it is the precise case in which his surrender was stipulated by treaty. Of this extraordinary dilemma, then, the gentleman from New York is, himself, perfectly at liberty to retain either horn. He has chosen to consider it as a crime, and says it has been made a crime by treaty, and is punished by sending the offender out of the country.

The gentleman is incorrect in every part of his statement. Murder on board a British frigate is not a crime created by treaty. It would have been a crime of precisely the same magnitude had the treaty never been formed. It is not punished by sending the offender out of the United States. The experience of this unfortunate criminal, who was hung and gibbeted, evinced to him that the punishment of his crime was of a much more serious nature than mere banishment from the United States.

The gentleman from Pennsylvania (Albert Gallatin) and the gentleman from Virginia (John Nicholas) have both contended that this was a case proper for the decision of the courts, because points of law occurred, and points of law must have been decided in its determination.

The points of law which must have been decided, are stated by the gentleman from Pennsylvania to be, first, a question whether the offence was committed within the British jurisdiction; and, secondly, whether the crime charged was comprehended within the treaty.

It is true, sir, these points of law must have occurred, and must have been decided; but it by no means follows that they could only have been decided in court. A variety of legal questions must present themselves in the performance of every part of Executive duty, but these questions are not therefore to be decided in court. Whether a patent for land shall issue or not is always a question of law, but not a question which must necessarily be carried into court. The gentleman from Pennsylvania seems to have permitted himself to have been misled by the misrepresentation of the Constitution made in the resolutions of the gentleman from New York; and, in consequence of being so misled, his observations have the appearance of endeavoring to fit the Constitution to his arguments, instead of adapting his arguments to the Constitution.

When the gentleman has proved that these are questions of law, and that they must have been decided by the President, he has not advanced a single step towards proving that they were improper for Executive decision. The question whether vessels captured within three miles of the American coast, or by privateers fitted out in the American ports, were legally captured or not, and whether the American Government was bound to restore them, if in its power, were questions of law; but they were questions of political law, proper to be decided, and they were decided by the Executive, and not by the courts.

The *casus fœderis* of the guaranty was a question of law, but no man could have hazarded the opinion that such a question must be carried into court, and can only be there decided. So the *casus fœderis*, under the twenty-seventh article of the treaty with Great Britain, is a question of law, but of political law. The question to be decided is, whether the particular case proposed be one in which the nation has bound itself to act, and this is a question depending on principles never submitted to courts.

If a murder should be committed within the United States, and the murderer should seek an asylum in Britain, the question whether the *casus fœderis* of the twenty-seventh article had occurred, so that his delivery ought to be demanded, would be a question of law, but no man would say it was a question which ought to be decided in the courts.

When, therefore, the gentleman from Pennsylvania has established, that in delivering up Thomas Nash, points of law were decided by the President, he has established a position which in no degree whatever aids his argument.

The case was in its nature a national demand made upon the nation. The parties were the two nations. They cannot come into court to litigate their claims, nor can a court decide on them. Of consequence, the demand is not a case for judicial cognizance.

The President is the sole organ of the nation in its external relations, and its sole representative with foreign nations. Of consequence, the demand of a foreign nation can only be made on him.

He possesses the whole Executive power. He holds and directs the force of the nation. Of consequence, any act to be performed by the force of the nation is to be performed through him.

He is charged to execute the laws. A treaty is declared to be a law. He must then execute a treaty, where he, and he alone, possesses the means of executing it.

The treaty, which is a law, enjoins the performance of a particular object. The person who is to perform this object is marked out by the Constitution, since the person is named who conducts the foreign intercourse, and is to take care that the laws be faithfully executed. The means by which it is to be performed, the force of the nation, are in the hands of this person. Ought not this person to perform the object, although the particular mode of using the means has not been prescribed? Congress, unquestionably, may prescribe the mode, and Congress may devolve on others the whole execution of the contract; but, till this be done, it seems the duty of the Executive department to execute the contract by any means it possesses.

The gentleman from Pennsylvania contends that, although this should be properly an Executive duty, yet it cannot be performed until Congress shall direct the mode of performance. He says that, although the jurisdiction of the courts is extended by the Constitution to all cases of admiralty and maritime jurisdiction, yet if the courts had been created without any express assignment of jurisdiction, they could not have taken cognizance of cases expressly allotted to them by the Constitution. The Executive, he says, can, no more than courts, supply a legislative omission.

It is not admitted that, in the case stated, courts could not have taken jurisdiction. The contrary is believed to have been the correct opinion. And although the Executive cannot supply a total Legislative omission, yet it is not admitted, or believed that there is such a total omission in this case.

The treaty, stipulating that a murderer shall be delivered up to justice, is as obligatory as an act of Congress making the same declaration. If, then, there was an act of Congress in the words of the treaty, declaring that a person who had committed murder within the jurisdiction of Britain, and sought an asylum within the territory of the United States, should be delivered up by the United States, on the demand of His Britannic Majesty, and such evidence of his criminality, as would have justified his commitment for trial, had the offence been here committed; could the President, who is bound to execute the laws, have justified the refusal to deliver up the criminal, by saying, that the Legislature had totally omitted to provide for the case?

The Executive is not only the Constitutional department, but seems to be the proper department to which the power in question may most wisely and most safely be confided.

The department which is entrusted with the whole foreign intercourse of the nation, with the negotiation of all its treaties, with the power of demanding a reciprocal performance of the article, which is accountable to the nation for the violation of its engagements with foreign nations, and for the consequences resulting from such violation, seems the proper department to be entrusted with the execution of a national contract like that under consideration.

If, at any time, policy may temper the strict execution of the contract, where may that political discretion be placed so safely as in the department whose duty it is to understand precisely the state of the political intercourse and connexion between the United States and foreign nations, to understand the manner in which the particular stipulation is explained and performed by foreign nations, and to understand completely the state of the Union?

This department, too, independent of judicial aid, which may, perhaps, in some instances, be called in, is furnished with a great law officer, whose duty it is to understand and to advise when the *casus fœderis* occurs. And if the President should cause to be arrested under the treaty an individual who was so circumstanced as not to be properly the object of such an arrest, he may perhaps bring the question of the legality of his arrest before a judge, by a writ of habeas corpus.

It is then demonstrated, that, according to the principles of the American Government, the question whether the nation has or has not bound itself to deliver up any individual, charged with having committed murder or forgery within the jurisdiction of Britain, is a question the power to decide which rests alone with the Executive department.

It remains to inquire whether, in exercising this power, and in performing the duty it enjoins, the President has committed an unauthorized and dangerous interference with judicial decisions. . . .

Gentlemen had considered it as an offence against judicial authority, and a violation of judicial rights to withdraw from their sentence a criminal against whom a prosecution had been commenced. They had treated the subject as if it was the privilege of courts to condemn to death the guilty wretch arraigned at their bar, and that to intercept the judgment was to violate the privilege. Nothing can be more incorrect than this view of the case. It is not the privilege, it is the sad duty of courts to administer criminal judgment. It is a duty to be performed at the demand of the nation, and with which the nation has a right to dispense. If judgment of death is to be pronounced, it must be at the prosecution of the nation, and the nation may at will stop that prosecution. In this respect the President expresses constitutionally the will of the nation; and may rightfully, as was done in the case at Trenton, enter a *nolle prosequi*, or direct that the criminal be prosecuted no farther. This is no interference with judicial decisions, nor any invasion of the province of a court. It is the exercise of an indubitable and a Constitutional power. Had the President directed the Judge at Charleston to decide for or against his own jurisdiction, to condemn or acquit the prisoner, this would have been a dangerous interference with judicial decisions, and ought to have been resisted. But no such direction has been given, nor any such decision been required. If the President determined that Thomas Nash ought to have been delivered up to the British Government for a murder committed on board a British frigate, provided evidence of the fact was adduced, it was a question which duty obliged him to determine, and which he determined rightly. If, in consequence of this determination, he arrested the proceedings of a court on a national prosecution, he had a right to arrest and to stop them, and the exercise of this right was a necessary consequence of the determination of the principal question. In conforming to this decision, the court has left open the question of its jurisdiction. Should another prosecution of the same sort be commenced, which should not be suspended but continued by the Executive, the case of Thomas Nash would not bind as a precedent against the jurisdiction of the court. If it should even prove that, in the opinion of the Executive, a murder committed on board a foreign fleet was not within the jurisdiction of the court, it would prove nothing more; and though this opinion might rightfully induce the Executive to exercise its power over the prosecution, yet if the prosecution was continued, it would have no influence with the court in deciding on its jurisdiction. . . .

It has then been demonstrated—

1st. That the case of Thomas Nash, as stated to the President, was completely within the twenty-seventh article of the treaty between the United States and Great Britain.

2d. That this question was proper for Executive, and not for Judicial decision; and,

3d. That in deciding it, the President is not chargeable with an interference with Judicial decisions.

After trespassing so long, Mr. MARSHALL said, on the patience of the House, in arguing what had appeared to him to be the material points growing out of the resolutions, he regretted the necessity of detaining them still longer for the purpose of noticing an observation which appeared not to be considered by the gentleman who made it as belonging to the argument.

The subject introduced by this observation, however, was so calculated to interest the public feelings, that he must be excused for stating his opinion on it.

The gentleman from Pennsylvania had said that an impressed American seaman, who should commit homicide for the purpose of liberating himself from the vessel in which he was confined, ought not to be given up as a murderer. In this,

Mr. M. said, he concurred entirely with that gentleman. He believed the opinion to be unquestionably correct, as were the reasons that gentleman had given in support of it. He had never heard any American avow a contrary sentiment, nor did he believe a contrary sentiment could find a place in the bosom of any American. He could not pretend, and did not pretend to know the opinion of the Executive on this subject, because he had never heard the opinions of that department; but he felt the most perfect conviction, founded on the general conduct of the Government, that it could never surrender an impressed American to the nation which, in making the impressment, had committed a national injury.

This belief was in no degree shaken by the conduct of the Executive in this particular case.

In his own mind, it was a sufficient defence of the President from an imputation of this kind, that the fact of Thomas Nash being an impressed American was obviously not contemplated by him in the decision he made on the principles of the case. Consequently, if a new circumstance occurred, which would essentially change the case decided by the President, the Judge ought not to have acted under that decision, but the new circumstance ought to have been stated. Satisfactory as this defence might appear, he should not resort to it, because to some it might seem a subterfuge. He defended the conduct of the President on other and still stronger ground.

The President had decided that a murder committed on board a British frigate on the high seas, was within the jurisdiction of that nation, and consequently within the twenty-seventh article of its treaty with the United States. He therefore directed Thomas Nash to be delivered to the British Minister, if satisfactory evidence of the murder should be adduced. The sufficiency of the evidence was submitted entirely to the Judge.

If Thomas Nash had committed a murder, the decision was that he should be surrendered to the British Minister; but if he had not committed a murder, he was not to be surrendered.

Had Thomas Nash been an impressed American, the homicide on board the Hermione would, most certainly, not have been a murder.

The act of impressing an American is an act of lawless violence. The confinement on board a vessel is a continuation of the violence, and an additional outrage. Death committed within the United States, in resisting such violence, would not have been murder, and the person giving the wound could not have been treated as a murderer. Thomas Nash was only to have been delivered up to justice on such evidence as, had the fact been committed within the United States, would have been sufficient to have induced his commitment and trial for murder. Of consequence, the decision of the President was so expressed as to exclude the case of an impressed American liberating himself by homicide. He concluded with observing, that he had already too long availed himself of the indulgence of the House to venture farther on that indulgence by recapitulating or reinforcing the arguments which had already been urged.

Part Two

THE JURISDICTION
OF THE SUPREME COURT

6. *Judicial Review of Congress*

MARBURY v. MADISON (1803)

(1 Cranch 137)

The Constitution itself made no mention of judicial review of acts
of Congress, and the discussions in the Constitutional Convention of
1787 were completely irrelevant. Alexander Hamilton asserted in
the seventy-eighth *Federalist* paper that the Supreme Court would
have this jurisdiction, but since Hamilton was not present when the
convention examined the judicial article (Article III), his contention was thus based on hearsay. In short, there is no conclusive
evidence that the framers of the Constitution either did or did not
intend the judiciary to oversee the work of Congress. The best cir-
cumstantial evidence, however, suggests the judicial review of congressional measures was a necessary component of the total package;
without this barrier the intricate requirements of constitutional
amendment (ratification by two-thirds of each house of Congress
plus three-fourths of the state legislatures) would have become
meaningless. Without judicial review, a President working with a
congressional majority could have amended the Constitution at
his pleasure—and the Constitution would hardly have been the "supreme law of the land" as Article VI proclaimed.

Attempting to read the minds of the dead is an intriguing pastime, though somewhat unempirical. In this context it is scarcely necessary, since practice rapidly outran theory: the ink was hardly dry on the Constitution before different groups were asking the courts to declare that measures they found undesirable were unconstitutional. For example, Jeffersonian lawyers tried to get federal judges to declare the Alien and Sedition Acts of 1798 violative of the Constitution (on states' rights grounds). When this failed, Jefferson and Madison secured passage of the Kentucky and Virginia Resolutions of 1798–99 declaring the Alien and Sedition Acts to be a monstrous invasion of states' rights.

In *Marbury v. Madison*, the shoe was on the other foot: the defeated Federalists were attempting to get the Supreme Court to take action against the Jefferson administration. The political background of this case almost defies belief—it was a circus of sorts. Early in 1801, after the election of 1800 had memorialized the failure of the Federalist Party and brought to the new capital on the Potomac both Jefferson as President and Jeffersonian majorities in Congress, the "lame duck" Federalist Congress quickly passed the Judiciary Act of 1801. This act was designed to increase the number of circuit judges and justices of the peace. President John Adams designated Federalist stalwarts to fill the posts, but his Secretary of State, John Marshall, was not able to deliver all the commissions before he left office in March.

The incoming President Jefferson ordered his new Secretary of State not to deliver any of the remaining commissions, and Congress repealed the Judiciary Act of 1801. These actions seemingly contravened the constitutional stipulation of the tenure of judges—the new circuit judges presumably appointed for life under the Federalist statute simply found their jobs abolished! Congress also changed the schedule of the Supreme Court so the latter would not convene until October 1803!

The first challenge to this drastic policy came in *Marbury v. Madison*. William Marbury, whose commission as Justice of the Peace of the District of Columbia had been signed by President

Adams and sealed by Secretary of State Marshall, came before the Supreme Court with a sad tale: his commission had never been delivered to him by Marshall's successor, Secretary of State James Madison. He claimed that he had been deprived of his property and office and asked the Court to issue to the Secretary of State a writ of mandamus—a legal command that the commission be transmitted.

John Marshall, recently appointed Chief Justice of the Supreme Court (in fact, for the last six weeks of the Adams administration he had occupied both his old position as Secretary of State and his new one—but at only one salary), was in a difficult position. He had to rule on a case where he, as Secretary, had been personally involved. Moreover, Marshall, as an outstanding Federalist and a rugged political in-fighter, had long been a thorn in Jefferson's side. Thus he had to act with great circumspection. Rumor had it that the Jeffersonians were only awaiting a plausible pretext to launch impeachment action against the Chief Justice and a number of his political associates. (They did in fact impeach Justice Samuel Chase of the Supreme Court, but the Senate failed to convict by the necessary two-thirds majority.)

Marshall, however, was determined to try to find out what did happen to the commission (perhaps he was curious?), and this led to a unique episode in American legal annals: the United States Attorney General pleaded the Fifth Amendment privilege against self-incrimination! It so happened that Attorney General Levi Lincoln had been acting Secretary of State in the first weeks of the Jefferson administration while Madison was visiting his sick father. When Madison returned, Lincoln took up his own function as Attorney General and, in the course of events, appeared before the Supreme Court to defend the government against Marbury's charge. Since it was Lincoln who probably threw Marbury's commission into the fire, and since the Court could hold that this was a criminal action, the Attorney General quite properly refused to reply to the Chief Justice's interrogation on the ground that he "might criminate (*sic*) himself." Marshall told him he was quite right and passed on to other matters.

In this decision the Chief Justice conducted a two-level defense. On the first level—the seemingly unconstitutional disregard of judicial tenure—he was clearly outgunned and chose discretion as the better part of valor. But on the second level, where he could prevent escalation, Marshall successfully executed a tour de force and left the Jeffersonians in stunned dismay. After utilizing his opinion to give Jefferson and his cohorts a severe lecture on the meaning of constitutionalism and confirming Marbury in the latter's view that he had been most foully treated by Jefferson, Marshall ruled that Marbury would have to take his problem elsewhere because the statute giving the Supreme Court jurisdiction in this matter (Section 13 of the Judiciary Act of 1789) was unconstitutional. Congress, in other words, had improperly granted the Court the right to issue a mandamus in this area because its act expanded the area of original jurisdiction of the Court beyond that stipulated by Article III of the Constitution. (The power to issue writs of mandamus was neither then nor is it now considered to be a way to enlarge jurisdiction; mandamus and other similar writs can merely implement existing jurisdiction, and Section 13 did no more than confer the power to issue writs where jurisdiction existed.) Marshall argued that if Congress were allowed to "give this court . . . original jurisdiction where the constitution has declared it shall be appellate," the distribution of jurisdiction prescribed by the Constitution would be without substance. He ruled that since the Constitution was superior to all statutes, a law conflicting with it was unconstitutional.

However tortured the logic that supported it, the outcome was a victory for the Court. Although in tactical terms it limited its own area of jurisdiction, rather than that of the President or Congress, in strategic terms it asserted the Court's right to review acts of Congress.

OPINION OF THE COURT.—At the last term, on the affidavits then read and filed with the clerk, a rule was granted in this case, requiring the secretary of state to show cause why a *mandamus* should not issue, directing him to deliver to William Marbury his commission as a justice of the peace for the county of Washington, in the district of Columbia.

No cause has been shown, and the present motion is for a *mandamus.* The peculiar delicacy of this case, the novelty of some of its circumstances, and the real difficulty attending the points which occur in it, require a complete exposition of the principles on which the opinion to be given by the court is founded. These principles have been, on the side of the applicant, very ably argued at the bar. In rendering the opinion of the court, there will be some departure in form, though not in substance, from the points stated in that argument.

In the order in which the court has viewed this subject, the following questions have been considered and decided: 1st. Has the applicant a right to the commission he demands? 2d. If he has a right, and that right has been violated, do the laws of his country afford him a remedy? 3d. If they do afford him a remedy, is it a *mandamus* issuing from this court?

The first object of inquiry is—Has the applicant a right to the commission he demands? His right originates in an act of congress passed in February 1801, concerning the district of Columbia. . . .

It appears, from the affidavits, that, in compliance with this law, a commission for William Marbury, as a justice of peace for the county of Washington, was signed by John Adams, then President of the United States; after which, the seal of the United States was affixed to it; but the commission has never reached the person for whom it was made out. In order to determine whether he is entitled to his commission, it becomes necessary to inquire, whether he has been appointed to the office. For if he has been appointed, the law continues him in office for five years, and he is entitled to the possession of those evidences of office, which, being completed, became his property.

The 2d section of the 2d article of the constitution declares, that "the president shall nominate, and by and with the advice and consent of the senate, shall appoint ambassadors, other public ministers and consuls, and all other officers of the United States, whose appointments are not otherwise provided for." The 3d section declares, that "he shall commission all the officers of the United States."

An act of congress directs the secretary of state to keep the seal of the United States, "to make out and record, and affix the said seal to all civil commissions to officers of the United States, to be appointed by the president, by and with the consent of the senate, or by the president alone; provided, that the said seal shall not be affixed to any commission, before the same shall have been signed by the president of the United States.

These are the clauses of the constitution and laws of the United States, which affect this part of the case. They seem to contemplate three distinct operations: 1st. The nomination: this is the sole act of the president, and is completely voluntary. 2d. The appointment: this is also the act of the president, and is also a voluntary act, though it can only be performed by and with the advice and consent of the senate. 3d. The commission: to grant a commission to a person appointed, might, perhaps, be deemed a duty enjoined by the constitution. "He shall," says that instrument, "commission all the officers of the United States." . . .

This is an appointment made by the president, by and with the advice and consent of the senate, and is evidenced by no act but the commission itself. In such a case, therefore, the commission and the appointment seem inseparable; it being almost impossible to show an appointment, otherwise than by providing the existence of a commission; still the commission is not necessarily the appointment, though conclusive evidence of it.

But at what stage, does it amount to this conclusive evidence? The answer to this question seems an obvious one. The appointment being the sole act of the president, must be completely evidenced, when it is shown that he has done everything to be performed by him. Should the commission, instead of being evidence of an appointment, even be considered as constituting the appointment itself; still, it would be made, when the last act to be done by the president was performed, or, at farthest, when the commission was complete.

The last act to be done by the president is the signature of the commission: he has then acted on the advice and consent of the senate to his own nomination. The time for deliberation has then passed: he has decided. His judgment, on the advice and consent of the senate, concurring with his nomination, has been made, and the officer is appointed. This appointment is evidenced by an open unequivocal act; and being the last act required from the person making it, necessarily excludes the idea of its being, so far as respects the appointment, an inchoate and incomplete transaction.

Some point of time must be taken, when the power of the executive over an officer, not removable at his will, must cease. That point of time must be, when the constitutional power of appointment has been exercised. And this power has been exercised, when the last act, required from the person possessing the power, has been performed: this last act is the signature of the commission. This idea seems to have prevailed with the legislature, when the act passed converting the department of foreign affairs into the department of state. By that act, it is enacted, that the secretary of state shall keep the seal of the United States, "and shall make out and record, and shall affix the said seal to all civil commissions to officers of the United States, to be appointed by the president;" "provided, that the said seal shall not be affixed to any commission, before the same shall have been signed by the President of the United States; nor to any other instrument or act, without the special warrant of the president therefor."

The signature is a warrant for affixing the great seal to the commission; and the great seal is only to be affixed to an instrument which is complete. It attests, by an act, supposed to be of public notoriety, the verity of the presidential signature. It is never to be affixed, until the commission is signed, because the signature, which gives force and effect to the commission, is conclusive evidence that the appointment is made.

The commission being signed, the subsequent duty of the secretary of state is prescribed by law, and not to be guided by the will of the president. He is to affix the seal of the United States to the commission, and is to record it. This is not a proceeding which may be varied, if the judgment of the executive shall suggest one more eligible; but is a precise course accurately marked out by law, and is to be strictly pursued. It is the duty of the secretary of state, to conform to the law, and in this he is an officer of the United States, bound to obey the laws. He acts, in this respect, as has been very properly stated at the bar, under the authority of law, and not by the instructions of the president. It is a ministerial act, which the law enjoins on a particular officer for a particular purpose.

If it should be supposed, that the solemnity of affixing the seal is necessary, not only to the validity of the commission, but even to the completion of an appointment, still, when the seal is affixed, the appointment is made, and the commission is valid. No other solemnity is required by law; no other act is to be performed on the part of government. All that the executive can do, to invest the person with his office, is done; and unless the appointment be then made, the executive cannot make one without the co-operation of others.

After searching anxiously for the principles on which a contrary opinion may be supported, none have been found, which appear of sufficient force to maintain the opposite doctrine. Such as the imagination of the court could suggest, have been very deliberately examined, and after allowing them all the weight which it appears possible to give them, they do not shake the opinion which has been formed. In considering this question, it has been conjectured, that the commission may have been assimilated to a deed, to the validity of which delivery is essential. This idea is founded on the supposition, that the commission is not merely evidence of an appointment, but is itself the actual appointment; a supposition by no means unquestionable. But for the purpose of examining this objection fairly, let it be conceded, that the principle claimed for its support is established.

The appointment being, under the constitution, to be made by the president, personally, the delivery of the deed of appointment, if necessary to its completion, must be made by the president also. It is not necessary, that the delivery should be made personally to the grantee of the office: it never is so made. The law would seem to contemplate, that it should be made to the secretary of state, since it directs the secretary to affix the seal to the commission, after it shall have been signed by the president. If, then, the act of delivery be necessary to give validity to the commission, it has been delivered, when executed and given to the secretary, for the purpose of being sealed, recorded and transmitted to the party. . . .

It has also occurred as possible, and barely possible, that the transmission of the commission, and the acceptance thereof, might be deemed necessary to complete the right of the plaintiff. The transmission of the commission is a practice, directed by convenience, but not by law. It cannot, therefore, be necessary to constitute the appointment, which must precede it, and which is the mere act of the president. If the executive required that every person appointed to an office should himself take means to procure his commission, the appointment would not be the less valid on that account. The appointment is the sole act of the president; the transmission of the commission is the sole act of the officer to whom that duty is assigned, and may be accelerated or retarded by circumstances which can have no influence on the appointment. A commission is transmitted to a person already appointed; not to a person to be appointed or not, as the letter inclosing the commission should happen to get into the post-office and reach him in safety, or to miscarry.

It may have some tendency to elucidate this point, to inquire, whether the possession of the original commission be indispensably necessary to authorize a person, appointed to any office, to perform the duties of that office. If it was necessary, then a loss of the commission would lose the office. Not only negligence, but accident or fraud, fire or theft, might deprive an individual of his office. In such a case, I presume, it could not be doubted, but that a copy from the record of the office of the secretary of state would be, to every intent and purpose, equal to the original: the act of congress has expressly made it so. To give that copy validity, it would not be necessary to prove that the original had been transmitted and afterwards lost. The copy would be complete evidence that the original had existed, and that the appointment had been made, but not that the original had been transmitted. If, indeed, it should appear, that the original had been mislaid in the office of state, that circumstance would not affect the operation of the copy. When all the requisites have been performed, which authorize a recording officer to record any instrument whatever, and the order for that purpose has been given, the instrument is, in law, considered as recorded, although the manual labor of inserting it in a book kept for that purpose may not have been performed. In the case of commissions, the law orders the secretary of state to record them. When, therefore, they are signed and sealed, the order for their being recorded is given; and whether inserted in the book or not, they are in law recorded.

A copy of this record is declared equal to the original, and the fees to be paid by a person requiring a copy are ascertained by law. Can a keeper of a public record erase therefrom a commission which has been recorded? Or can he refuse a copy thereof to a person demanding it on the terms prescribed by law? Such a copy would, equally with the original, authorize the justice of peace to proceed in the performance of his duty, because it would, equally with the original, attest his appointment.

If the transmission of a commission be not considered as necessary to give validity to an appointment, still less is its acceptance. The appointment is the sole act of the president; the acceptance is the sole act of the officer, and is, in plain common sense, posterior to the appointment. As he may resign, so may he refuse to accept: but neither the one nor the other is capable of rendering the appointment a nonentity.

That this is the understanding of the government, is apparent from the whole tenor of its conduct. A commission bears date, and the salary of the officer commences, from his appointment; not from the transmission or acceptance of his commission. When a person appointed to any office refuses to accept that office, the successor is nominated in the place of the person who has declined to accept, and not in the place of the person who had been previously in office, and had created the original vacancy.

It is, therefore, decidedly the opinion of the court, that when a commission has been signed by the president, the appointment is made; and that the commission is complete, when the seal of the United States has been affixed to it by the secretary of state.

Where an officer is removable at the will of the executive, the circumstance which completes his appointment is of no concern; because the act is at any time revocable; and the commission may be arrested, if still in the office. But when the officer is not removable at the will of the executive, the appointment is not revocable, and cannot be annulled: it has conferred legal rights which cannot be resumed. The discretion of the executive is to be exercised, until the appointment has been made. But having once made the appointment, his power over the office is terminated, in all cases where, by law, the officer is not removable by him. The right to the office is then in the person appointed, and he has the absolute unconditional power of accepting or rejecting it.

Mr. Marbury, then, since his commission was signed by the president, and sealed by the secretary of state, was appointed; and as the law creating the office, gave the officer a right to hold for five years, independent of the executive, the appointment was not revocable, but vested in the officer legal rights, which are protected by the laws of his country. To withhold his commission, therefore, is an act deemed by the court not warranted by law, but violative of a vested legal right.

2. This brings us to the second inquiry; which is: If he has a right, and that right has been violated, do the laws of his country afford him a remedy? The very essence of civil liberty certainly consists in the right of every individual to claim the protection of the laws, whenever he receives an injury. One of the first duties of government is to afford that protection. In Great Britain, the king himself is sued in the respectful form of a petition, and he never fails to comply with the judgment of his court. . . .

The government of the United States has been emphatically termed a government of laws, and not of men. It will certainly cease to deserve this high appellation, if the laws furnish no remedy for the violation of a vested legal right. If this obloquy is to be cast on the jurisprudence of our country, it must arise from the peculiar character of the case.

It behooves us, then, to inquire whether there be in its composition any ingredient which shall exempt it from legal investigation, or exclude the injured party from legal redress. In pursuing this inquiry, the first question which presents itself is, whether this can be arranged with that class of cases which come under the description of *damnum absque injuria;* a loss without an injury. This description of cases never has been considered, and it is believed, never can be considered, as comprehending offices of trust, of honor or of profit. The office of justice of peace in the district of Columbia is such an office; it is, therefore, worthy of the attention and guardianship of the laws. It has received that attention and guardianship: it has been created by special act of congress, and has been secured, so far as the laws can give security, to the person appointed to fill it, for five years. It is not, then, on account of the worthlessness of the thing pursued, that the injured party can be alleged to be without remedy.

Is it in the nature of the transaction? Is the act of delivering or withholding a commission to be considered as a mere political act, belonging to the executive department alone, for the performance of which entire confidence is placed by our constitution in the supreme executive; and for any misconduct respecting which, the injured individual has no remedy? That there may be such cases is not to be questioned; but that every act of duty, to be performed in any of the great departments of government, constitutes such a case, is not to be admitted.

By the act concerning invalids, passed in June 1794 (1 U. S. Stat. 392), the secretary at war is ordered to place on the pension list, all persons whose names are contained in a report previously made by him to congress. If he should refuse to do so, would the wounded veteran be without remedy? Is it to be contended, that where the law, in precise terms, directs the performance of an act, in which an individual is interested, the law is incapable of securing obedience to its mandate? Is it on account of the character of the person against whom the complaint is made? Is it to be contended that the heads of departments are not amenable to the laws of their country? Whatever the practice on particular occasions may be, the theory of this principle will certainly never be maintained. No act of the legislature confers so extraordinary a privilege, nor can it derive countenance from the doctrines of the common law. . . .

By the act passed in 1796, authorizing the sale of the lands above the mouth of Kentucky river (1 U. S. Stat. 464), the purchaser, on paying his purchase-money, becomes completely entitled to the property purchased; and on producing to the secretary of state the receipt of the treasurer, upon a certificate required by the law, the president of the United States is authorized to grant him a patent. It is further enacted, that all patents shall be countersigned by the secretary of state, and recorded in his office. If the secretary of state should choose to withhold this patent; or, the patent being lost, should refuse a copy of it; can it be imagined, that the law furnishes to the injured person no remedy? It is not believed, that any person whatever would attempt to maintain such a proposition.

It follows, then, that the question, whether the legality of an act of the head of a department be examinable in a court of justice or not, must always depend on the nature of that act. If some acts be examinable, and others not, there must be some rule of law to guide the court in the exercise of its jurisdiction. In some instances, there may be difficulty in applying the rule to particular cases; but there cannot, it is believed, be much difficulty in laying down the rule.

By the constitution of the United States, the president is invested with certain important political powers, in the exercise of which he is to use his own discretion, and is accountable only to his country in his political character, and to his own conscience. To aid him in the performance of these duties, he is authorized to appoint certain officers, who act by his authority, and in conformity with his orders. In such cases, their acts are his acts; and whatever opinion may be entertained of the manner in which executive discretion may be used, still there exists, and can exist, no power to control that discretion. The subjects are political: they respect the nation, not individual rights, and being entrusted to the executive, the decision of the executive is conclusive. The application of this remark will be perceived, by adverting to the act of congress for establishing the department of foreign affairs. This officer, as his duties were prescribed by that act, is to conform precisely to the will of the president; he is the mere organ by whom that will is communicated. The acts of such an officer, as an officer, can never be examinable by the courts. But when the legislature proceeds to impose on that officer other duties; when he is directed peremptorily to perform certain acts; when the rights of individuals are dependent on the performance of those acts; he is so far the officer of the law; is amenable to the laws for his conduct; and cannot, at his discretion, sport away the vested rights of others.

The conclusion from this reasoning is, that where the heads of departments are the political or confidential agents of the executive, merely to execute the will of the president, or rather to act in cases in which the executive possesses a constitutional or legal discretion, nothing can be more perfectly clear, than that their acts are only politically examinable. But where a specific duty is assigned by law, and individual rights depend upon the performance of that duty, it seems equally clear, that the individual who considers himself injured, has a right to resort to the laws of his country for a remedy.

If this be the rule, let us inquire, how it applies to the case under the consideration of the court. The power of nominating to the senate, and the power of appointing the person nominated, are political powers, to be exercised by the president, according to his own discretion. When he has made an appointment, he has exercised his whole power, and his discretion has been completely applied to the case. If, by law, the officer be removable at the will of the president, then a new appointment may be immediately made, and the rights of the officer are terminated. But as a fact which has existed, cannot be made never to have existed, the appointment cannot be annihilated; and consequently, if the officer is by law not removable at the will of the president, the rights he has acquired are protected by the law, and are not resumable by the president. They cannot be extinguished by executive authority, and he has the privilege of asserting them in like manner, as if they had been derived from any other source.

The question whether a right has vested or not, is, in its

nature, judicial, and must be tried by the judicial authority. If, for example, Mr. Marbury had taken the oaths of a magistrate, and proceeded to act as one; in consequence of which, a suit has been instituted against him, in which his defence had depended on his being a magistrate, the validity of his appointment must have been determined by judicial authority. So, if he conceives that, by virtue of his appointment, he has a legal right either to the commission which has been made out for him, or to a copy of that commission, it is equally a question examinable in a court, and the decision of the court upon it must depend on the opinion entertained of his appointment. That question has been discussed, and the opinion is, that the latest point of time which can be taken as that at which the appointment was complete, and evidenced, was when, after the signature of the president, the seal of the United States was affixed to the commission.

It is, then, the opinion of the Court: 1st. That by signing the commission of Mr. Marbury, the President of the United States appointed him a justice of peace for the county of Washington, in the district of Columbia; and that the seal of the United States, affixed thereto by the secretary of state, is conclusive testimony of the verity of the signature, and of the completion of the appointment; and that the appointment conferred on him a legal right to the office for the space of five years. 2d. That, having this legal title to the office, he has a consequent right to the commission; a refusal to deliver which is a plain violation of that right, for which the laws of his country afford him a remedy.

3. It remains to be inquired whether he is entitled to the remedy for which he applies? This depends on—1st. The nature of the writ applied for; and 2d. The power of this court.

1st. The nature of the writ. Blackstone, in the 3d volume of his Commentaries, page 110, defines a *mandamus* to be "a command issuing in the king's name, from the court of king's bench, and directed to any person, corporation or inferior court of judicature, within the king's dominions, requiring them to do some particular thing therein specified, which appertains to their office and duty, and which the court of king's bench has previously determined, or at least supposes, to be consonant to right and justice."

LORD MANSFIELD, in 3 Burr. 1267, in the case of *The King* v. *Baker et al.*, states, with much precision and explicitness, the cases in which this writ may be used. "Whenever," says that very able judge, "there is a right to execute an office, perform a service, or exercise a franchise (more especially if it be in a matter of public concern, or attended with profit), and a person is kept out of possession, or dispossessed of such right, and has no other specific legal remedy, this court ought to assist by *mandamus*, upon reasons of justice, as the writ expresses, and upon reasons of public policy, to preserve peace, order and good government." In the same case, he says, "this writ ought to be used upon all occasions where the law has established no specific remedy, and where in justice and good government there ought to be one." . . .

This writ, if awarded, would be directed to an officer of government, and its mandate to him would be, to use the words of Blackstone, "to do a particular thing therein specified, which appertains to his office and duty, and which the court has previously determined, or at least supposes, to be consonant to right and justice." Or, in the words of Lord MANSFIELD, the applicant, in this case, has a right to execute an office of public concern, and is kept out of possession of that right. These circumstances certainly concur in this case.

Still, to render the *mandamus* a proper remedy, the officer to whom it is to be directed, must be one to whom, on legal principles, such writ may be directed; and the person applying for it must be without any other specific and legal remedy.

1. With respect to the officer to whom it would be directed. The intimate political relation subsisting between the president of the United States and the heads of departments, necessarily

renders any legal investigation of the acts of one of those high officers peculiarly irksome, as well as delicate; and excites some hesitation with respect to the propriety of entering into such investigation. Impressions are often received, without much reflection or examination, and it is not wonderful, that in such a case as this, the assertion, by an individual, of his legal claims in a court of justice, to which claims it is the duty of that court to attend, should at first view be considered by some, as an attempt to intrude into the cabinet, and to intermeddle with the prerogatives of the executive.

It is scarcely necessary for the court to disclaim all pretensions to such a jurisdiction. An extravagance, so absurd and excessive, could not have been entertained for a moment. The province of the court is, solely, to decide on the rights of individuals, not to inquire how the executive, or executive officers, perform duties in which they have a discretion. Questions in their nature political, or which are, by the constitution and laws, submitted to the executive, can never be made in this court.

But, if this be not such a question; if, so far from being an intrusion into the secrets of the cabinet, it respects a paper which, according to law, is upon record, and to a copy of which the law gives a right, on the payment of ten cents; if it be no intermeddling with a subject over which the executive can be considered as having exercised any control; what is there, in the exalted station of the officer, which shall bar a citizen from asserting, in a court of justice, his legal rights, or shall forbid a court to listen to the claim, or to issue a *mandamus*, directing the performance of a duty, not depending on executive discretion, but on particular acts of congress, and the general principles of law?

If one of the heads of departments commits any illegal act, under color of his office, by which an individual sustains an injury, it cannot be pretended, that his office alone exempts him from being sued in the ordinary mode of proceeding, and being compelled to obey the judgment of the law. How then, can his office exempt him from this particular mode of deciding on the legality of his conduct, if the case be such a case as would, were any other individual the party complained of, authorize the process?

It is not by the office of the person to whom the writ is directed, but the nature of the thing to be done, that the propriety or impropriety of issuing a *mandamus* is to be determined. Where the head of a department acts in a case, in which executive discretion is to be exercised; in which he is the mere organ of executive will; it is again repeated, that any application to a court to control, in any respect, his conduct would be rejected without hesitation. But where he is directed by law to do a certain act, affecting the absolute rights of individuals, in the performance of which he is not placed under the particular direction of the president, and the performance of which the president cannot lawfully forbid, and therefore, is never presumed to have forbidden; as, for example, to record a commission or a patent for land, which has received all the legal solemnities; or to give a copy of such record; in such cases, it is not perceived, on what ground the courts of the country are further excused from the duty of giving judgment that right be done to an injured individual, than if the same services were to be performed by a person not the head of a department. . . .

It is true, that the *mandamus,* now moved for, is not for the performance of an act expressly enjoined by statute. It is to deliver a commission; on which subject, the acts of congress are silent. This difference is not considered as affecting the case. It has already been stated, that the applicant has, to that commission, a vested legal right, of which the executive cannot deprive him. He has been appointed to an office, from which he is not removable at the will of the executive; and being so appointed, he has a right to the commission which the secretary has received from the president for his use. The act of congress does not indeed order the secretary of state to send it to him, but it is placed in his hands for the person entitled to it; and cannot be more lawfully withheld by him, than by any other person. . . .

This, then, is a plain case for a *mandamus,* either to deliver the commission, or a copy of it from the record; and it only remains to be inquired, whether it can issue from this court?

The act to establish the judicial courts of the United States authorizes the supreme court, "to issue writs of *mandamus,* in cases warranted by the principles and usages of law, to any courts appointed or persons holding office, under the authority of the United States." The secretary of state, being a person holding an office under the authority of the United States, is precisely within the letter of this description; and if this court is not authorized to issue a writ of *mandamus* to such an officer it must be because the law is unconstitutional, and therefore, absolutely incapable of conferring the authority, and assigning the duties which its words purport to confer and assign.

The constitution vests the whole judicial power of the United States in one supreme court, and such inferior courts as congress shall, from time to time, ordain and establish. This power is expressly extended to all cases arising under the laws of the United States; and consequently, in some form, may be exercised over the present case; because the right claimed is given by a law of the United States.

In the distribution of this power, it is declared, that "the supreme court shall have original jurisdiction, in all cases affecting ambassadors, other public ministers and consuls, and those in which a state shall be a party. In all other cases, the supreme court shall have appellate jurisdiction." It has been insisted, at the bar, that as the original grant of jurisdiction to the supreme and inferior courts, is general, and the clause, assigning original jurisdiction to the supreme court, contains no negative or restrictive words, the power remains to the legislature, to assign original jurisdiction to that court, in other cases than those specified in the article which has been recited; provided those cases belong to the judicial power of the United States

If it had been intended to leave it in the discretion of the legislature, to apportion the judicial power between the supreme and inferior courts, according to the will of that body, it would certainly have been useless to have proceeded further than to have defined the judicial power, and the tribunals in which it should be vested. The subsequent part of the section is mere surplusage—is entirely without meaning, if such is to be the construction. If congress remains at liberty to give this court appellate jurisdiction, where the constitution has declared their jurisdiction shall be original; and original jurisdiction where the constitution has declared it shall be appellate; the distribution of jurisdiction, made in the constitution, is form without substance. Affirmative words are often, in their operation, negative of other objects than those affirmed; and in this case, a negative or exclusive sense must be given to them, or they have no operation at all.

It cannot be presumed, that any clause in the constitution is intended to be without effect; and therefore, such a construction is inadmissible, unless the words require it. If the solicitude of the convention, respecting our peace with foreign powers, induced a provision that the supreme court should take original jurisdiction in cases which might be supposed to affect them; yet the clause would have proceeded no further than to provide for such cases, if no further restriction on the powers of congress had been intended. That they should have appellate jurisdiction in all other cases, with such exceptions as congress might make, is no restriction; unless the words be deemed exclusive of original jurisdiction.

When an instrument organizing, fundamentally, a judicial system, divides it into one supreme, and so many inferior courts as the legislature may ordain and establish; then enumerates its powers, and proceeds so far to distribute them, as to define the jurisdiction of the supreme court, by declaring the cases in which it shall take original jurisdiction, and that in others it shall take appellate jurisdiction, the plain import of the words seems to be, that in one class of cases, its jurisdiction is original, and not appellate; in the other, it is appellate, and not original. If any other construction would render the clause inoperative, that is an additional reason for rejecting such other construction, and for adhering to their obvious meaning. To enable this court, then, to issue a *mandamus*, it must be shown to be an exercise of appellate jurisdiction, or to be necessary to enable them to exercise appellate jurisdiction.

It has been stated at the bar, that the appellate jurisdiction may be exercised in a variety of forms, and that if it be the will of the legislature that a *mandamus* should be used for that purpose, that will must be obeyed. This is true, yet the jurisdiction must be appellate, not original. It is the essential criterion of appellate jurisdiction, that it revises and corrects the proceedings in a cause already instituted, and does not create that cause. Although, therefore, a *mandamus* may be directed to courts, yet to issue such a writ to an officer, for the delivery of a paper, is, in effect, the same as to sustain an original action for that paper, and therefore, seems not to belong to appellate, but to original jurisdiction. Neither is it necessary in such a case as this, to enable the court to exercise its appellate jurisdiction. The authority, therefore, given to the supreme court by the act establishing the judicial courts of the United States, to issue writs of *mandamus* to public officers, appears not to be warranted by the constitution; and it becomes necessary to inquire, whether a jurisdiction so conferred can be exercised.

The question, whether an act, repugnant to the constitution, can become the law of the land, is a question deeply interesting to the United States; but happily, not of an intricacy proportioned to its interest. It seems only necessary to recognise certain principles, supposed to have been long and well established, to decide it. That the people have an original right to establish, for their future government, such principles as, in their opinion, shall most conduce to their own happiness, is the basis on which the whole American fabric has been erected. The exercise of this original right is a very great exertion; nor can it, nor ought it, to be frequently repeated. The principles, therefore, so established, are deemed fundamental: and as the authority from which they proceed is supreme, and can seldom act, they are designed to be permanent.

This original and supreme will organizes the government, and assigns to different departments their respective powers. It may either stop here, or establish certain limits not to be transcended by those departments. The government of the United States is of the latter description. The powers of the legislature are defined and limited; and that those limits may not be mistaken or forgotten, the constitution is written. To what purpose are powers limited, and to what purpose is that limitation committed to writing, if these limits may, at any time, be passed by those intended to be restrained? The distinction between a government with limited and unlimited powers is abolished, if those limits do not confine the persons on whom they are imposed, and if acts prohibited and acts allowed, are of equal obligation. It is a proposition too plain to be contested, that the constitution controls any legislative act repugnant to it; or that the legislature may alter the constitution by an ordinary act.

Between these alternatives, there is no middle ground. The constitution is either a superior paramount law, unchangeable by ordinary means, or it is on a level with ordinary legislative acts, and, like other acts, is alterable when the legislature shall please to alter it. If the former part of the alternative be true, then a legislative act, contrary to the constitution, is not law: if the latter part be true, then written constitutions are absurd attempts, on the part of the people, to limit a power, in its own nature, illimitable.

Certainly, all those who have framed written constitutions contemplate them as forming the fundamental and paramount law of the nation, and consequently, the theory of every such government must be, that an act of the legislature, repugnant to the constitution, is void. This theory is essentially attached to a written constitution, and is, consequently, to be considered, by this court, as one of the fundamental principles of our society. It is not, therefore, to be lost sight of, in the further consideration of this subject.

If an act of the legislature, repugnant to the constitution, is void, does it, notwithstanding its invalidity, bind the courts, and oblige them to give it effect? Or, in other words, though it be not law, does it constitute a rule as operative as if it was a law? This would be to overthrow, in fact, what was established in theory, and would seem, at first view, an absurdity too gross to be insisted on. It shall, however, receive a more attentive consideration.

It is, emphatically, the province and duty of the judicial department, to say what the law is. Those who apply the rule to particular cases, must of necessity expound and interpret that rule. If two laws conflict with each other, the courts must decide on the operation of each. So, if a law be in opposition to the constitution; if both the law and the constitution apply to a particular case, so that the court must either decide that case, conformable to the law, disregarding the constitution; or conformable to the constitution, disregarding the law; the court must determine which of these conflicting rules governs the case: this is of the very essence of judicial duty. If then, the courts are to regard the constitution, and the constitution is superior to any ordinary act of the legislature, the constitution and not such ordinary act, must govern the case to which they both apply.

Those, then, who controvert the principle, that the constitution is to be considered, in court, as a paramount law, are reduced to the necessity of maintaining that courts must close their eyes on the constitution, and see only the law. This doctrine would subvert the very foundation of all written constitutions. It would declare that an act which, according to the principles and theory of our government, is entirely void, is yet, in practice, completely obligatory. It would declare, that if the legislature shall do what is expressly forbidden, such act, notwithstanding the express prohibition, is in reality effectual. It would be giving to the legislature a practical and real omnipotence, with the same breath which professes to restrict their powers within narrow limits. It is prescribing limits, and declaring that those limits may be passed at pleasure. That it thus reduces to nothing, what we have deemed the greatest improvement on political institutions, a written constitution, would, of itself, be sufficient, in America, where written constitutions have been viewed with so much reverence, for rejecting the construction. But the peculiar expressions of the constitution of the United States furnish additional arguments in favor of its rejection. The judicial power of the United States is extended to all cases arising under the constitution. Could it be the intention of those who gave this power, to say, that in using it, the constitution should not be looked into? That a case arising under the constitution should be decided, without examining the instrument under which it arises? This is too extravagant to be maintained. In some cases, then, the constitution must be looked into by the judges. And if they can open it at all, what part of it are they forbidden to read or to obey?

There are many other parts of the constitution which serve to illustrate this subject. It is declared, that "no tax or duty shall be laid on articles exported from any state." Suppose, a duty on the export of cotton, of tobacco or of flour; and a suit instituted to recover it. Ought judgment to be rendered in such a case? ought the judges to close their eyes on the constitution, and only see the law?

The constitution declares "that no bill of attainder or *ex post facto* law shall be passed." If, however, such a bill should be passed, and a person should be prosecuted under it; must the court condemn to death those victims whom the constitution endeavors to preserve?

"No person," says the constitution, "shall be convicted of treason, unless on the testimony of two witnesses to the same *overt* act, or on confession in open court." Here, the language of the constitution is addressed especially to the courts. It prescribes, directly for them, a rule of evidence not to be departed from. If the legislature should change that rule, and declare one witness, or a confession out of court, sufficient for conviction, must the constitutional principle yield to the legislative act?

From these, and many other selections which might be made, it is apparent, that the framers of the constitution contemplated that instrument as a rule for the government of courts, as well as of the legislature. Why otherwise does it direct the judges to take an oath to support it? This oath certainly applies in an especial manner, to their conduct in their official character. How immoral to impose it on them, if they were to be used as the instruments, and the knowing instruments, for violating what they swear to support!

The oath of office, too, imposed by the legislature, is completely demonstrative of the legislative opinion on this subject. It is in these words: "I do solemnly swear, that I will administer justice, without respect to persons, and do equal right to the poor and to the rich; and that I will faithfully and impartially discharge all the duties incumbent on me as——, according to the best of my abilities and understanding, agreeably to the constitution and laws of the United States." Why does a judge swear to discharge his duties agreeably to the constitution of the United States, if that constitution forms no rule for his government? if it is closed upon him, and cannot be inspected by him? If such be the real state of things, this is worse than solemn mockery. To prescribe, or to take this oath, becomes equally a crime.

It is also not entirely unworthy of observation, that in declaring what shall be the supreme law of the land, the constitution itself is first mentioned; and not the laws of the United States, generally, but those only which shall be made in pursuance of the constitution, have that rank.

Thus, the particular phraseology of the constitution of the United States confirms and strengthens the principle, supposed to be essential to all written constitutions, that a law repugnant to the constitution is void; and that courts, as well as other departments, are bound by that instrument.

The rule must be discharged.

7. Judicial Review Over the States

COHENS v. VIRGINIA (1821)

(6 Wheaton 264)

Marshall took the occasion in the following case to reaffirm the Supreme Court's right to a monopoly in final constitutional interpretation. The specific congressional grant of that monopoly was Section 25 of the Judiciary Act of 1789, which (to oversimplify a bit) authorized the Supreme Court to review any state-court decision challenging the validity of federal authority. Justice Story had already sustained the constitutionality of Section 25 five years earlier over the objections of Virginia in *Martin v. Hunter's Lessee* (1816). But here once again Virginia presented (with some minor embellishments) the same argument, one which Marshall correctly regarded as a foundation for constitutional nihilism. The federal courts, in the Virginian view, had no authority to review the interpretations of constitutional questions reached by the judges of the "sovereign states." Virginia frankly admitted that without one final arbiter several conflicting schools of constitutional interpretation might well emerge, but that such tension was an "irremedial mischief" built into the system. With the recent secessionist rhetoric over the Missouri Compromise still in mind, the Chief Justice adamantly refused to silence the *national* tribunal. Without Section 25, there would be no independent voice to rebut the party line of disunion.

The instant case hardly deserved the pitched battle between the forces of nationalism and states' rights fought in its honor. For the plaintiffs, the Cohen brothers, had committed no more horrendous a crime than selling in Virginia a few tickets for a Washington, D.C., lottery. But the sale violated a Virginia ordinance intended to ban competition with the state's own lotteries. The local Norfolk court indulgently fined the brothers the minimum penalty for this economic crime against the state—$100. Then counsel for the Cohens appealed to the Supreme Court, allegedly to recover the paltry fine although the appeal bore all the signs of a contrived case designed to accomplish far more than the recovery of a trivial $100. To represent the hapless Cohens there appeared a procession of the highest paid lawyers in the country, who pegged the appeal upon a purported conflict between a state law and a Congressional statute, (Congress was ultimately responsible for authorizing the Washington lottery whose operations—it was asserted—had been illicitly checked by the Virginia statute.)

To protect the Cohens' entrepreneurial rights, their counsel urged the supremacy of national statutes and the monopoly control that the Supreme Court had to have in interpreting the constitutional foundations of that supremacy. To protect Virginia's lottery monopoly, counsel for the state insisted upon open competition in constitutional interpretation! Virginia contended that, properly understood, "state sovereignty" barred the Supreme Court from even hearing the case. Thus Marshall had first to establish the jurisdiction of the Supreme Court to call a state before it in a case in which the validity of a congressional statute had possibly been denied. Marshall summoned his resources for the task and the result was literally stunning: even his staunchest admirers were startled by the extent to which he subsumed his conclusions in his premises.

After resolving the jurisdictional controversy in *Cohens v. Virginia* in his favor, Marshall turned to the merits of the case, the concrete issues which had supplied the pretext for his vindication of the Court's authority over the non-sovereign states. (The merits could be reached because Marshall had just casually redefined judicial review to extend to all cases in which "the correct decision depends on the construction of either" the Constitution or a law of the United States.) The Cohens, it should be recalled, had been selling tickets for a lottery authorized by congressional statute; a decision on the merits therefore required a construction of a federal statute. To put it another way, Marshall—having held that Congress *could* protect the Cohens from Virginia—inquired whether this had been the congressional intent.

Marshall, fully cognizant of the barrage that Virginians and likeminded men would launch in retaliation for his assult on the ideological beachhead of states' rights, had no intention of providing the states' rights forces a "cause" to use in rallying forces to rescind Section 25 of the Judiciary Act. If the Court could be accused of subverting the entire structure of the state police power simply to protect a District of Columbia lottery, it would be difficult to mobilize public support in its behalf. But Marshall was far too shrewd to provide his vitriolic antagonist, Spencer Roane, Chief Justice of the Virginia Supreme Court, with such high-powered political explosives.

So Marshall characteristically advanced two steps forward (on the jurisdictional issue) and one step back (on the merits). With spectacular aplomb Marshall found no necessary conflict between the two statutes! The Washington lottery, a careful reading of the statute indicated, was only authorized to operate locally. Virginia had a perfect right, therefore, to fine the Cohens for trying to export a commodity restricted to local consumption. Virginia, in short, had jurisdiction over the brothers Cohen because Congress had permitted this exercise of "state sovereignty." Unfortunately, Roane (who had a poorly developed sense of humor) failed to appreciate this minor classic of statutory construction.

Mr. Chief Justice Marshall delivered the opinion of the court:

This is a writ of error to a judgment rendered in the Court of Hustings for the borough of Norfolk, on an information for selling lottery tickets, contrary to an act of the legislature of Virginia. In the state court, the defendant claimed the protection of an act of Congress. . . .

Judgment was rendered against the defendants; and the court in which it was rendered being the highest court of the state in which the cause was cognizable, the record has been brought into this court by a writ of error.

The defendant in error moves to dismiss this writ, for want of jurisdiction. . . .

1st. The first question to be considered is, whether the jurisdiction of this court is excluded by the character of the parties, one of them being a state, and the other a citizen of that state?

The second section of the third article of the constitution defines the extent of the judicial power of the United States. Jurisdiction is given to the courts of the Union in two classes of cases. In the first, their jurisdiction depends on the character of the cause, whoever may be the parties. This class comprehends "all cases in law and equity arising under this constitution, the laws of the United States, and treaties made, or which shall be made, under their authority." This clause extends the jurisdiction of the court to all the cases described, without making in its terms any exception whatever, and without any regard to the condition of the party. If there be any exception, it is to be implied against the express words of the article.

In the second class, the jurisdiction depends entirely on the character of the parties. In this are comprehended "controversies between two or more states, between a state and citizens of another state," "and between a state and foreign states, citizens or subjects." If these be the parties, it is entirely unimportant what may be the subject of controversy. Be it what it may, these parties have a constitutional right to come into the courts of the Union. . . .

The jurisdiction of the court, then, being extended by the letter of the constitution to all cases arising under it, or under the laws of the United States, it follows that those who would withdraw any case of this description from that jurisdiction, must sustain the exemption they claim on the spirit and true meaning of the constitution, which spirit and true meaning must be so apparent as to overrule the words which its framers have employed.

The counsel for the defendant in error have undertaken to do this; and have laid down the general proposition, that a sovereign independent state is not suable except by its own consent.

This general proposition will not be controverted. But its consent is not requisite in each particular case. It may be given in a general law. And if a state has surrendered any portion of its sovereignty, the question whether a liability to suit be a part of this portion, depends on the instrument by which the surrender is made. If, upon a just construction of that instrument, it shall appear that the state has submitted to be sued, then it has parted with this sovereign right of judging in every case on the justice of its own pretensions, and has entrusted that power to a tribunal in whose impartiality it confides. . . . The general government, though limited as to its objects, is supreme with respect to those objects. This principle is a part of the constitution; and if there be any who deny its necessity, none can deny its authority.

To this supreme government ample powers are confided; and if it were possible to doubt the great purposes for which they were so confided, the people of the United States have declared, that they are given "in order to form a more perfect union, establish justice, ensure domestic tranquility, provide for the common defense, promote the general welfare, and secure the blessings of liberty to themselves and their posterity."

With the ample powers confided to this supreme government, for these interesting purposes, are connected many express and important limitations on the sovereignty of the states, which are made for the same purposes. The powers of the Union, on the great subjects of war, peace, and commerce, and on many others, are in themselves limitations of the sovereignty of the states; but in addition to these, the sovereignty of the states is surrendered in many instances where the surrender can only operate to the benefit of the people, and where, perhaps, no other power is conferred on Congress than a conservative power to maintain the principles established in the constitution. The maintenance of these principles in their purity, is certainly among the great duties of the government. One of the instruments by which this duty may be peaceably performed, is the judicial department. It is authorized to decide all cases of every description, arising under the constitution or laws of the United States. From this general grant of jurisdiction, no exception is made of those cases in which a state may be a party. When we consider the situation of the government of the Union and of a state, in relation to each other; the nature of our constitution; the subordination of the state governments to that constitution; the great purpose for which jurisdiction over all cases arising under the constitution and laws of the United States is confided to the judicial department, are we at liberty to insert in this general grant, an exception of those cases in which a state may be a party? Will the spirit of the constitution justify this attempt to control its words? We think it will not. We think a case arising under the constitution or laws of the United States, is cognizable in the courts of the Union, whoever may be the parties to that case.

Had any doubt existed with respect to the just construction of this part of the section, that doubt would have been removed by the enumeration of those cases to which the jurisdiction of the federal courts is extended, in consequence of the character of the parties. In that enumeration, we find, "controversies between two or more states, between a state and citizen of another state," "and between a state and foreign states, citizens, or subjects." . . . The constitution gave to every person having a claim upon a state, a right to submit his case to the court of the nation. However unimportant his claim might be, however little the community might be interested in its decision, the framers of our constitution thought it necessary, for the purposes of justice, to provide a tribunal as superior to influence as possible, in which that claim might be decided. Can it be imagined, that the same persons considered a case involving the constitution of our country and the majesty of the laws—questions in which every American citizen must be deeply interested—as withdrawn from this tribunal, because a state is a party? . . .

The mischievous consequences of the construction contended for on the part of Virginia, are also entitled to great consideration. It would prostrate, it has been said, the government and its laws at the feet of every state in the Union. And would not this be its effect? What power of the government could be executed by its own means, in any state disposed to resist its execution by a course of legislation? The laws must be executed by individuals acting within the several states. If these individuals may be exposed to penalties, and if the courts of the Union cannot correct the judgments by which these penalties may be enforced, the course of the government may be, at any time, arrested by the will of one of its members. Each member will possess a veto on the will of the whole.

The answer which has been given to this argument, does not deny its truth, but insists that confidence is reposed, and may be safely reposed, in the state institutions; and that, if they shall ever become so insane or so wicked as to seek the destruction of the government, they may accomplish their object by refusing to perform the functions assigned to them. . . . The framers of the constitution were, indeed, unable to make any provisions which should protect that instrument against a general combination of the states, or of the people, for its destruction; and, conscious of this inability, they have not made the attempt. But they were able to provide against the operation of measures adopted in any one state, whose tendency might be to arrest the execution of the laws, and this it was the part of true wisdom to attempt. We think they have attempted it.

It has been also urged, as an additional objection to the jurisdiction of the court, that cases between a state and one of its own citizens, do not come within the general scope of the constitution; and were obviously never intended to be made cognizable in the federal courts. . . . If the constitution or laws may be violated by proceedings instituted by a state against its own citizens, and if that violation may be such as essentially to affect the constitution and the laws, such as to arrest the progress of government in its constitutional course, why should these cases, be excepted from that provision which expressly extends the judicial power of the Union to all cases arising under the constitution and laws?

After bestowing on this subject the most attentive consideration, the court can perceive no reason founded on the character of the parties for introducing an exception which the constitution has not made; and we think that the judicial power, as originally given, extends to all cases arising under the constitution or a law of the United States, whoever may be the parties.

It has been also contended, that this jurisdiction, if given, is original, and cannot be exercised in the appellate form.

The words of the constitution are, "in all cases affecting ambassadors, other public ministers, and consuls, and those in which a state shall be a party, the Supreme Court shall have original jurisdiction. In all the other cases before mentioned, the Supreme Court shall have appellate jurisdiction."

This distinction between original and appellate jurisdiction, excludes, we are told, in all cases, the exercise of the one where the other is given.

The constitution gives the Supreme Court original jurisdiction in certain enumerated cases, and gives it appellate jurisdiction in all others.

Among those in which jurisdiction must be exercised in the

appellate form, are cases arising under the constitution and laws of the United States. These provisions of the constitution are equally obligatory, and are to be equally respected. If a state be a party, the jurisdiction of this court is original; if the case arise under a constitution or a law, the jurisdiction is appellate. But a case to which a state is a party may arise under the constitution or a law of the United States. What rule is applicable to such a case? What, then, becomes the duty of the court? Certainly, we think, so to construe the constitution as to give effect to both provisions, as far as it is possible to reconcile them, and not to permit their seeming repugnancy to destroy each other. We must endeavor so to construe them as to preserve the true intent and meaning of the instrument. . . .

The constitution declares, that in cases where a state is a party, the Supreme Court shall have original jurisdiction; but does not say that its appellate jurisdiction shall not be exercised in cases where, from their nature, appellate jurisdiction is given, whether a state be or be not a party. It may be conceded, that where the case is of such a nature as to admit of its originating in the Supreme Court, it ought to originate there; but where, from its nature, it cannot originate in that court, these words ought not to be so construed as to require it. There are many cases in which it would be found extremely difficult, and subversive of the spirit of the constitution, to maintain the construction, that appellate jurisdiction cannot be exercised where one of the parties might sue or be sued in this court.

The constitution defines the jurisdiction of the Supreme Court, but does not define that of the inferior courts. Can it be affirmed, that a state might not sue the citizen of another state in a circuit court? Should the Circuit Court decide for or against its jurisdiction, should it dismiss the suit, or give judgment against the state, might not its decision be revised in the Supreme Court? The argument is, that it could not; and the very clause which is urged to prove that the Circuit Court could give no judgment in the case, is also urged to prove that its judgment is irreversible. A supervising court, whose peculiar province it is to correct the errors of an inferior court, has no power to correct a judgment given without jurisdiction, because, in the same case, that supervising court has original jurisdiction. Had negative words been employed, it would be difficult to give them this construction if they would admit of any other. But, without negative words, this irrational construction can never be maintained. . . . [Thus,] the original jurisdiction of the Supreme Court, in cases where a state is a party, refers to those cases in which, according to the grant of power made in the preceding clause, jurisdiction might be exercised in consequence of the character of the party, and an original suit might be instituted in any of the federal courts; not to those cases in which an original suit might not be instituted in a federal court. Of the last description, is every case between a state and its citizens, and, perhaps, every case in which a state is enforcing its penal laws. In such cases, therefore, the Supreme Court cannot take original jurisdiction. In every other case, that is, in every case to which the judicial power extends, and in which original jurisdiction is not expressly given, that judicial power shall be exercised in the appellate, and only in the appellate form. The original jurisdiction of this court cannot be enlarged, but its appellate jurisdiction may be exercised in every case cognizable under the third article of the constitution, in the federal courts, in which original jurisdiction cannot be exercised; and the extent of this judicial power is to be measured, not by giving the affirmative words of the distributive clause a negative operation in every possible case, but by giving their true meaning to the words which define its extent. . . .

We think, then, that, as the constitution originally stood, the appellate jurisdiction of this court, in all cases arising under the constitution, laws, or treaties of the United States, was not arrested by the circumstance that a state was a party.

This leads to a consideration of the 11th amendment.

It is in these words: "The judicial power of the United States shall not be construed to extend to any suit in law or equity commenced or prosecuted against one of the United States, by citizens of another state, or by citizens or subjects of any foreign state."

It is a part of our history, that, at the adoption of the constitution, all the states were greatly indebted; and the apprehension that these debts might be prosecuted in the federal courts, formed a very serious objection to that instrument. Suits were instituted; and the court maintained its jurisdiction. The alarm was general; and, to quiet the apprehensions that were so extensively entertained, this amendment was proposed in Congress, and adopted by the state legislatures. That its motive was not to maintain the sovereignty of a state from the degradation supposed to attend a compulsory appearance before the tribunal of the nation, may be inferred from the terms of the amendment. It does not comprehend controversies between two or more states, or between a state and a foreign state. The jurisdiction of the court still extends to these cases; and in these a state may still be sued. We must ascribe the amendment, then, to some other cause than the dignity of a state. There is no difficulty in finding this cause. Those who were inhibited from commencing a suit against a state, or from prosecuting one which might be commenced before the adoption of the amendment, were persons who might probably be its creditors. There was not much reason to fear that foreign or sister states would be creditors to any considerable amount, and there was reason to retain the jurisdiction of the court in those cases, because it might be essential to the preservation of peace. The amendment, therefore, extended to suits commenced or prosecuted by individuals, but not to those brought by states.

The first impression made on the mind by this amendment is, that it was intended for those cases, and for those only, in which some demand against a state is made by an individual in the courts of the Union. If we consider the causes to which it is to be traced, we are conducted to the same conclusion. A general interest might well be felt in leaving to a state the full power of consulting its convenience in the adjustment of its debts, or of other claims upon it; but no interest could be felt in so changing the relations between the whole and its parts, as to strip the government of the means of protecting, by the instrumentality of its courts, the constitution and laws from active violation. . . .

Under the judiciary act, the effect of a writ of error is simply to bring the record into court, and submit the judgment of the inferior tribunal to re-examination. It does not in any manner act upon the parties; it acts only on the record. It removes the record into the supervising tribunal. Where, then, a state obtains a judgment against an individual, and the court, rendering such judgment, overrules a defense set up under the constitution or laws of the United States, the transfer of this record into the Supreme Court, for the sole purpose of inquiring whether the judgment violates the constitution or laws of the United States, can with no propriety, we think, be denominated a suit commenced or prosecuted against the state whose judgment is so far re-examined. Nothing is demanded from the state. No claim against it of any description is asserted or prosecuted. The party is not to be restored to the possession of anything. Essentially, it is an appeal on a single point; and the defendant who appeals from a judgment rendered against him, is never said to commence or prosecute a suit against the plaintiff who has obtained the judgment. The writ of error is given rather than an appeal, because it is the more usual mode of removing suits at common law; and because, perhaps, it is more technically proper where a single point of law, and not the whole case, is to be re-examined. But an appeal might be given, and might be so regulated as to effect every purpose of a writ of error. The mode of removal is form, and not substance. Whether it be by writ of error or appeal, no claim is asserted, no demand is made by the original defendant; he only asserts the constitutional right to have his defense examined by that tribunal whose province it is to construe the constitution and laws of the Union. . . .

It is, then, the opinion of the court, that the defendant who removes a judgment rendered against him by a state court into this court, for the purpose of re-examining the question, whether that judgment be in violation of the constitution or laws of the United States, does not commence or prosecute a suit against the state, whatever may be its opinion where the effect of the writ may be to restore the party to the possession of a thing which he demands.

But should we in this be mistaken, the error does not affect the case now before the court. If this writ of error be a suit in the sense of the 11th amendment, it is not a suit commenced or prosecuted "by a citizen of another state, or by a citizen or subject of any foreign state." It is not, then, within the amendment, but is governed entirely by the constitution as originally framed, and we have already seen, that in its origin, the judicial power was extended to all cases arising under the constitution or laws of the United States, without respect to parties.

2d. The second objection to the jurisdiction of the court is, that its appellate power cannot be exercised, in any case, over the judgment of a state court.

This objection is sustained chiefly by arguments drawn from the supposed total separation of the judiciary of a state from that of the Union, and their entire independence of each other. The argument considers the federal judiciary as completely foreign to that of a state; and as being no more connected with it, in any respect whatever, than the court of a foreign state. . . .

To this argument, in all its forms, the same answer may be given. Let the nature and objects of our Union be considered; let the great fundamental principles, on which the fabric stands, be examined; and we think the result must be, that there is nothing so extravagantly absurd in giving to the court of the nation the power of revising the decisions of local tribunals on questions which affect the natiòn, as to require that words which import this power should be restricted by a forced construction. The question, then, must depend on the words themselves; and on their construction we shall be the more readily excused for not adding to the observations already made, because the subject was fully discussed and exhausted in the case of *Martin* v. *Hunter.*

3d. We come now to the third objection, which, though differently stated by the counsel, is substantially the same. One gentleman has said that the judiciary act does not give jurisdiction in the case.

The cause was argued in the state court, on a case agreed by the parties, which states the prosecution under a law for selling lottery tickets, which is set forth, and further states, the act of Congress by which the city of Washington was authorized to establish the lottery. It then states that the lottery was regularly established by virtue of the act, and concludes with referring to the court the questions, whether the act of Congress be valid? whether on its just construction, it constitutes a bar to the prosecution? and, whether the act of Assembly, on which the prosecution is founded, be not itself invalid? These questions were decided against the operation of the act of Congress, and in favor of the operation of the act of the state.

If the 25th section of the judiciary act be inspected, it will at once be perceived that it comprehends expressly the case under consideration.

But it is not upon the letter of the act that the gentleman who stated this point in this form, founds his argument. Both gentlemen concur substantially in their views of this part of the case. They deny that the act of Congress on which the plaintiff in error relies, is a law of the United States; or, if a law of the United States, is within the second clause of the sixth article.

In the enumeration of the powers of Congress, which is made in the 8th section of the first article, we find that of exercising exclusive legislation over such district as shall become the seat of government. This power, like all others which are specified, is conferred on Congress as the legislature of the Union; for, strip them of that character, and they would not possess it. In no other character can it be exercised. In legislating for the district, they necessarily preserve the character of the legislature of the Union; for, it is in that character alone that the constitution confers on them this power of exclusive legislation. This proposition need not be enforced.

The 2d clause of the 6th article declares, that "this constitution, and the laws of the United States, which shall be made in pursuance thereof, shall be the supreme law of the land."

The clause which gives exclusive jurisdiction is, unquestionably, a part of the constitution, and, as such, binds all the United States. Those who contend that acts of Congress, made in pursuance of this power, do not, like acts made in pursuance of other powers, bind the nation, ought to show some safe and clear rule which shall support this construction, and prove that an act of Congress, clothed in all the forms which attend other legislative acts, and passed in virtue of a power conferred on, and exercised by Congress, as the legislature of the Union, is not a law of the United States, and does not bind them. . . . [Counsel argued] that Congress, when legislating for the district, assumed a distinct character, and was reduced to a mere local legislature, whose laws could possess no obligation out of the ten miles square. . . .

[Marshall argued by way of counter-example that Congressional power over felonies committed in federal military installations might well extend outside the installations if the felon fled onto non-federal property, etc.]

Congress is not a local legislature, but exercises this particular power, like all its other powers, in its high character, as the legislature of the Union. The American people thought it a necessary power, and they conferred it for their own benefit.

Being so conferred, it carries with it all those incidental powers which are necessary to its complete and effectual execution.

Whether any particular law be designed to operate without the district or not, depends on the words of that law. If it be designed so to operate, then the question, whether the power so exercised be incidental to the power of exclusive legislation, and be warranted by the constitution, requires a consideration of that instrument. In such cases the constitution and the law must be compared and construed. This is the exercise of jurisdiction. It is the only exercise of it which is allowed in such a case. For the act of Congress directs, that "no other error shall be assigned or regarded as a ground of reversal, in any such case as aforesaid, than such as appears on the face of the record, and immediately respects the beforementioned questions of validity or construction of the said constitution, treaties," &c.

The whole merits of this case, then, consist in the construction of the constitution and the act of Congress. The jurisdiction of the court, if acknowledged, goes no further. This we are required to do without the exercise of jurisdiction.

The counsel for the state of Virginia have, in support of this motion, urged many arguments of great weight against the application of the act of Congress to such a case as this; but those arguments go to the construction of the constitution, or of the law, or of both; and seem, therefore, rather calculated to sustain their cause upon its merits, than to prove a failure of jurisdiction in the court.

After having bestowed upon this question the most deliberate consideration of which we are capable, the court is unanimously of opinion, that the objections to its jurisdiction are not sustained, and that the motion ought to be overruled.

The opinion of the court [on the merits] was delivered by *Mr. Chief Justice Marshall:*

This case was stated in the opinion given on the motion for

dismissing the writ of error for want of jurisdiction in the court. It now comes on to be decided on the question whether the Borough Court of Norfolk, in overruling the defense set up under the act of Congress, has misconstrued that act. It is in these words:

"The said corporation shall have full power to authorize the drawing of lotteries for effecting any important improvement in the city, which the ordinary funds or revenue thereof will not accomplish. Provided, that the sum to be raised in each year shall not exceed the amount of $10,000. And provided, also, that the object for which the money is intended to be raised shall be first submitted to the President of the United States, and shall be approved of by him."

Two questions arise on this act:

1st. Does it purport to authorize the corporation to force the sale of these lottery tickets in states where such sales may be prohibited by law? If it does.

2d. Is the law constitutional?

If the first question be answered in the affirmative, it will become necessary to consider the second. If it should be answered in the negative, it will be unnecessary, and consequently improper, to pursue any inquiries, which would then be merely speculative, respecting the power of Congress in the case.

In inquiring into the extent of the power granted to the corporation of Washington, we must first examine the words of the grant. We find in them no expression which looks beyond the limits of the city. The powers granted are all of them local in their nature, and all of them such as would, in the common course of things, if not necessarily, be exercised within the city. The subject on which Congress was employed when framing this act was a local subject; it was not the establishment of a lottery, but the formation of a separate body for the management of the internal affairs of the city, for its internal government, for its police. Congress must have considered itself as delegating to this corporate body powers for these objects, and for these objects solely. In delegating these powers, therefore, it seems reasonable to suppose that the mind of the legislature was directed to the city alone, to the action of the being they were creating within the city, and not to any extraterritorial operations. In describing the powers of such a being, no words of limitation need be used. They are limited by the subject. But, if it be intended to give its acts a binding efficacy beyond the natural limits of its power, and within the jurisdiction of a distinct power, we should expect to find, in the language of the incorporating act, some words indicating such intention.

Without such words, we cannot suppose that Congress designed to give to the acts of the corporation any other effect, beyond its limits, than attends every act having the sanction of local law, when anything depends upon it which is to be transacted elsewhere.

If this would be the reasonable construction of corporate powers generally, it is more especially proper in a case where an attempt is made so to exercise those powers as to control and limit the penal laws of a state. This is an operation which was not, we think, in the contemplation of the legislature, while incorporating the city of Washington.

To interfere with the penal laws of a state, where they are not leveled against the legitimate powers of the Union, but have for their sole object, the internal government of the country, is a very serious measure, which Congress cannot be supposed to adopt lightly, or inconsiderately. The motives for it must be serious and weighty. It would be taken deliberately, and the intention would be clearly and unequivocally expressed.

An act, such as that under consideration, ought not, we think, to be so construed as to imply this intention, unless its provisions were such as to render the construction inevitable.

We do not think it essential to the corporate power in question, that it should be exercised out of the city. Could the lottery be drawn in any state of the Union? Does the corporate power to authorize the drawing of a lottery imply a power to authorize its being drawn without the jurisdiction of a corporation, in a place where it may be prohibited by law? This, we think, would scarcely be asserted. And what clear legal distinction can be taken between a power to draw a lottery in a place where it is prohibited by law and a power to establish an office for the sale of tickets in a place where it is prohibited by law? It may be urged, that the place where the lottery is drawn is of no importance to the corporation, and therefore the act need not be so construed as to give power over the place, but that the right to sell tickets throughout the United States is of importance, and therefore ought to be implied.

That the power to sell tickets in every part of the United States might facilitate their sale, is not to be denied; but it does not follow that Congress designed, for the purpose of giving this increased facility, to overrule the penal laws of the several states. In the city of Washington, the great metropolis of the nation, visited by individuals from every part of the Union, tickets may be freely sold to all who are willing to purchase. Can it be affirmed that this is so limited a market that the incorporating act must be extended beyond its words, and made to conflict with the internal police of the states, unless it be construed to give a more extensive market?

It has been said that the states cannot make it unlawful to buy that which Congress has made it lawful to sell.

This proposition is not denied; and, therefore, the validity of a law punishing a citizen of Virginia for purchasing a ticket in the city of Washington might well be drawn into question. Such a law would be a direct attempt to counteract and defeat a measure authorized by the United States. But a law to punish the sale of lottery tickets in Virginia, is of a different character. Before we can impeach its validity, we must inquire whether Congress intended to empower this corporation to do any act within a state which the laws of that state might prohibit.

In addition to the very important circumstance, that the act contains no words indicating such intention, and that this extensive construction is not essential to the execution of the corporate power, the court cannot resist the conviction, that the intention ascribed to this act, had it existed, would have been executed by very different means from those which have been employed.

Had Congress intended to establish a lottery for those improvements in the city which are deemed national, the lottery itself would have become the subject of legislative consideration. It would be organized by law, and agents for its execution would be appointed by the President, or in such other manner as the law might direct. If such agents were to act out of the district, there would be, probably, some provision made for such a state of things, and in making such provisions Congress would examine its power to make them. The whole subject would be under the control of the government, or of persons appointed by the government.

But in this case no lottery is established by law, no control is exercised by the government over any which may be established. The lottery emanates from a corporate power. The corporation may authorize, or not authorize it, and may select the purposes to which the proceeds are to be applied. This corporation is a being intended for local objects only. All its capacities are limited to the city. This, as well as every other law it is capable of making, is a by-law, and, from its nature, is only co-extensive with the city. It is not probable that such an agent would be employed in the execution of a lottery established by Congress; but when it acts, not as the agent for carrying into effect a lottery established by Congress, but in its own corporate capacity, from its own corporate powers, it is reasonable to suppose that its acts were intended to partake of the nature of that capacity and of those powers; and, like all its other acts, be merely local in its nature.

The proceeds of these lotteries are to come in aid of the revenues of the city. These revenues are raised by laws whose operation is entirely local, and for objects which are also local; for no person will suppose, that the President's house, the Capitol, the Navy Yard, or other public institution, was to be benefited by these lotteries, or was to form a charge on the city revenue. Coming in aid of the city revenue, they are of the same character with it; the mere creature of a corporate power.

The circumstances, that the lottery cannot be drawn without the permission of the President, and that this resource is to be used only for important improvements, have been relied on as giving to this corporate power a more extensive operation than is given to those with which it is associated. We do not think so.

The President has no agency in the lottery. It does not originate with him, nor is the improvement to which its profits are to be applied to be selected by him. Congress has not enlarged the corporate power by restricting its exercise to cases of which the President might approve.

We very readily admit, that the act establishing the seat of government, and the act appointing commissioners to superintend the public buildings, are laws of universal obligation. We admit, too, that the laws of any state to defeat the loan authorized by Congress, would have been void, as would have been any attempt to arrest the progress of the canal, or of any other measure which Congress may adopt. These, and all other laws relative to the district, have the authority which may be claimed by other acts of the national legislature; but their extent is to be determined by those rules of construction which are applicable to all laws. The act incorporating the city of Washington is, unquestionably, of universal obligation; but the extent of the corporate powers conferred by that act, is to be determined by those considerations which belong to the case.

Whether we consider the general character of a law incorporating a city, the objects for which such law is usually made, or the words in which this particular power is conferred, we arrive at the same result. The corporation was merely empowered to authorize the drawing of lotteries; and the mind of Congress was not directed to any provision for the sale of the tickets beyond the limits of the corporation. That subject does not seem to have been taken into view. It is the unanimous opinion of the court, that the law cannot be construed to embrace it.

Judgment affirmed.

8. *Diversity Jurisdiction: The District of Columbia*

HEPBURN v. ELLZEY (1804)

(2 Cranch 445)

Residence in the District of Columbia conferred only the chance to observe Washington politics, not access to the federal courts. In the following case Marshall informed District residents that unless Congress corrected their anomalous legal status—that of stateless United States citizens—they could not bring diversity suits in the federal courts, *i.e.*, they could not initiate action under that section of Article III of the Constitution which confers jurisdiction upon federal courts in lawsuits between citizens of different states. Marshall's ruling that the District is not a state is still law today. Congress finally in 1940 got around to granting District residents access to the federal courts in diversity jurisdiction, but Marshall's rule that the District is not a state was not challenged by a majority of the Supreme Court when in 1949 the 1940 statute was sustained. A majority of the justices simply sustained the statute without agreeing on the reasons for its constitutionality.

Marshall, Ch. J., delivered the opinion of the Court.

The question in this case is, whether the plaintiffs, as residents of the District of Columbia, can maintain an action in the circuit court of the United States for the district of Virginia.

This depends on the act of Congress describing the jurisdiction of that court. That act gives jurisdiction to the circuit courts in cases between a citizen of the state in which the suit is brought, and a citizen of another state. To support the jurisdiction in this case, therefore, it must appear that Columbia is a state.

On the part of the plaintiffs it has been urged that Columbia is a distinct political society; and is, therefore, "a state" according to the definitions of writers on general law.

This is true. But as the act of Congress obviously uses the word "state" in reference to that term as used in the constitution, it becomes necessary to inquire whether Columbia is a state in the sense of that instrument. The result of that examination is a conviction that the members of the American confederacy only are the states contemplated in the constitution. . . .

[T]he word state is used in the constitution as designating a member of the union, and excludes from the term the signification attached to it by writers on the law of nations. When the same term which has been used plainly in this limited sense in the articles respecting the legislative and executive departments, is also employed in that which respects the judicial department, it must be understood as retaining the sense originally given to it. . . .

It is true that as citizens of the United States, and of that particular district which is subject to the jurisdiction of Congress, it is extraordinary that the courts of the United States, which are open to aliens, and to the citizens of every state in the union, should be closed upon them. But this is a subject for legislative, not for judicial consideration.

The opinion to be certified to the circuit court is, that that court has no jurisdiction in the case.

9. *Diversity Jurisdiction: The Territories*

NEW ORLEANS v. WINTER (1816)

(1 Wheaton 91)

Residents of the territories fell into the same category as the residents of the District of Columbia: there was no access to the federal courts in diversity jurisdiction. Marshall maintained that territories lacked the defining characteristics of states.

Marshall, Ch. J., delivered the opinion of the court, and, after stating the facts, proceeded as follows:

The proceedings of the court, therefore, is arrested *in limine,* by a question respecting its jurisdiction. In the case of *Hepburn & Dundas* v. *Ellzey,* this court determined, on mature consideration, that a citizen of the District of Columbia could not maintain a suit in the Circuit Court of the United States. That opinion is still retained.

It has been attempted to distinguish a territory from the District of Columbia; but the court is of opinion that this distinction cannot be maintained. They may differ in many respects, but neither of them is a state, in the sense in which that term is used in the constitution. Every reason assigned for the opinion of the court, that a citizen of Columbia was not capable of suing in the courts of the United States, under the judiciary act, is equally applicable to a citizen of a territory. Gabriel Winter then, being a citizen of the Mississippi territory, was incapable of maintaining a suit alone in the Circuit Court of Louisiana. Is his case mended by being associated with others who are capable of suing in that court? In the case of *Strawbridge et al.* v. *Curtis et al.* it was decided that where a joint interest is prosecuted, the jurisdiction cannot be sustained, unless each individual be entitled to claim that jurisdiction. In this case it has been doubted whether the parties might elect to sue jointly or severally. However this may be, having elected to sue jointly, the court is incapable of distinguishing their case, so far as respects jurisdiction, from one in which they were compelled to unite. The Circuit Court of Louisiana, therefore, had no jurisdiction of the cause, and their judgment must, on that account, be reversed, and the petition dismissed.

Judgment reversed.

10. *Diversity Jurisdiction: Corporations*

BANK OF THE UNITED STATES
v. DEVEAUX (1809)

(5 Cranch 61)

In the following opinion Marshall disallowed the contention that the Bank of the United States, a corporation chartered by Congress, had the right to sue in the federal courts. According to Marshall, the Judiciary Act conferred jurisdiction on the circuit courts only for "controversies between citizens of different states." Since a corporation per se was not a citizen in the conventional sense, it had no diversity access to the federal courts. Thus, corporations could sue and be sued only in state courts. The bank, however, preferred the more hospitable atmosphere in federal courtrooms; the states had from the outset demonstrated their antagonism to the fiscal offspring of Hamilton's "Leviathan." In fact, this case arose as a test of the constitutionality of a Georgia statute taxing the branches of the bank; the suit was against the sheriff who had collected the tax. Marshall was not ready to take this particular test and, in effect, postponed the day of constitutional reckoning until an analogous situation reappeared before the court ten years later. (See *McCulloch v. Maryland* on following pages.)

But Marshall proceeded to circumvent the barricades he had just built. First, he noted that the bank could be admitted to the federal courts only if Congress explicitly conferred that right. (Congress took the hint when rechartering the bank, and this explicit enlargement of federal jurisdiction was then sustained by Marshall in *Osborn v. Bank.*) Second, a corporation could institute action in the federal courts through a narrow side door if the *members* of the corporation had the right credentials. Members of a corporation could sue "in their corporate character, by their corporate name, for a corporate right" *provided* that they were all citizens of the same state. Did not this concession by Marshall undermine the logic he had employed to chase away the "metaphysicians" of the bank? The answer depended upon the utility of the concession. As corporations grew in size and in number, they could easily draw stockholders from every state in the Union. In the light of Marshall's ruling, this heterogeneity meant that the normal corporation lacked the proper credentials for access to the federal courts.

Indeed, for thirty-five years the federal courts were virtually barred from hearing diversity suits involving corporations (except, of course, those involving the Bank of the United States or its branches, for which a special congressional provision was made) until Marshall's ruling—that corporations per se are not "citizens"— was overruled in *Louisville, Cincinnati, and Charleston R.R. v. Letson* (1844).

Marshall, Ch. J., delivered the opinion of the court as follows: . . .

The jurisdiction of this court being limited, so far as respects the character of the parties in this particular case, "to controversies between citizens of different states," both parties must be citizens, to come within the description.

That invisible, intangible, and artificial being, that mere

legal entity, a corporation aggregate, is certainly not a citizen; and, consequently, cannot sue or be sued in the courts of the United States, unless the rights of the members, in this respect, can be exercised in their corporate name. If the corporation be considered as a mere faculty, and not as a company of individuals, who, in transacting their joint concerns, may use a legal name, they must be excluded from the courts of the Union. . . .

Aliens, or citizens of different states . . . can [not] be supposed to be less the objects of constitutional provision, because they are allowed to sue by a corporate name. That name, indeed, cannot be an alien or a citizen; but the persons whom it represents may be the one or the other; and the controversy is, in fact and in law, between those persons suing in their corporate character, by their corporate name, for a corporate right, and the individual against whom the suit may be instituted. Substantially and essentially, the parties in such a case, where the members of the corporation are aliens, or citizens of a different state from the opposite party, come within the spirit and terms of the jurisdiction conferred by the constitution on the national tribunals.

Such has been the universal understanding on the subject. Repeatedly has this court decided causes between a corporation and an individual without feeling a doubt respecting its jurisdiction. Those decisions are not cited as authority; for they were made without considering this particular point; but they have much weight, as they show that this point neither occurred to the bar or the bench; and that the common understanding of intelligent men is in favor of the right of incorporated aliens, or citizens of a different state from the defendant, to sue in the national courts. It is by a course of acute metaphysical and abtruse reasoning, which has been most ably employed on this occasion, that this opinion is shaken. . . .

If, then, the Congress of the United States had, in terms, enacted that incorporated aliens might sue a citizen, or that the incorporated citizens of one state might sue a citizen of another state, in the federal courts, by its corporate name, this court would not have felt itself justified in declaring that such a law transcended the constitution. . . .

If the constitution would authorize Congress to give the courts of the Union jurisdiction in this case, in consequence of the character of the members of the corporation, then the judicial act ought to be construed to give it. For the term citizen ought to be understood as it is used in the constitution, and as it is used in other laws. That is, to describe the real persons who come into court, in this case, under their corporate name. . . .

If a corporation may sue in the courts of the Union, the court is of opinion that the averment in this case is sufficient.

Being authorized to sue in their corporate name, they could make the averment, and it must apply to the plaintiffs as individuals, because it could not be true as applied to the corporation.

Part Three

CONTRACTS
AND STATE AUTHORITY

11. *Land Grants Are Charters*

FLETCHER v. PECK (1810)
(6 Cranch 87)

This opinion is significant in constitutional history both for its interpretation of the contract clause and for the precedent-making invalidation of a state statute. The origins of the case were as eccentric as the law it proclaimed. It began in 1795 when Georgia sold the western part of her territory—presently Alabama and Mississippi—for less than a penny and a half an acre, a sale to four companies of land speculators which was not exactly above board even by the lax standards of that day. A substantial number of the legislators were promised shares in the land companies as a reward for favorable votes. The citizenry became enraged at so much corruption (particularly at so low a price) and at the next election threw out the rascals. The new legislature promptly rescinded the grant as fraudulently obtained, although it should be added there were no criminal indictments of those involved. In a ceremony on the capitol stairs, the leader of the campaign for repeal burned all the records of the grant; the latter was declared utterly void.

A further ironic element was provided by the fact that Georgia had no right to sell much of the land in the first place: it was Indian land protected by federal treaties! In order to avoid trouble with the Indians, Congress in 1803 convinced Georgia to cede her claim to the western territory to the federal government. As partial payment for the cession, Congress agreed to set aside five million acres to cover claims against the state. A commission, composed of Jefferson's Cabinet, suggested in a report to Congress that the reserved lands be sold with the proceeds to be distributed to innocent purchasers, victimized by the land companies. A group of New Englanders who had bought an interest in the four original, now propertyless, speculating companies formed a lobby to persuade Congress to adopt the policy recommendations in the report.

But Congressman John Randolph, fulminating against President Jefferson at length, blocked action on the report for several years. Besides being unwilling to sanction the original corruption of the Georgia legislature, Randolph was incensed at one point that the Postmaster-General was dispensing patronage on the floor of Congress to those who would favor the report. (Gideon Granger, the Postmaster-General, was moonlighting as chief lobbyist for the New England speculators.) Blocked in Congress, the lobby designed an ingenious test case between two "innocent purchasers" to challenge the validity of the Georgian rescinding act. The most distinguished constitutional lawyers in the nation (including Joseph Story—appointed Associate Justice in 1811—and John Quincy Adams) appeared in the case, a fact which Justice William Johnson noted in his partial dissent in the following touching tribute: "It appeared to me to be strong evidence, upon the face of it, of being a mere feigned case. . . . My confidence, however, in the respectable gentlemen who have been engaged for the parties, has induced me to abandon my scruples, in the belief that they would never consent to impose a mere feigned case upon this Court."

Marshall held that the Georgia legislature's rescinding act was null and void as an unconstitutional violation of the contract clause. He refused to recognize the relevance of the corruption of the Georgia legislature on two grounds: (1) it would be imprudent for the Court to investigate the motives of legislators, and (2) if corruption were admitted as justifiable cause for rescinding the grant, innocent purchasers would suffer. Marshall evidently thought little of the maxim: "let the buyer beware," perhaps because of his own experience in land speculation. The Chief Justice clearly abandoned the common law tradition at this juncture, for fraud was long recognized as a ground for annulment of contracts. But he was not through with revising common law; he further asserted that a land grant by a legislature was a contract, albeit a rather unusual one.

There is no evidence to support the proposition that the Founders had intended to subsume land grants under the contract clause. In fact, Marshall appears to have been less than certain about the relevance of the contract clause. He obviously wanted to nullify the rescinding act, but he was not sure that his reading of the contract clause was sufficient. So he invoked the principles of natural law for cosmic reinforcement. Thus, at the end of his rhetorical journey he held that the Georgia rescinding act was void *either* for violating the principles of free government or for violating the contract clause! *Fletcher v. Peck* is seldom utilized in the law schools as a model of neutral principles of constitutional law.

The holding was in practical terms a "dead letter" at the moment of its appearance: Georgia no longer held the land. But the New England lobbyists could and did claim that they had the Constitution on their side. Eventually in 1814 Congress appropriated $5,000,-000 to compensate the "innocent purchasers."

MARSHALL, C. J., delivered the opinion of the court as follows: . . .

This suit was instituted on several covenants contained in a deed made by John Peck, the defendant in error, conveying to Robert Fletcher, the plaintiff in error, certain lands which were part of a large purchase made by James Gunn and others, in the year 1795, from the State of Georgia, the contract for which was made in the form of a bill passed by the legislature of that State.

The first count in the declaration set forth a breach in the second covenant contained in the deed. The covenant is, "that the legislature of the State of Georgia, at the time of passing the act of sale aforesaid, had good right to sell and dispose of the same in manner pointed out by the said act." The breach assigned is, that the legislature had no power to sell.

The plea in bar sets forth the constitution of the State of Georgia, and avers that the lands sold by the defendant to the plaintiff, were within that State. It then sets forth the granting act, and avers the power of the legislature to sell and dispose of the premises as pointed out by the act.

To this plea the plaintiff below demurred, and the defendant joined in demurrer.

That the legislature of Georgia, unless restrained by its own constitution, possesses the power of disposing of the unappropriated lands within its own limits, in such manner as its own judgment shall dictate, is a proposition not to be controverted. The only question, then, presented by this demurrer, for the consideration of the court, is this, did the then constitution of the State of Georgia prohibit the legislature to dispose of the lands, which were the subject of this contract, in the manner stipulated by the contract?

The question, whether a law be void for its repugnancy to the constitution, is, at all times, a question of much delicacy, which ought seldom, if ever, to be decided in the affirmative, in a doubtful case. The court, when impelled by duty to render such a judgment, would be unworthy of its station, could it be unmindful of the solemn obligations which that station imposes. But it is not on slight implication and vague conjecture that the legislature is to be pronounced to have transcended its powers, and its acts to be considered as void. The opposition between the constitution and the law should be such that the judge feels a clear and strong conviction of their incompatibility with each other.

In this case the court can perceive no such opposition. In

the constitution of Georgia, adopted in the year 1789, the court can perceive no restriction on the legislative power, which inhibits the passage of the act of 1795. They cannot say that, in passing that act, the legislature has transcended its powers, and violated the constitution.

In overruling the demurrer, therefore, to the first plea, the circuit court committed no error.

The 3d covenant is, that all the title which the State of Georgia ever had in the premises had been legally conveyed to John Peck, the grantor.

The 2d count assigns, in substance, as a breach of this covenant, that the original grantees from the State of Georgia promised and assured divers members of the legislature, then sitting in general assembly, that if the said members would assent to, and vote for, the passing of the act, and if the said bill should pass, such members should have a share of, and be interested in, all the lands purchased from the said State by virtue of such law. And that divers of the said members, to whom the said promises were made, were unduly influenced thereby, and, under such influence, did vote for the passing of the said bill; by reason whereof the said law was a nullity, &c., and so the title of the State of Georgia did not pass to the said Peck, &c.

The plea to this count, after protesting that the promises it alleges were not made, avers, that until after the purchase made from the original grantees by James Greenleaf, under whom the said Peck claims, neither the said James Greenleaf, nor the said Peck, nor any of the mesne vendors between the said Greenleaf and Peck, had any notice or knowledge that any such promises or assurances were made by the said original grantees, or either of them, to any of the members of the legislature of the State of Georgia.

To this plea the plaintiff demurred generally, and the defendant joined in the demurrer.

That corruption should find its way into the governments of our infant republics, and contaminate the very source of legislation, or that impure motives should contribute to the passage of a law, or the formation of a legislative contract, are circumstances most deeply to be deplored. How far a court of justice would, in any case, be competent, on proceedings instituted by the State itself, to vacate a contract thus formed, and to annul rights acquired, under that contract, by third persons having no notice of the improper means by which it was obtained, is a question which the court would approach with much circumspection. It may well be doubted how far the validity of a law depends upon the motives of its framers, and how far the particular inducements, operating on members of the supreme sovereign power of a State, to the formation of a contract by that power, are examinable in a court of justice. If the principle be conceded, that an act of the supreme sovereign power might be declared null by a court, in consequence of the means which procured it, still would there be much difficulty in saying to what extent those means must be applied to produce this effect. Must it be direct corruption, or would interest or undue influence of any kind be sufficient? Must the vitiating cause operate on a majority, or on what number of the members? Would the act be null, whatever might be the wish of the nation, or would its obligation or nullity depend upon the public sentiment?

If the majority of the legislature be corrupted, it may well be doubted, whether it be within the province of the judiciary to control their conduct, and, if less than a majority act from impure motives, the principle by which judicial interference would be regulated, is not clearly discerned.

Whatever difficulties this subject might present, when viewed under aspects of which it may be susceptible, this court can perceive none in the particular pleadings now under consideration. . . .

The case, as made out in the pleadings, is simply this. One individual who holds lands in the State of Georgia, under a deed covenanting that the title of Georgia was in the grantor, brings an action of covenant upon this deed, and assigns, as a breach, that some of the members of the legislature were induced to vote in favor of the law, which constituted the contract, by being promised an interest in it, and that therefore the act is a mere nullity.

This solemn question cannot be brought thus collaterally and incidentally before the court. It would be indecent, in the extreme, upon a private contract, between two individuals, to enter into an inquiry respecting the corruption of the sovereign power of a State. If the title be plainly deduced from a legislative act, which the legislature might constitutionally pass, if the act be clothed with all the requisite forms of a law, a court, sitting as a court of law, cannot sustain a suit brought by one individual against another founded on the allegation that the act is a nullity, in consequence of the impure motives which influenced certain members of the legislature which passed the law.

The circuit court, therefore, did right in overruling this demurrer.

The 4th covenant in the deed is, that the title to the premises has been, in no way, constitutionally or legally impaired by virtue of any subsequent act of any subsequent legislature of the State of Georgia.

The third count recites the undue means practised on certain members of the legislature, as stated in the second count, and then alleges that, in consequence of these practices and of other causes, a subsequent legislature passed an act annulling and rescinding the law under which the conveyance to the original grantees was made, declaring that conveyance void, and asserting the title of the State to the lands it contained. The count proceeds to recite at large, this rescinding act, and concludes with averring that, by reason of this act, the title of the said Peck in the premises was constitutionally and legally impaired, and rendered null and void.

After protesting, as before, that no such promises were made as stated in this count, the defendant again pleads that himself and the first purchaser under the original grantees, and all intermediate holders of the property, were purchasers without notice.

To this plea there is a demurrer and joinder.

The importance and the difficulty of the questions presented by these pleadings, are deeply felt by the court.

The lands in controversy vested absolutely in James Gunn and others, the original grantees, by the conveyance of the governor, made in pursuance of an act of assembly to which the legislature was fully competent. Being thus in full possession of the legal estate, they, for a valuable consideration, conveyed portions of the land to those who were willing to purchase. If the original transaction was infected with fraud, these purchasers did not participate in it, and had no notice of it. They were innocent. Yet the legislature of Georgia has involved them in the fate of the first parties to the transaction, and, if the act be valid, has annihilated their rights also.

The legislature of Georgia was a party to this transaction; and for a party to pronounce its own deed invalid, whatever cause may be assigned for its invalidity, must be considered as a mere act of power which must find its vindication in a train of reasoning not often heard in courts of justice.

If the legislature felt itself absolved from those rules of property which are common to all the citizens of the United States, and from those principles of equity which are acknowledged in all our courts, its act is to be supported by its power alone, and the same power may devest any other individual of his lands, if it shall be the will of the legislature so to exert it.

It is not intended to speak with disrespect of the legislature of Georgia, or of its acts. Far from it. The question is a general question, and is treated as one. For although such powerful objections to a legislative grant, as are alleged against this, may not again exist, yet the principle, on which alone this rescinding act is to be supported, may be applied to every case to which it shall be the will of any legislature to apply it. The principle is this: that a legislature may, by its own act, devest the vested estate of any man whatever, for reasons which shall, by itself, be deemed sufficient.

In this case the legislature may have had ample proof that the original grant was obtained by practices which can never be too much reprobated, and which would have justified its abrogation so far as respected those to whom crime was imputable. But the grant, when issued, conveyed an estate in fee-simple to the grantee, clothed with all the solemnities which law can bestow. This estate was transferable; and those who purchased parts of it were not stained by that guilt which infected the original transaction. Their case is not distinguishable from the ordinary case of purchasers of a legal estate without knowledge of any secret fraud which might have led to the emanation of the original grant. According to the well-known course of equity, their rights could not be affected by such fraud. Their situation was the same, their title was the same, with that of every other member of the community who holds land by regular conveyances from the original patentee.

Is the power of the legislature competent to the annihilation of such title, and to a resumption of the property thus held?

The principle asserted is, that one legislature is competent to repeal any act which a former legislature was competent to pass; and that one legislature cannot abridge the powers of a succeeding legislature.

The correctness of this principle, so far as respects general legislation, can never be controverted. But if an act be done under a law, a succeeding legislature cannot undo it. The past cannot be recalled by the most absolute power. Conveyances have been made, those conveyances have vested legal estates, and, if those estates may be seized by the sovereign authority, still, that they originally vested is a fact, and cannot cease to be a fact.

When, then, a law is in its nature a contract, when absolute rights have vested under that contract, a repeal of the law cannot devest those rights; and the act of annulling them, if legitimate, is rendered so by a power applicable to the case of every individual in the community.

It may well be doubted whether the nature of society and of government does not prescribe some limits to the legislative power; and if any be prescribed, where are they to be found, if the property of an individual, fairly and honestly acquired, may be seized without compensation.

To the legislature all legislative power is granted; but the question, whether the act of transferring the property of an individual to the public, be in the nature of the legislative power, is well worthy of serious reflection.

It is the peculiar province of the legislature to prescribe general rules for the government of society; the application of those rules to individuals in society would seem to be the duty of other departments. How far the power of giving the law may involve every other power, in cases where the constitution is silent, never has been, and perhaps never can be, definitely stated.

The validity of this rescinding act, then, might well be doubted, were Georgia a single sovereign power. But Georgia cannot be viewed as a single, unconnected, sovereign power, on whose legislature no other restrictions are imposed than may be found in its own constitution. She is a part of a large empire; she is a member of the American Union; and that union has a constitution the supremacy of which all acknowledge, and which imposes limits to the legislatures of the several States, which none claim a right to pass. The constitution of the United States declares that no State shall pass any bill of attainder, *ex post facto* law, or law impairing the obligation of contracts.

Does the case now under consideration come within this prohibitory section of the constitution?

In considering this very interesting question, we immediately ask ourselves what is a contract? Is a grant a contract?

A contract is a compact between two or more parties, and is either executory or executed. An executory contract is one in which a party binds himself to do, or not to do, a particular thing; such was the law under which the conveyance was made by the governor. A contract executed is one in which the object of contract is performed; and this, says Blackstone, differs in nothing from a grant. The contract between Georgia and the purchasers was executed by the grant. A contract executed, as well as one which is executory, contains obligations binding on the parties. A grant, in its own nature, amounts to an extinguishment of the right of the grantor, and implies a contract not to reassert that right. A party is, therefore, always estopped by his own grant.

Since, then, in fact, a grant is a contract executed, the obligation of which still continues, and since the constitution uses the general term contract, without distinguishing between those which are executory and those which are executed, it must be construed to comprehend the latter as well as the former. A law annulling conveyances between individuals, and declaring that the grantors should stand seized of their former estates, notwithstanding those grants, would be as repugnant to the constitution as a law discharging the vendors of property from the obligation of executing their contracts by conveyances. It would be strange if a contract to convey was secured by the constitution, while an absolute conveyance remained unprotected.

If, under a fair construction of the constitution, grants are comprehended under the term contracts, is a grant from the State excluded from the operation of the provision? Is the clause to be considered as inhibiting the State from impairing the obligation of contracts between two individuals, but as excluding from that inhibition contracts made with itself?

The words themselves contain no such distinction. They are

general, and are applicable to contracts of every description. If contracts made with the State are to be exempted from their operation, the exception must arise from the character of the contracting party, not from the words which are employed.

Whatever respect might have been felt for the state sovereignties, it is not to be disguised that the framers of the constitution viewed, with some apprehension, the violent acts which might grow out of the feelings of the moment; and that the people of the United States, in adopting that instrument, have manifested a determination to shield themselves and their property from the effects of those sudden and strong passions to which men are exposed. The restrictions on the legislative power of the States are obviously founded in this sentiment; and the Constitution of the United States contains what may be deemed a bill of rights for the people of each State.

No State shall pass any bill of attainder, *ex post facto* law, or law impairing the obligation of contracts.

A bill of attainder may affect the life of an individual, or may confiscate his property, or may do both.

In this form the power of the legislature over the lives and fortunes of individuals is expressly restrained. What motive, then, for implying, in words which import a general prohibition to impair the obligation of contracts, an exception in favor of the right to impair the obligation of those contracts into which the State may enter?

The State legislatures can pass no *ex post facto* law. An *ex post facto* law is one which renders an act punishable in a manner in which it was not punishable when it was committed. Such a law may inflict penalties on the person, or may inflict pecuniary penalties which swell the public treasury. The legislature is then prohibited from passing a law by which a man's estate, or any part of it, shall be seized for a crime which was not declared, by some previous law, to render him liable to that punishment. Why, then, should violence be done to the natural meaning of words for the purpose of leaving to the legislature the power of seizing, for public use, the estate of an individual in the form of a law annulling the title by which he holds that estate? The court can perceive no sufficient grounds for making that distinction. This rescinding act would have the effect of an *ex post facto* law. It forfeits the estate of Fletcher for a crime not committed by himself, but by those from whom he purchased. This cannot be effected in the form of an *ex post facto* law, or bill of attainder; why, then, is it allowable in the form of a law annulling the original grant?

The argument in favor of presuming an intention to except a case, not excepted by the words of the constitution, is susceptible of some illustration from a principle originally ingrafted in that instrument, though no longer a part of it. The constitution, as passed, gave the courts of the United States jurisdiction in suits brought against individual States. A State, then, which violated its own contract, was suable in the courts of the United States for that violation. Would it have been a defence in such a suit to say that the State had passed a law absolving itself from the contract? It is scarcely to be conceived that such a defence could be set up. And yet, if a State is neither restrained by the general principles of our political institutions, nor by the words of the constitution, from impairing the obligation of its own contracts, such a defence would be a valid one. This feature is no longer found in the constitution; but it aids in the construction of those clauses with which it was originally associated.

It is, then, the unanimous opinion of the court, that, in this case, the estate having passed into the hands of a purchaser for a valuable consideration, without notice, the State of Georgia was restrained, either by general principles which are common to our free institutions, or by the particular provisions of the Constitution of the United States, from passing a law whereby the estate of the plaintiff in the premises so purchased could be constitutionally and legally impaired and rendered null and void.

In overruling the demurrer to the 3d plea, therefore, there is no error. . . .

12. *Charters Are Contracts*

DARTMOUTH COLLEGE v. WOODWARD (1819)

(4 Wheaton 517)

Marshall continued to extend the coverage of the contract clause to novel categories. In the opinion that follows, he improvised (upon a theme provided by Daniel Webster and Joseph Hopkinson, counsel for the college) the doctrine that corporate charters are contracts and as such are beyond legislative infringement. Oddly enough, the beneficiary of his largesse was hardly an industrial or commercial corporation. Rather it was a small college in New Hampshire originally established as a seminary for the local Indians. The case basically involved a faction fight between the founder's son, John Wheelock, and the Board of Trustees that took on partisan coloration. Outnumbered by the board, Wheelock appealed to his Republican compatriots who had just won an overwhelming victory in the election of 1815. Coming to his rescue, they proceeded to "nationalize" the college. The administrative superstructure of the college was so reorganized that the former Federalist-dominated board was packed and put under the supervisory control of the governor and his council.

The case came on appeal to the Supreme Court under Section 25 of the Judiciary Act on a writ of error to vindicate the purged trustees. They had unsuccessfully tried to regain possession of the account books, seal, and records of the college in the state courts. (Woodward was the secretary-treasurer of the college, who had aligned himself with the new trustees and kept the materials in question.) In a masterful display of creative constitutionalism Marshall vetoed the state's reorganization plan and returned the college to private life.

Marshall's line of argument demonstrated his capacity for adopting an advanced position. Webster as counsel for the old board spent most of his brief arguing the more moderate view that the charter was a franchise, conferring a vested interest to the trustees subject to abrogation for cause. That is, he did not push the notion that a private corporation had total autonomy vis-à-vis the police power of the state. Even though Webster, in an emotional peroration, did weep that "it is a small college, but there are those who love it," he concentrated his analytical effort on the point that the college was a private charity as against the state's view that it was a regulatable public institution.

Marshall accepted the definition of the college as a private charity, but he went on to establish a much broader constitutional point. With respect to the intention of the founders, the Chief Justice rejoined that the burden of proof lay upon those who would assert that the founders, had they only thought of the Dartmouth situation, would have excluded the college from the protection of the contract clause. For his part, he had no doubt that the corporate charter was a contract. Indeed, he begged the question! "It can require no argument to prove that the circumstances of this case constitute a contract." (Aside from his unnerving ahistoricism, he was guilty of rearranging the facts—the circumstances of the case were not as he presented them: see J. M. Shirley, *The Dartmouth College Causes and the Supreme Court* (1879).) For all that, his new law of contract prohibited the states from altering the terms of corporate charters in a fashion parallel to his handling of land grants in *Fletcher v. Peck* and *New Jersey v. Wilson.* Although Marshall advised the states in the future to be more careful in drawing up and conferring charters, the real effect of the decision was a mad, no–holds–barred scramble for charters. If a railroad magnate could bribe a legislature for a prize charter, he had Marshall to thank for guaranteeing the illegality of second thoughts by new legislators. Needless to say, the American industrial revolution owed much of its nutrient support to this remarkable interpretation of a charter, one wholly at variance with the traditions of English law.

The opinion of the court was delivered by MARSHALL, Ch. J. —This is an action of trover, brought by the Trustees of Dartmouth College against William H. Woodward, in the state court of New Hampshire, for the book of records, corporate seal, and other corporate property, to which the plaintiffs allege themselves to be entitled. A special verdict, after setting out the rights of the parties, finds for the defendant, if certain acts of the legislature of New Hampshire, passed on the 27th of June, and on the 18th of December 1816, be valid, and binding on the trustees, without their assent, and not repugnant to the constitution of the United States; otherwise, it finds for the plaintiffs. . . . The superior court of judicature of New Hampshire rendered a judgment upon this verdict for the defendant, which judgment has been brought before this court by writ of error. The single question now to be considered is, do the acts to which the verdict refers violate the constitution of the United States?

This court can be insensible neither to the magnitude nor delicacy of this question. The validity of a legislative act is to be examined; and the opinion of the highest law tribunal of a state is to be revised—an opinion which carries with it intrinsic evidence of the diligence, of the ability, and the integrity, with which it was formed. On more than one occasion, this court has expressed the cautious circumspection with which it approaches the consideration of such questions; and has declared, that in no doubtful case, would it pronounce a legislative act to be contrary to the constitution. But the American people have said, in the constitution of the United States, that "no state shall pass any bill of attainder, *ex post facto* law, or law impairing the obligation of contracts." In the same instrument, they have also said, "that the judicial power shall extend to all cases in law and equity arising under the constitution." On the judges of this court, then, is imposed the high and solemn duty of protecting, from even legislative violation, those contracts which the constitution of our country has placed beyond legislative control; and, however irksome the task may be, this is a duty from which we dare not shrink.

The title of the plaintiffs originates in a charter dated the 13th day of December, in the year 1769, incorporating twelve persons therein mentioned, by the name of "The Trustees of Dartmouth College," granting to them and their successors the usual corporate privileges and powers, and authorizing the trustees, who are to govern the college, to fill up all vacancies which may be created in their own body.

The defendant claims under three acts of the legislature of New Hampshire, the most material of which was passed on the 27th of June 1816, and is entitled, "an act to amend the charter, and enlarge and improve the corporation of Dartmouth College." Among other alterations in the charter, this act increases the number of trustees to twenty-one, gives the appointment of the additional members to the executive of the state, and creates a board of overseers, with power to inspect and control the most important acts of the trustees. This board consists of twenty-five persons. The president of the senate, the speaker of the house of representatives, of New Hampshire, and the governor and lieutenant-governor of Vermont, for the time being, are to be members *ex officio*. The board is to be completed by the governor and council of New Hampshire, who are also empowered to fill all vacancies which may occur. The acts of the 18th and 26th of December are supplemental to that of the 27th of June, and are principally intended to carry that act into effect. The majority of the trustees of the college have refused to accept this amended charter, and have brought this suit for the corporate property, which is in possession of a person holding by virtue of the acts which have been stated.

It can require no argument to prove, that the circumstances of this case constitute a contract. An application is made to the crown for a charter to incorporate a religious and literary institution. In the application, it is stated, that large contributions have been made for the object, which will be conferred on the corporation, as soon as it shall be created. The charter is granted, and on its faith the property is conveyed. Surely, in this transaction every ingredient of a complete and legitimate contract is to be found. The points for consideration are, 1. Is this contract protected by the constitution of the United States? 2. Is it impaired by the acts under which the defendant holds? . . .

That the framers of the constitution did not intend to restrain the states in the regulation of their civil institutions, adopted for internal government, and that the instrument they have given us, is not to be so construed, may be admitted. The provision of the constitution never has been understood to embrace other contracts, than those which respect property, or some object of value, and confer rights which may be asserted in a court of justice. . . .

The parties in this case differ less on general principles, less on the true construction of the constitution in the abstract, than on the application of those principles to this case, and on the true construction of the charter of 1769. This is the point on which the cause essentially depends. If the act of incorporation be a grant of political power, if it create a civil institution, to be employed in the administration of the government, or if the funds of the college be public property, or if the state of New Hampshire, as a government, be alone interested in its transactions, the subject is one in which the legislature of the state may act according to its own judgment, unrestrained by any limitation of its power imposed by the constitution of the United States. . . .

Whence, then, can be derived the idea, that Dartmouth

College has become a public institution, and its trustees public officers, exercising powers conferred by the public for public objects? Not from the source whence its funds were drawn; for its foundation is purely private and eleemosynary—not from the application of those funds; for money may be given for education, and the persons receiving it do not, by being employed in the education of youth, become members of the civil government. Is it from the act of incorporation? Let this subject be considered.

A corporation is an artificial being, invisible, intangible, and existing only in contemplation of law. Being the mere creature of law, it possesses only those properties which the charter of its creation confers upon it, either expressly, or as incidental to its very existence. These are such as are supposed best calculated to effect the object for which it was created. Among the most important are immortality, and, if the expression may be allowed, individuality; properties, by which a perpetual succession of many persons are considered as the same, and may act as a single individual. They enable a corporation to manage its own affairs, and to hold property, without the perplexing intricacies, the hazardous and endless necessity, of perpetual conveyances for the purpose of transmitting it from hand to hand. It is chiefly for the purpose of clothing bodies of men, in succession, with these qualities and capacities, that corporations were invented, and are in use. By these means, a perpetual succession of individuals are capable of acting for the promotion of the particular object, like one immortal being. But this being does not share in the civil government of the country, unless that be the purpose for which it was created. Its immortality no more confers on it political power, or a political character, than immortality would confer such power or character on a natural person. It is no more a state instrument, than a natural person exercising the same powers would be. If, then, a natural person, employed by individuals in the education of youth, or for the government of a seminary in

which youth is educated, would not become a public officer,
or be considered as a member of the civil government, how
is it, that this artificial being, created by law, for the purpose
of being employed by the same individuals, for the same purposes, should become a part of the civil government of the
country? Is it because its existence, its capacities, its powers,
are given by law? Because the government has given it the
power to take and to hold property, in a particular form, and
for particular purposes, has the government a consequent right
substantially to change that form, or to vary the purposes to
which the property is to be applied? This principle has never
been asserted or recognised, and is supported by no authority.
Can it derive aid from reason?

The objects for which a corporation is created are universally such as the government wishes to promote. They are
deemed beneficial to the country; and this benefit constitutes
the consideration, and in most cases, the sole consideration of
the grant. In most eleemosynary institutions, the object would
be difficult, perhaps unattainable, without the aid of a charter of
incorporation. Charitable or public-spirited individuals, desirous of making permanent appropriations for charitable or
other useful purposes, find it impossible to effect their design
securely and certainly, without an incorporating act. They apply to the government, state their beneficial object, and offer
to advance the money necessary for its accomplishment, provided the government will confer on the instrument which is to
execute their designs the capacity to execute them. The proposition is considered and approved. The benefit to the public is
considered as an ample compensation for the faculty it confers,
and the corporation is created. If the advantages to the public
constitute a full compensation for the faculty it gives, there
can be no reason for exacting a further compensation, by claim-
ing a right to exercise over this artificial being, a power which
changes its nature, and touches the fund, for the security and
application of which it was created. There can be no reason

for implying in a charter, given for a valuable consideration, a power which is not only not expressed, but is in direct contradiction to its express stipulations.

From the fact, then, that a charter of incorporation has been granted, nothing can be inferred, which changes the character of the institution, or transfers to the government any new power over it. The character of civil institutions does not grow out of their incorporation, but out of the manner in which they are formed, and the objects for which they are created. The right to change them is not founded on their being incorporated, but on their being the instruments of government, created for its purposes. The same institutions, created for the same objects, though not incorporated, would be public institutions, and, of course, be controllable by the legislature. The incorporating act neither gives nor prevents this control. Neither, in reason, can the incorporating act change the character of a private eleemosynary institution.

We are next led to the inquiry, for whose benefit the property given to Dartmouth College was secured? The counsel for the defendant have insisted, that the beneficial interest is in the people of New Hampshire. . . .

The particular interests of New Hampshire never entered into the mind of the donors, never constituted a motive for their donation. The propagation of the Christian religion among the savages, and the dissemination of useful knowledge among the youth of the country, were the avowed and the sole objects of their contributions. In these, New Hampshire would participate; but nothing particular or exclusive was intended for her. Even the site of the college was selected, not for the sake of New Hampshire, but because it was "most subservient to the great ends in view," and because liberal donations of land were offered by the proprietors, on condition that the institution should be there established. The real advantages from the location of the college, are, perhaps, not less considerable to those on the west, than to those on the east side of Connecticut river. The clause which constitutes the incorporation, and expresses the objects for which it was made, declares those objects to be the instruction of the Indians, "and also of English youth, and any others." So that the objects of the contributors, and the incorporating act, were the same; the promotion of Christianity, and of education generally, not the interests of New Hampshire particularly. . . .

Yet a question remains to be considered, of more real difficulty, on which more doubt has been entertained, than on all that have been discussed. The founders of the college, at least, those whose contributions were in money, have parted with the property bestowed upon it, and their representatives have no interest in that property. The donors of land are equally without interest, so long as the corporation shall exist. Could they be found, they are unaffected by any alteration in its constitution, and probably regardless of its form, or even of its existence. The students are fluctuating, and no individual among our youth has a vested interest in the institution, which can be asserted in a court of justice. Neither the founders of the college, nor the youth for whose benefit it was founded, complain of the alteration made in its charter, or think themselves injured by it. The trustees alone complain, and the trustees have no beneficial interest to be protected. Can this be such a contract, as the constitution intended to withdraw from the power of state legislation? Contracts, the parties to which have a vested beneficial interest, and those only, it has been said, are the objects about which the constitution is solicitous, and to which its protection is extended.

The court has bestowed on this argument the most deliberate consideration, and the result will be stated. Dr. Wheelock, acting for himself, and for those who, at his solicitation, had made contributions to his school, applied for this charter, as the instrument which should enable him, and them, to perpetuate their beneficent intention. It was granted. An artificial, immortal being, was created by the crown, capable of receiving and distributing for ever, according to the will of the donors, the donations which should be made to it. On this being, the contributions which had been collected were immediately bestowed. These gifts were made, not indeed to make a profit for the donors, or their posterity, but for something, in their opinion, of inestimable value; for something which they deemed a full equivalent for the money with which it was purchased. The consideration for which they stipulated, is the perpetual application of the fund to its object, in the mode prescribed by themselves. Their descendants may take no interest in the preservation of this consideration. But in this respect their descendants are not their representatives; they are represented by the corporation. The corporation is the assignee of their rights, stands in their place, and distributes their bounty, as they would themselves have distributed it, had they been immortal. So, with respect to the students who are to derive learning from this source; the corporation is a trustee for them also. Their potential rights, which, taken distributively, are imperceptible, amount collectively to a most important interest. These are, in the aggregate, to be exercised, asserted and protected, by the corporation. They were as completely out of the donors, at the instant of their being vested in the corporation, and as incapable of being asserted by the students, as at present. . . .

If the insignificance of the object does not require that we should exclude contracts respecting it from the protection of the constitution; neither, as we conceive, is the policy of leaving them subject to legislative alteration so apparent, as to require a forced construction of that instrument, in order to effect it. . . . The motives for such an exception must be very powerful, to justify the construction which makes it.

The motives suggested at the bar grow out of the original appointment of the trustees, which is supposed to have been in a spirit hostile to the genius of our government, and the presumption, that if allowed to continue themselves, they now are, and must remain for ever, what they originally were. Hence is inferred the necessity of applying to this corporation, and to other similar corporations, the correcting and improving hand of the legislature. It has been urged repeatedly, and certainly with a degree of earnestness which attracted attention, that the trustees, deriving their power from a regal source, must, necessarily, partake of the spirit of their origin; and that their first principles, unimproved by that resplendent light which has been shed around them, must continue to govern the college, and to guide the students.

Before we inquire into the influence which this argument ought to have on the constitutional question, it may not be amiss to examine the fact on which it rests. The first trustees were undoubtedly named in the charter, by the crown; but at whose suggestion were they named? By whom were they selected? The charter informs us. Dr. Wheelock had represented, "that for many weighty reasons, it would be expedient, that the gentlemen whom he had already nominated, in his last will, to be trustees in America, should be of the corporation now proposed." When, afterwards, the trustees are named in the charter, can it be doubted, that the persons mentioned by Dr. Wheelock in his will were appointed? Some were probably added by the crown, with the approbation of Dr. Wheelock. Among these, is the doctor himself. If any others were appointed, at the instance of the crown, they are the governor, three members of the council, and the speaker of the house of representatives of the colony of New Hampshire. The stations filled by these persons ought to rescue them from any other imputation than too great a dependence on the crown. If, in the revolution that followed, they acted under the influence of this sentiment, they must have ceased to be trustees; if they took part with their countrymen, the imputation, which suspicion might excite, would no longer attach to them. The original trustees, then, or most of them, were named by Dr. Wheelock, and those who were added to his nomination, most probably, with his approbation, were among the most eminent and respectable individuals in New Hampshire.

The opinion of the court, after mature deliberation, is, that this is a contract, the obligation of which cannot be impaired, without violating the constitution of the United States. This opinion appears to us to be equally supported by reason, and by the former decisions of this court.

2. We next proceed to the inquiry, whether its obligation has been impaired by those acts of the legislature of New Hampshire, to which the special verdict refers? . . .

By the revolution, the duties, as well as the powers, of government devolved on the people of New Hampshire. It is admitted, that among the latter was comprehended the transcendent power of parliament, as well as that of the executive department. It is too clear, to require the support of argument, that all contracts and rights respecting property, remained unchanged by the revolution. The obligations, then, which were created by the charter to Dartmouth College, were the same in the new, that they had been in the old government. The power of the government was also the same. A repeal of this charter, at any time prior to the adoption of the present constitution of the United States, would have been an extraordinary and unprecedented act of power, but one which could have been contested only by the restrictions upon the legislature, to be found in the constitution of the state. But the constitution of the United States has imposed this additional limitation, that the legislature of a state shall pass no act "impairing the obligation of contracts." . . .

On the effect of this law, two opinions cannot be entertained. Between acting directly, and acting through the agency of trustees and overseers, no essential difference is perceived. The whole power of governing the college is transferred from trustees, appointed according to the will of the founder, expressed in the charter, to the executive of New Hampshire. The management and application of the funds of this eleemosynary institution, which are placed by the donors in the hands of trustees named in the charter, and empowered to perpetuate themselves, are placed by this act under the control of the government of the state. The will of the state is

substituted for the will of the donors, in every essential operation of the college. This is not an immaterial change. The
founders of the college contracted, not merely for the perpetual application of the funds which they gave, to the objects
for which those funds were given; they contracted also, to secure that application by the constitution of the corporation.
They contracted for a system, which should, so far as human
foresight can provide, retain for ever the government of the
literary institution they had formed, in the hands of persons
approved by themselves. This system is totally changed. The
charter of 1769 exists no longer. It is re-organized; and re-
organized in such a manner, as to convert a literary institution,
moulded according to the will of its founders, and placed
under the control of private literary men, into a machine entirely subservient to the will of government. This may be for
the advantage of this college in particular, and may be for the
advantage of literature in general; but it is not according to
the will of the donors, and is subversive of that contract, on the
faith of which their property was given. . . .

It results from this opinion, that the acts of the legislature
of New Hampshire, which are stated in the special verdict
found in this cause, are repugnant to the constitution of the
United States; and that the judgment on this special verdict
ought to have been for the plaintiffs. The judgment of the state
court must, therefore, be reversed.

13. *Tax Exemption in Contracts, I*

NEW JERSEY v. WILSON (1812)

(7 Cranch 164)

Here Marshall applied the doctrine of *Fletcher v. Peck*—a state is
bound by its contracts—to invalidate a state statute that rescinded a

tax exemption purportedly linked to a colonial legislature's land grant. His zeal for protecting the inviolability of contracts from the hands of state legislators caused him to rule, in effect, that states could irretrievably whittle away their tax base through short-sighted grants of tax-exempt lands. Presumably states were now forewarned to stipulate limitations upon the exemptions, e.g., by stating that when the original party sold the land, the exemption terminated. But Marshall was unwilling to assume that any such stipulations for the benefit of the state had been implied in original grants. In the case at bar, the legislature seemed to have intended that the exemption go to the party and not to the land, but he replied that since there was no explicit statement of any such intention, none would be assumed.

The state simply ignored the holding and continued to tax the parcel of land at issue. Indeed, for seventy-five years the successive owners paid the tax until somebody (probably an enterprising attorney) stumbled across the Marshall opinion. The issue was then reopened, but the Supreme Court in *New Jersey v. Wright* (1886) upheld the state's right to tax on the ground that acquiescence in the tax by the owners over decades implied a surrender of the exemption: as the legal maxim runs, they had "slept upon their rights." The doctrine of the original case was not disturbed, although the Court suggested that if the case were then coming up for the first time, it would be held that the taxing power of the state could only be impaired by explicit legislative provision. By 1830 Marshall had, himself, reached a similar position. (See *Providence Bank v. Billings*, on following pages.)

Marshall, Ch. J., delivered the opinion of the court as follows: . . . In October, 1804, the legislature passed an act repealing that section of the act of August, 1758, which exempts the lands therein mentioned from taxes. The lands were then assessed, and the taxes demanded. The plaintiffs, [who purchased what was formerly a tax-free Indian reservation], thinking themselves injured by this assessment, brought the case before the courts in the manner prescribed by the laws of New Jersey, and in the highest court of the state the validity of the repealing act was affirmed and the land declared liable to taxation. The cause is brought into this court by writ of error, and the question here to be decided is, does the act of 1804 violate the constitution of the United States?

The constitution of the United States declares that no state shall "pass any bill of attainder, *ex post facto* law, or law impairing the obligation of contracts. . . .

The question, then, is narrowed to the inquiry whether in the case stated, a contract existed, and whether that contract is violated by the act of 1804.

Every requisite to the formation of a contract is found in the proceedings between the then colony of New Jersey and the Indians. The subject was a purchase on the part of the government of extensive claims of the Indians, the extinguishment of which would quiet the title to a large portion of the province. A proposition to this effect is made, the terms stipulated, the consideration agreed upon, which is a tract of land with the privilege of exemption from taxation; and then, in consideration of the arrangement previously made, one of which this act of assembly is stated to be, the Indians execute their deed of cession. This is certainly a contract clothed in forms of unusual solemnity. The privilege, though for the benefit of the Indians, is annexed, by the terms which create it, to the land itself, not to their persons. It is for their advantage that it should be annexed to the land, because, in the event of a sale on which alone the question could become material, the value would be enhanced by it.

It is not doubted but that the state of New Jersey might have insisted on a surrender of this privilege as the sole condition on which a sale of the property should be allowed. But this condition has not been insisted on. The land has been sold, with the assent of the state, with all its privileges and immunities. The purchaser succeeds, with the assent of the state, to all the rights of the Indians. He stands, with respect to this land, in their place, and claims the benefit of their contract. This contract is certainly impaired by a law which would annul this essential part of it.

14. *Natural Law and Contracts*

OGDEN v. SAUNDERS (1827)

(12 Wheaton 213)

Only once did Marshall write a dissent from "the Court opinion" on a question of constitutional law. This next opinion marks the occasion. Perhaps the dissent may be regarded as the perfect expression (or perhaps the epitaph) of early nineteenth century conservative jurisprudence. For here Marshall discoursed on the "higher law" character of the contract clause, which in his reading incorporated an absolute prohibition of state interference with the execution of private contracts. As the oracle of natural law, the Supreme Court was bound, in effect, to disallow all state statutes purporting to alter the terms of contractual agreements. Furthermore, Marshall insisted that the proper interpretation of the contract clause precluded state statutes aimed at limiting *future* contracts.

Speaking for the Court, he had already ruled in *Sturges v. Crowninshield* (1819) that state statutes affecting contracts entered into prior to the passage of the relevant legislation did impair the obligations of contracts in violation of the Constitution. However, in that case he deliberately went beyond the case at bar to suggest that the contract clause operated prospectively as well—the argument of the following dissent. In fact, the confusion and dismay generated by his *obiter dictum* in *Sturges* prompted the challenge to it in *Ogden v. Saunders*.

A majority of one repudiated the Marshallian apparatus of natural law by ruling that state statutory stipulations could be read into the terms of future contracts. The majority of the Court believed the source of contract law to be in positive or municipal law, not in natural law. The disagreement between the majority and Marshall only superficially turned on the abstract status of contract law; at issue there was, of course, a serious dispute over public policy, and the legal questions were symbolic of this controversy. The majority of the Court believed that states could legitimately pass bankruptcy laws to mitigate the position of the insolvent debtor; Marshall, on the other hand, adamantly opposed state laws absolving debtors of their contractual obligations. In his view, state interference would necessarily invite financial instability. His natural law dogmas nicely meshed with his convictions about a sound economy. But at the dawn of Jacksonian Democracy, Marshall's viewpoint was decidedly unpopular, and the Court rejected the Chief Justice's economic postulates. On the closely allied issue of federalism versus states' rights, the majority was of the view that in the absence of a congressional bankruptcy statute the states could exercise jurisdiction. Unfortunately, the predominant view on this last point is far from clear, for each member of the majority wrote a separate opinion.

Marshall, however, was in the minority on but one of the major issues of the case. The New York statute had not only affected intrastate contracts, but it also asserted jurisdiction over contracts to which a citizen of another state was a party. A different majority, speaking through Justice Johnson, invalidated this part of the statute on the ground that the state had no jurisdiction over persons and property in other states. Thus, the law of contract which survived the fracas permitted courts to read state statutory "reservation clauses" into future private contracts between citizens of the same state. Note that on the general issue of banning state law mitigating contractual obligations, the Chief Justice lost to a majority of Justices Johnson, Trimble, Washington, and Thompson. But on the specific issue of the invalidity of the New York bankruptcy statute for its outreach to citizens of other states, Marshall carried the day; Johnson provided the swing vote, with Trimble, Thompson, and Washington in dissent.

Mr. Chief Justice MARSHALL. It 'is well known that the court has been divided in opinion on this case. Three judges, Mr. Justice Duvall, Mr. Justice Story, and myself, do not concur in the judgment which has been pronounced. . . .

The single question for consideration is, whether the act of the State of New York is consistent with or repugnant to the constitution of the United States? . . .

The provision of the constitution is that "no State shall pass any law" "impairing the obligation of contracts." The plaintiff in error contends that this provision inhibits the passage of retrospective laws only—of such as act on contracts in existence at their passage. The defendant in error maintains that it comprehends all future laws, whether prospective or retrospective, and withdraws every contract from State legislation the obligation of which has become complete.

That there is an essential difference in principle between laws which act on past and those which act on future contracts; that those of the first description can seldom be justified, while those of the last are proper subjects of ordinary legislative discretion, must be admitted. A constitutional restriction, therefore, on the power to pass laws of the one class may very well consist with entire legislative freedom respecting those of the other. Yet, when we consider the nature of our Union; that it is intended to make us, in a great measure, one people, as to commercial objects; that, so far as respects the intercommunication of individuals, the lines of separation between States are, in many respects, obliterated; it would not be a matter of surprise, if, on the delicate subject of contracts once formed, the interference of State legislation should be greatly abridged, or entirely forbidden. In the nature of the provision, then, there seems to be nothing which ought to influence our construction of the words; and, in making that construction, the whole clause, which consists of a single sentence, is to be taken together, and the intention is to be collected from the whole.

The first paragraph of the tenth section of the first article, which comprehends the provision under consideration, contains an enumeration of those cases in which the action of the State legislature is entirely prohibited. The second enumerates those in which the prohibition is modified. The first paragraph, consisting of total prohibitions, comprehends two classes of powers. Those of the first are political and general in their nature, being an exercise of sovereignty without affecting the rights of individuals. These are, the powers "to enter into any treaty, alliance, or confederation; grant letters of marque or reprisal, coin money, emit bills of credit."

The second class of prohibited laws comprehends those whose operation consists in their action on individuals. These are, laws which make anything but gold and silver coin a tender in payment of debts, bills of attainder, *ex post facto* laws, or laws impairing the obligation of contracts, or which grant any title of nobility.

In all these cases, whether the thing prohibited be the exercise of mere political power, or legislative action on individuals, the prohibition is complete and total. There is no exception from it. Legislation of every description is comprehended within it. A State is as entirely forbidden to pass laws impairing the obligation of contracts, as to make treaties, or coin money. The question recurs, what is a law impairing the obligation of contracts? . . .

So much of this prohibition as restrains the power of the States to punish offenders in criminal cases, the prohibition to pass bills of attainder and *ex post facto* laws, is, in its very terms, confined to pre-existing cases. A bill of attainder can be only for crimes already committed; and a law is not *ex post facto* unless it looks back to an act done before its passage. Language is incapable of expressing in plainer terms, that the mind of the Convention was directed to retroactive legislation. The thing forbidden is retroaction. But that part of the clause which relates to the civil transactions of individuals is expressed in more general terms; in terms which comprehend, in their ordinary signification, cases which occur after, as well as those which occur before, the passage of the act. It forbids a State to make anything but gold and silver coin a tender in payment of debts, or to pass any law impairing the obligation of contracts. These prohibitions relate to kindred subjects. They contemplate legislative interference with private rights, and restrain that interference. In construing that part of the clause which respects tender laws, a distinction has never been attempted between debts existing at the time the law may be passed, and debts afterwards created. The prohibition has been considered as total. . . .

What, then, was the original legal obligation of the contract now under the consideration of the Court?

The plaintiff in error insists that the law enters into the contract so completely as to become a constituent part of it; that it is to be construed as if it contained an express stipulation to be discharged, should the debtor become insolvent, by the surrender of all his property for the benefit of his creditors, in pursuance of the act of the legislature.

This is, unquestionably, pressing the argument very far; and the establishment of the principle leads inevitably to consequences which would affect society deeply and seriously.

Had an express condition been inserted in the contract, declaring that the debtor might be discharged from it at any time by surrendering all his property to his creditors, this condition would have bound the creditor. It would have constituted the obligation of his contract; and a legislative act annulling the condition would impair the contract. Such an act would, as is admitted by all, be unconstitutional, because it operates on pre-existing agreements. If a law authorizing debtors to discharge themselves from their debts by surrendering their property enters into the contract, and forms a part of it, if it is equivalent to a stipulation between the parties, no repeal of the law can affect contracts made during its existence. The effort to give it that effect would impair their obligation. The counsel for the plaintiff perceive and avow this consequence, in effect, when they contend that to deny the operation of the law on the contract under consideration is to impair its obligation. Are gentlemen prepared to say that an insolvent law, once enacted, must, to a considerable extent, be permanent? that the Legislature is incapable of varying it so far as respects existing contracts? . . .

If one law enters into all subsequent contracts, so does every other law which relates to the subject. A legislative act, then, declaring that all contracts should be subject to legislative control, and should be discharged as the legislature might prescribe, would become a component part of every contract, and be one of its conditions. Thus one of the most important features in the constitution of the United States, one which the state of the times most urgently required, one on which the good and the wise reposed confidently for securing the prosperity and harmony of our citizens, would lie prostrate, and be construed into an inanimate, inoperative, unmeaning clause.

Gentlemen are struck with the enormity of this result, and deny that their principle leads to it. They distinguish, or attempt to distinguish, between the incorporation of a general law, such as has been stated, and the incorporation of a particular law, such as the insolvent law of New York, into the contract. But will reason sustain this distinction? They say that men cannot be supposed to agree to so indefinite an article as such a general law would be, but may well be supposed to agree to an article, reasonable in itself, and the full extent of which is understood.

But the principle contended for does not make the insertion of this new term or condition into the contract to depend upon its reasonableness. It is inserted because the legislature has so enacted. If the enactment of the legislature becomes a condition of the contract because it is an enactment, then it is a high prerogative, indeed, to decide that one enactment shall enter the contract, while another, proceeding from the same authority, shall be excluded from it. . . .

We have, then, no hesitation in saying that, however law may act upon contracts, it does not enter into them and become a part of the agreement. The effect of such a principle would be a mischievous abridgement of legislative power over subjects within the proper jurisdiction of states by arresting their power to repeal or modify such laws with respect to existing contracts.

But although the argument is not sustainable in this form, it assumes another in which it is more plausible. Contract, it is said, being the creature of society, derives its obligation from the law; and although the law may not enter into the agreement so as to form a constituent part of it, still it acts externally upon the contract, and determines how far the principle of coercion shall be applied to it; and this being universally understood, no individual can complain justly of its application to himself, in a case where it was known when the contract was formed.

This argument has been illustrated by references to the statutes of frauds, of usury, and of limitations. The construction of the words in the constitution respecting contracts, for which the defendants contend, would, it has been said, withdraw all these subjects from State legislation. The acknowledgment that they remain within it is urged as an admission that contract is not withdrawn by the constitution, but remains under State control, subject to this restriction only, that no law shall be passed impairing the obligation of contracts in existence at its passage.

The defendants maintain that an error lies at the very foundation of this argument. It assumes that contract is the mere creature of society, and derives all its obligation from human legislation; that it is not the stipulation an individual makes which binds him, but some declaration of the supreme power of a State to which he belongs, that he shall perform what he has undertaken to perform; that, though this original declaration may be lost in remote antiquity, it must be presumed as the origin of the obligation of contracts. This postulate the defendants deny, and, we think, with great reason.

It is an argument of no inconsiderable weight against it that we find no trace of such an enactment. So far back as human research carries us, we find the judicial power, as a part of the executive, administering justice by the application of remedies to violated rights, or broken contracts. We find that power applying these remedies on the idea of a pre-existing obligation on every man to do what he has promised on consideration to do; that the breach of this obligation is an injury for which the injured party has a just claim to compensation, and that society ought to afford him a remedy for that injury. We find allusions to the mode of acquiring property, but we find no allusion, from the earliest time, to any supposed act of the governing power giving obligation to contracts. On the contrary, the proceedings respecting them, of which we know anything, evince the idea of a pre-existing intrinsic obligation which human law enforces. If, on tracing the right to contract, and the obligations created by contract, to their source, we find them to exist anterior to and independent of society, we may reasonably conclude that those original and pre-existing principles are, like many other natural rights, brought with man into society; and although they may be controlled are not given by human legislation. . . .

In our system, the legislature of a State is the supreme power, in all cases where its action is not restrained by the constitution of the United States. Where it is so restrained, the legislature ceases to be the supreme power, and its acts are not law. It is, then, begging the question to say that, because contracts may be discharged by a law previously enacted, this contract may be discharged by this act of the legislature of New York; for the question returns upon us, is this act a law? Is it consistent with, or repugnant to, the constitution of the United States? This question is to be solved only by the constitution itself.

In examining it, we readily admit, that the whole subject of contracts is under the control of society, and that all the power of society over it resides in the State legislatures, except in those special cases where restraint is imposed by the constitution of the United States. The particular restraint now under consideration is on the power to impair the obligation of contracts. The extent of this restraint cannot be ascertained by showing that the legislature may prescribe the circumstances on which the original validity of a contract shall be made to depend. If the legislative will be that certain agreements shall be in writing, that they shall be sealed, that they shall be attested by a certain number of witnesses, that they shall be recorded, or that they shall assume any prescribed form, before they become obligatory, all these are regulations which society may rightfully make, and which do not come within the restrictions of the constitution, because they do not *impair* the obligation of the contract. The obligation must exist before it can be impaired; and a prohibition to impair it when made does not imply an inability to prescribe those circumstances which shall create its obligation. The statutes of frauds, therefore, which have been enacted in the several States, and which are acknowledged to flow from the proper exercise of State sovereignty, prescribe regulations which must precede the obligation of the contract, and, consequently, cannot impair that obligation. Acts of this description, therefore, are most clearly not within the prohibition of the constitution. . . .

The counsel for the plaintiff in error insist that the right to regulate the remedy and to modify the obligation of the contract are the same; that obligation and remedy are identical, that they are synonymous,—two words conveying the same idea. . . .

[T]he right to contract is the attribute of a free agent, and that he may rightfully coerce performance from another free agent who violates his faith. Contracts have, consequently, an intrinsic obligation. When men come into society they can no longer exercise this original and natural right of coercion. It would be incompatible with general peace, and is, therefore, surrendered. Society prohibits the use of private, individual coercion, and gives in its place a more safe and more certain remedy. But the right to contract is not surrendered with the right to coerce performance. It is still incident to that degree of free agency which the laws leave to every individual, and the obligation of the contract is a necessary consequence of the right to make it. Laws regulate this right, but where not regulated it is retained in its original extent. Obligation and remedy, then, are not identical; they originate at different times, and are derived from different sources. . . .

But we are told that the power of the State over the remedy may be used to the destruction of all beneficial results from the right; and hence it is inferred that the construction which maintains the inviolability of the obligation must be extended to the power of regulating the remedy.

The difficulty which this view of the subject presents does not proceed from the identity or connection of right and remedy, but from the existence of distinct governments acting on kindred subjects. The constitution contemplates restraint as to the obligation of contracts, not as to the application of remedy. If this restraint affects a power which the constitution did not mean to touch, it can only be when that power is used as an instrument of hostility to invade the inviolability of contract, which is placed beyond its reach. A State may use many of its acknowledged powers in such manner as to come in conflict with the provisions of the constitution. Thus, the power over its domestic police, the power to regulate commerce purely internal, may be so exercised as to interfere with regulations of commerce with foreign nations or between the States. In such cases, the power which is supreme must control that which is not supreme, when they come in conflict. But this principle does not involve any self-contradiction, or deny the existence of the several powers in the respective governments. So, if a State shall not merely modify or withhold a particular remedy, but shall apply it in such manner as to extinguish the obligation without performance, it would be an abuse of power which could scarcely be misunderstood, but which would not prove that remedy could not be regulated without regulating obligation.

The counsel for the plaintiff in error put a case of more difficulty, and urge it as a conclusive argument against the existence of a distinct line dividing obligation from remedy. It is this. The law affords remedy by giving execution against the person or the property, or both. The same power which can withdraw the remedy against the person can withdraw that against the property, or that against both, and thus effectually defeat the obligation. The constitution, we are told, deals not with form, but with substance; and cannot be presumed, if it designed to protect the obligation of contracts from State legislation, to have left it thus obviously exposed to destruction.

The answer is, that if the law goes farther, and annuls the obligation without affording the remedy which satisfies it, if its action on the remedy be such as palpably to impair the obligation of the contract, the very case arises which we suppose to be within the constitution. If it leaves the obligation untouched, but withholds the remedy, or affords one which is merely nominal, it is like all other cases of misgovernment, and leaves the debtor still liable to his creditor, should he be found, or should his property be found, where the laws afford a remedy. . . .

We perceive, then, no reason for the opinion that the prohibition "to pass any law impairing the obligation of contracts" is incompatible with the fair exercise of that discretion, which the State legislatures possess, in common with all governments, to regulate the remedies afforded by their own Courts. We think, that obligation and remedy are distinguishable from each other. That the first is created by the act of the parties, the last is afforded by government. The words of the restriction we have been considering countenance, we think, this idea. No State shall "pass any law impairing the obligation of contracts." These words seem to us to import, that the obligation is intrinsic, that it is created by the contract itself, not that it is dependent on the laws made to enforce it. When we advert to the course of reading generally pursued by American statesmen in early life, we must suppose that the framers of our constitution were intimately acquainted with the writings of those wise and learned men whose treatises on the laws of nature and nations have guided public opinion on the subjects of obligation and contract. If we turn to those treatises, we find them to concur in the declaration that contracts possess an original, intrinsic obligation, derived from the acts of free agents, and not given by government. We must suppose that the framers of our constitution took the same view of the subject, and the language they have used confirms this opinion.

The propositions we have endeavoured to maintain, of the truth of which we are ourselves convinced, are these:

That the words of the clause in the constitution which we are considering, taken in their natural obvious sense, admit of a prospective, as well as of a retrospective, operation;

That an act of the legislature does not enter into the contract, and become one of the conditions stipulated by the parties; nor does it act externally on the agreement, unless it have the full force of law;

That contracts derive their obligation from the act of the parties, not from the grant of government; and the right of government to regulate the manner in which they shall be formed, or to prohibit such as may be against the policy of the State, is entirely consistent with their inviolability after they have been formed;

That the obligation of a contract is not identified with the means which government may furnish to enforce it; and that a prohibition to pass any law impairing it does not imply a prohibition to vary the remedy; nor does a power to vary the remedy imply a power to impair the obligation derived from the act of the parties.

We cannot look back to the history of the times when the august spectacle was exhibited of the assemblage of a whole people by their representatives in Convention, in order to unite thirteen independent sovereignties under one government, so far as might be necessary for the purposes of union, without being sensible of the great importance which was at that time attached to the tenth section of the first article. The power of changing the relative situation of debtor and creditor, of interfering with contracts, a power which comes home to every man, touches the interest of all, and controls the conduct of every individual in those things which he supposes to be proper for his own exclusive management, had been used to such an excess by the State legislatures as to break in upon the ordinary intercourse of society, and destroy all confidence between man and man. The mischief had become so great, so alarming, as not only to impair commercial intercourse, and threaten the existence of credit, but to sap the morals of the people, and destroy the sanctity of private faith. To guard against the continuance of the evil was an object of deep interest with all the truly wise, as well as the virtuous, of this great community, and was one of the important benefits expected from a reform of the government.

To impose restraints on State legislation as respected this delicate and interesting subject, was thought necessary by all those patriots who could take an enlightened and comprehensive view of our situation; and the principle obtained an early admission into the various schemes of government which were submitted to the Convention. In framing an instrument which was intended to be perpetual, the presumption is strong that every important principle introduced into it is intended to be perpetual also; that a principle expressed in terms to operate in all future time is intended so to operate. But, if the construction for which the plaintiff's counsel contend be the true one, the constitution will have imposed a restriction, in language indicating perpetuity, which every State in the Union may elude at pleasure. The obligation of contracts in force, at any given time, is but of short duration; and, if the inhibition be of retrospective laws only, a very short lapse of time will remove every subject on which the act is forbidden to operate, and make this provision of the constitution so far useless. Instead of introducing a great principle, prohibiting all laws of this obnoxious character, the constitution will only suspend their operation for a moment, or except from it pre-existing cases. The object would scarcely seem to be of sufficient importance to have found a place in that instrument.

This construction would change the character of the provision, and convert an inhibition to pass laws impairing the obligation of contracts into an inhibition to pass retrospective laws. Had this been the intention of the Convention, is it not reasonable to believe that it would have been so expressed? . . .

It is also worthy of consideration that those laws which had effected all that mischief the constitution intended to prevent were prospective, as well as retrospective, in their operation. They embraced future contracts as well as those previously formed. There is the less reason for imputing to the Convention an intention, not manifested by their language, to confine a restriction, intended to guard against the recurrence of those mischiefs, to retrospective legislation. For these reasons, we are of opinion that, on this point, the District Court of Louisiana has decided rightly.

15. *Tax Exemptions in Contracts, II*

PROVIDENCE BANK v. BILLINGS (1830)

(4 Peters 514)

The opinion below marks a decided retreat from the principles of *New Jersey v. Wilson* and *Dartmouth College*. Marshall, in essence, reversed his usual presumption employed in construing the obligation of contracts. Now the benefit of the doubt went to the state rather than, as formerly, to the contracting party. This case arose from a state tax upon the capital stock of a state-chartered bank, imposed after the bank had been set up. Marshall sustained the statute on the ground that tax exemptions could not by implication be read into corporate charters. He expressed in passing sentiments which were remote from those in *Fletcher v. Peck*: "The interest, wisdom, and justice of the representative body, and its relations with its constituents, furnish the only security, where there is no express contract, against unjust and excessive taxation, as well as against unwise legislation generally." But the Chief Justice had to make such concessions in order to "deliver the opinion of the Court."

Undoubtedly, the recent appointees to the Court were totally unsympathetic to any interpretation of the contract clause which diminished the tax and police powers of the states. (These justices may be classified as "strict constructionists," but the other side of that coin must be remembered: it showed a broad construction of state powers.) Thus, with a majority of the Court opposed to Marshall's own reading of the contract clause, the Chief Justice was forced to play another tune if he were still to be the piper. Perhaps as piper he could stress some themes more than others. But he was also decidedly more concerned with pursuing a policy of cooperation with his brethren to secure judicial review than with displaying his ideological grievances in public. He understood that an openly divided Court would only provide critics of judicial review with leverage to widen the gap between factions to the point of deadlock and perhaps jurisprudential chaos—such as that which in fact later occurred in the Taney Court.

Mr. Chief Justice MARSHALL delivered the opinion of the Court: . . .

In 1822 the legislature of Rhode Island passed "an act imposing a duty on licensed persons and others, and bodies corporate within the state;" in which, among other things, it is enacted "that there shall be paid, for the use of the state, by each and every bank within the state, except the Bank of the United States, the sum of fifty cents on each and every thousand dollars of the capital stock actually paid in." This tax was afterwards augmented to one dollar and twenty-five cents. . . .

It has been settled that a contract entered into between a state and an individual is as fully protected by the tenth section of the first article of the constitution as a contract between two individuals; and it is not denied that a charter incorporating a bank is a contract. Is this contract impaired by taxing the banks of the state?

This question is to be answered by the charter itself.

It contains no stipulation promising exemption from taxation. The state, then, has made no express contract which has been impaired by the act of which the plaintiffs complain. No words have been found in the charter which, in themselves, would justify the opinion that the power of taxation was in the view of either of the parties; and that an exemption of it was intended, though not expressed. The plaintiffs find great difficulty in showing that the charter contains a promise, either express or implied, not to tax the bank. . . .

The great object of an incorporation is to bestow the character and properties of individuality on a collective and changing body of men. This capacity is always given to such a body. Any privileges which may exempt it from the burdens common to individuals do not flow necessarily from the charter, but must be expressed in it, or they do not exist.

If the power of taxation is inconsistent with the charter, because it may be so exercised as to destroy the object for which the charter is given, it is equally inconsistent with every other charter, because it is equally capable of working the destruction of the objects for which every other charter is given. If the grant of a power to trade in money to a given amount implies an exemption of the stock in trade from taxation, because the tax may absorb all the profits, then the grant of any other thing implies the same exemption, for that thing may be taxed to an extent which will render it totally unprofitable to the grantee. Land, for example, has in many, perhaps in all, the states been granted by government since the adoption of the constitution. This grant is a contract, the object of which is that the profits issuing from it shall inure to the benefit of the grantee. Yet the power of taxation may be carried so far as to absorb these profits. Does this impair the obligation of the contract? The idea is rejected by all, and the proposition appears so extravagant that it is difficult to admit any resemblance in the cases. And yet, if the proposition for which the plaintiffs contend be true, it carries us to this point. That proposition is, that a power which is in itself capable of being exerted to the total destruction of the grant, is inconsistent with the grant, and is, therefore, impliedly relinquished by the grantor, though the language of the instrument contains no allusion to the subject. If this be an abstract truth, it may be supposed universal. But it is not universal, and therefore its truth cannot be admitted, in these broad terms, in any case. We must look for the exemption in the language of the instrument, and, if we do not find it there, it would be going very far to insert it by construction.

The power of legislation, and, consequently, of taxation, operates on all the persons and property belonging to the body politic. This is an original principle, which has its foundation in society itself. It is granted by all, for the benefit of all. It resides in government as a part of itself, and need not be reserved, when property of any description, or the right to use it in any manner, is granted to individuals or corporate bodies. However absolute the right of an individual may be, it is still in the nature of that right that it must bear a portion of the public burdens; and that portion must be determined by the legislature. This vital power may be abused; but the constitution of the United States was not intended to furnish the corrective for every abuse of power which may be committed by the state governments. The interest, wisdom, and justice of the representative body, and its relations with its constituents, furnish the only security, where there is no express contract, against unjust and excessive taxation, as well as against unwise legislation generally. This principle was laid down in the case of *M'Cullough* vs. *The State of Maryland,* and in *Osborn et al.* vs. *The Bank of the United States.* Both those cases, we think, proceeded on the admission that an incorporated bank, unless its charter shall express the exemption, is no more exempted from taxation than an unincorporated company would be, carrying on the same business. . . .

We have reflected seriously on this case, and are of opinion that the act of the legislature of Rhode Island, passed in 1822, imposing a duty on licensed persons and others, and bodies corporate within the state, does not impair the obligation of the contract created by the charter granted to the plaintiffs in error. It is therefore the opinion of this court that there is no error in the judgment of the supreme judicial court for the state of Rhode Island, affirming the judgment of the circuit court in this case; and the same is affirmed; and the cause is remanded to the said supreme judicial court that its judgment may be finally entered.

Part Four

THE PROTECTION
OF FEDERAL FINANCE

16. *The Union as Preferred Creditor*

U. S. v. FISHER (1804)

(2 Cranch 358)

The significance of the following opinion rests in the argument Marshall used to sustain the validity of a federal statute. The technical question of the case (does the federal government have "first crack" at insolvent debtors?) is not of any great historical interest. But in defending the congressional statute which arrogated to the federal government the status of preferred creditor, Marshall advanced for the first time his "broad construction" of congressional power: Congress has the right under the Constitution to select "any means which are in fact conducive to the exercise of a power granted by the Constitution." Notice that this was fourteen years before the more familiar statements of *McCulloch v. Maryland* (1819).

The Chief Justice then utilized the standard items in his preassembled construction kit. The first tool, the necessary and proper clause, sanctioned the selection of "any means" to effect a given "power." The second tool was used to unearth that given power. In the instant case, Marshall deduced the power to collect a debt from insolvent debtors from the power, explicitly granted to Congress, to pay federal obligations. With such exegetical talent a derivative power could be ingeniously improvised on the spot for coping with an *ad hoc* problem.

The states, however, objected to waiting until the federal government finished its action against the insolvent debtor. To dispose of this objection to the *means* Congress had chosen, the Chief Justice pulled out the third tool in his kit: the supremacy clause. The supremacy of federal law was perhaps a "mischief" of the system; nonetheless, the states had to be satisfied with second place. Finally, although the doctrinal innovations are of lasting significance, it might be of some trivial interest to note that here (as in *Marbury v. Madison*) Marshall took the opportunity to sanction judicially his previous political accomplishments: As a congressman he had shared major responsibility for drafting the Bankruptcy Act, the federal statute on which this case turned!

Marshall, Ch. J., delivered the opinion of the Court. The question in this case is, whether the United States, as holders of a protested bill of exchange, which has been negotiated in the ordinary course of trade, are entitled to be preferred to the general creditors, where the debtor becomes bankrupt.

The claim to this preference is founded on the 5th section of the act, entitled "An act to provide more effectually for the settlement of accounts between the United States and receivers of public money." . . . The section is in these words: "And be it further enacted, that where any revenue officer, or other person, hereafter becoming indebted to the United States, by bond or otherwise, shall become insolvent, or where the estate of any deceased debtor, in the hands of executors or administrators, shall be insufficient to pay all the debts due from the deceased, the debt due to the United States shall be first satisfied; and the priority hereby established shall be deemed to extend, as well to cases in which a debtor, not having sufficient property to pay all his debts, shall make a voluntary assignment thereof, or in which the estate and effects of an absconding, concealed, or absent debtor, shall be attached by process of law, as to cases in which an act of legal bankruptcy shall be committed."

That these words, taken in their natural and usual sense, would embrace the case before the court, seems not to be controverted. "Any revenue officer, or other person, hereafter becoming indebted to the United States by bond or otherwise," is a description of persons, which, if neither explained nor restricted by other words or circumstances, would comprehend every debtor of the public, however his debt might have been contracted. . . .

If the act has attempted to give the United States a preference in the case before the court, it remains to inquire whether the constitution obstructs its operation.

To the general observations made on this subject, it will only be observed, that as the court can never be unmindful of the solemn duty imposed on the judicial department when a claim is supported by an act which conflicts with the constitution, so the court can never be unmindful of its duty to obey laws which are authorized by that instrument.

In the case at bar, the preference claimed by the United States is not prohibited; but it has been truly said that under a constitution conferring specific powers, the power contended for must be granted, or it cannot be exercised.

It is claimed under the authority to make all laws which shall be necessary and proper to carry into execution the powers vested by the constitution in the government of the United States, or in any department or officer thereof.

In construing this clause it would be incorrect, and would produce endless difficulties, if the opinion should be maintained that no law was authorized which was not indispensably necessary to give effect to a specified power.

Where various systems might be adopted for that purpose, it might be said with respect to each, that it was not necessary, because the end might be obtained by other means. Congress must possess the choice of means, and must be empowered to use any means which are in fact conducive to the exercise of a power granted by the constitution.

The government is to pay the debt of the union, and must be authorized to use the means which appear to itself most eligible to effect that object. It has, consequently, a right to make remittances by bills or otherwise, and to take those precautions which will render the transaction safe.

This claim of priority on the part of the United States will, it has been said, interfere with the right of the state sovereignties respecting the dignity of debts, and will defeat the measures they have a right to adopt to secure themselves against delinquencies on the part of their own revenue officers.

But this is an objection to the constitution itself. The mischief suggested, so far as it can really happen, is the necessary consequence of the supremacy of the laws of the United States on all subjects to which the legislative power of Congress extends. . . .

Judgment reversed.

17. *Implied Powers:*
The Bank of the United States

McCULLOCH v. MARYLAND (1819)

(4 Wheaton 316)

Depending upon one's sensibilities, the following opinion is either stately jurisprudence or a spectacular coup. In either case, Marshall clearly wrote for the anthologies. Once and for all the Court revealed the expansive scope of the powers conferred by the Constitution upon the national government. The opinion was primarily built upon inferences drawn from implications with semantic distinctions as basic premises. Although the argument was rather complex, the objective was simple: to interpret the Constitution to give Congress all the authority it would ever need for meeting as yet unforeseeable "crises of human affairs." In sanctioning such plenary authority, Marshall spoke as the oracle of a sovereign people who have ordained a Constitution for all times. If the scope of governmental authority was breathtaking, it was justified by the Chief Justice's remark that, after all, "it is a *constitution* we are expounding."

After this preliminary invocation, Marshall announced the famed doctrine of implied powers. Drawing heavily on the position brilliantly developed by Alexander Hamilton in his original defense of the constitutionality of the bank, he ruled that the "necessary and proper" clause affords Congress the authority to work its will. That is, Congress may implement the objectives of the enumerated powers with whatever means are "plainly adapted" or "appropriate." Thus, the argument turned upon the appropriateness of various synonyms for the words "necessary" and proper." The so-called strict constructionists (following Jefferson's attack on the constitutionality of the Bank in 1791) insisted that "necessary" meant "absolutely necessary" and nothing more permissive, but Marshall repudiated this school of linguistic analysis as hamstringing the government of a sovereign people.

Marshall next developed another line of argument later called by some the doctrine of "resulting powers." He claimed that Congress could justify legislative policy by utilizing a mixture of enumerated powers. Thus, when Congress or the Court desired a particular legislative program but could not locate an appropriate enumerated power in constitutional justification, the acceptable solution would be to invoke a combination of enumerated powers. Paradoxically enough, in announcing this rule of construction the Court voluntarily limited the scope of its review over Congress. A Constitution capable of such breadth of interpretation could hardly serve as an effective check on legislative authority. Of course, the Court could (and later would) alter this tolerant principle of construction, but as the Marshall canons stood Congress hardly needed to concern itself with judicial intervention in policy questions.

The final point in Marshall's argument rested upon the "supremacy clause." He declared that congressional policy under his principles of construction voided all inferior state action. The whole argument was then applied to defend the constitutionality of the Bank of the United States. Congress, utilizing a group of enumerated powers including *inter alia* the war power, had the authority to incorporate the bank. Therefore, the states had no right to tax notes of the bank, for the "power to tax involves the power to destroy" a legitimate national institution. On its face, this last statement seems to be an exaggerated form of the "camel's nose under the tent" argument, but in this instance many states were literally quite prepared to tax the branch banks right into oblivion.

The state authorities in the South and West were outraged by the opinion, but they attacked the holding more persistently than they did the reasoning. The populations of these states, seized with the fever of speculation, blamed the bank for all the economic distresses of the day. When the bank imposed tight currency and credit restrictions, the over-inflated state banks which promoted speculation collapsed, bringing down with them the hopes of immediate wealth of imprudent investors. This is not to say that the officers of the bank were all virtuous and financially responsible: McCulloch, the cashier of the Baltimore Bank, had just embezzled over one and a quarter million dollars to cover his own investment portfolio.

In the face of Marshall's opinion, Ohio took direct action: the state cleaned out the vaults of the branch bank for non-payment of taxes. When the federal authorities recovered the money from the state treasurer, the local newspapers inveighed against the national government for depriving the state of property without due process! This episode in Ohio provided an opportunity for Marshall to reissue and reemphasize his *McCulloch* opinion in *Osborn v. the Bank* (1824). The Chief Justice also felt it necessary to publish a series of anonymous articles in defense of *McCulloch* against the attacks of Spencer Roane of Virginia (unfortunately the publisher—as Marshall told Justice Story who had asked for reprints—garbled his essays to the edge of incoherence).

Yet in the furor, Marshall had gained implicit support for his position on judicial review when the states criticized the Court for *not* striking down the incorporation of the bank as an unconstitutional exercise of congressional power. If Marshall's Court was conceded the authority to review acts of Congress, then surely opposition to judicial oversight of acts of the states was a losing theoretical cause.

MARSHALL, Ch. J., delivered the opinion of the court.—In the case now to be determined, the defendant, a sovereign state, denies the obligation of a law enacted by the legislature of the Union, and the plaintiff, on his part, contests the validity of an act which has been passed by the legislature of that state. The constitution of our country, in its most interesting and vital parts, is to be considered; the conflicting powers of the government of the Union and of its members, as marked in that constitution, are to be discussed; and an opinion given, which may essentially influence the great operations of the government. No tribunal can approach such a question without a deep sense of its importance, and of the awful responsibility involved in its decision. But it must be decided peacefully, or remain a source of hostile legislation, perhaps, of hostility of a still more serious nature; and if it is to be so decided, by this tribunal alone can the decision be made. On the supreme court of the United States has the constitution of our country devolved this important duty.

The first question made in the cause is—had congress power to incorporate a bank? . . . The power now contested was exercised by the first congress elected under the present constitution. The bill for incorporating the Bank of the United States did not steal upon an unsuspecting legislature, and pass unobserved. Its principle was completely understood, and was opposed with equal zeal and ability. After being resisted, first, in the fair and open field of debate, and afterwards, in the executive cabinet, with as much persevering talent as any measure has ever experienced, and being supported by arguments which convinced minds as pure and as intelligent as this country can boast, it became a law. The original act was permitted to expire; but a short experience of the embarrassments to which the refusal to revive it exposed the government, convinced those who were most prejudiced against the measure of its necessity, and induced the passage of the present law. It would require no ordinary share of intrepidity, to assert that a measure adopted under these circumstances, was a bold and plain usurpation, to which the constitution gave no countenance. . . .

In discussing this question, the counsel for the state of Maryland have deemed it of some importance, in the construction of the constitution, to consider that instrument, not as emanating from the people, but as the act of sovereign and independent states. The powers of the general government, it has been said, are delegated by the states, who alone are truly sovereign; and must be exercised in subordination to the states, who alone possess supreme dominion. It would be difficult to sustain this proposition. The convention which framed the constitution was indeed elected by the state legislatures. But the instrument, when it came from their hands, was a mere proposal, without obligation, or pretensions to it. It was reported to the then existing congress of the United States, with a request that it might "be submitted to a convention of delegates, chosen in each state by the people thereof, under the recommendation of its legislature, for their assent and ratification." This mode of proceeding was adopted; and by the convention, by congress, and by the state legislatures, the instrument was submitted to the *people*. They acted upon it in the only manner in which they can act safely, effectively and wisely, on such a subject, by assembling in convention. It is true, they assembled in their several states—and where else should they have assembled? No political dreamer was ever wild enough to think of breaking down the lines which separate the states, and of compounding the American people into one common mass. Of consequence, when they act, they act in their states. But the measures they adopt do not, on that account, cease to be the measures of the people themselves, or become the measures of the state governments.

From these conventions, the constitution derives its whole authority. The government proceeds directly from the people; is "ordained and established," in the name of the people; and is declared to be ordained, "in order to form a more perfect union, establish justice, insure domestic tranquillity, and secure the blessings of liberty to themselves and to their posterity." The assent of the states, in their sovereign capacity, is implied, in calling a convention, and thus submitting that instrument to the people. But the people were at perfect liberty to accept or reject it; and their act was final. It required not the affirmance, and could not be negatived, by the state governments. The constitution, when thus adopted, was of complete obligation, and bound the state sovereignties. . . . The government of the Union, then . . . is, emphatically and truly, a government of the people. In form, and in substance, it emanates from them. Its powers are granted by them, and are to be exercised directly on them, and for their benefit.

This government is acknowledged by all, to be one of enumerated powers. . . . But the question respecting the extent of the powers actually granted, is perpetually arising, and will probably continue to arise, so long as our system shall exist. In discussing these questions, the conflicting powers of the general and state governments must be brought into view, and the supremacy of their respective laws, when they are in opposition, must be settled.

If any one proposition could command the universal assent of mankind, we might expect it would be this—that the government of the Union, though limited in its powers, is supreme within its sphere of action. This would seem to result, necessarily, from its nature. It is the government of all; its powers are delegated by all; it represents all, and acts for all. Though any one state may be willing to control its operations, no state is willing to allow others to control them. The nation, on those subjects on which it can act, must necessarily bind its component parts. But this question is not left to mere reason: the people have, in express terms, decided it, by saying, "this constitution, and the laws of the United States, which shall be made in pursuance thereof," "shall be the supreme law of the land," and by requiring that the members of the state legislatures, and the officers of the executive and judicial departments of the states, shall take the oath of fidelity to it. The government of the United States, then, though limited in its powers, is supreme; and its laws, when made in pursuance of the constitution, form the supreme law of the land, "anything in the constitution or laws of any state to the contrary notwithstanding."

Among the enumerated powers, we do not find that of establishing a bank or creating a corporation. But there is no phrase in the instrument which, like the articles of confederation, excludes incidental or implied powers; and which requires that everything granted shall be expressly and minutely described. Even the 10th amendment, which was framed for the purpose of quieting the excessive jealousies which had been excited, omits the word "expressly," and declares only, that the powers "not delegated to the United States, nor prohibited to the states, are reserved to the states or to the people;" thus leaving the question, whether the particular power which may become the subject of contest, has been delegated to the one government, or prohibited to the other, to depend on a fair construction of the whole instrument. . . . A constitution, to contain an accurate detail of all the subdivisions of which its great powers will admit, and of all the means by which they may be carried into execution, would partake of the prolixity of a legal code, and could scarcely be embraced by the human mind. It would, probably, never be understood by the public. Its nature, therefore, requires, that only its great outlines should be marked, its important objects designated, and the minor ingredients which compose those objects, be deducted from the nature of the objects themselves. That this idea was entertained by the framers of the American constitution, is not only to be inferred from the nature of the instrument, but from the language. Why else were some of the limitations, found in the 9th section of the 1st article, introduced? It is also, in some degree, warranted, by their having omitted to use any restrictive term which might prevent its receiving a fair and just interpretation. In considering this question, then, we must never forget that it is a *constitution* we are expounding.

Although, among the enumerated powers of government, we do not find the word "bank" or "incorporation," we find the great powers, to lay and collect taxes; to borrow money; to regulate commerce; to declare and conduct a war; and to raise and support armies and navies. The sword and the purse, all the external relations, and no inconsiderable portion of the industry of the nation, are intrusted to its government. . . . [and] a government, intrusted with such ample powers, on the due execution of which the happiness and prosperity of the nation so vitally depends, must also be intrusted with ample means for their execution. The power being given, it is the interest of the nation to facilitate its execution. It can never be their interest, and cannot be presumed to have been their intention, to clog and embarrass its execution, by withholding the most appropriate means. . . . The exigencies of the nation may require, that the treasure raised in the north should be transported to the south, that raised in the east, conveyed to the west, or that this order should be reversed. Is that construction of the constitution to be preferred, which would render these operations difficult, hazardous and expensive? Can we adopt that construction (unless the words imperiously require it), which would impute to the framers of that instrument, when granting these powers for the public good, the intention of impeding their exercise, by withholding a choice of means? If, indeed, such be the mandate of the constitution, we have only to obey; but that instrument does not profess to enumerate the means by which the powers it confers may be executed; nor does it prohibit the creation of a corporation, if the existence of such a being be essential, to the beneficial exercise of those powers. It is, then, the subject of fair inquiry, how far such means may be employed.

It is not denied, that the powers given to the government imply the ordinary means of execution. That, for example, of raising revenue, and applying it to national purposes, is admitted to imply the power of conveying money from place to place, as the exigencies of the nation may require, and of employing the usual means of conveyance. But it is denied, that the government has its choice of means; or, that it may employ the most convenient means, if, to employ them, it be necessary to erect a corporation. On what foundation does this argument rest? On this alone: the power of creating a corporation, is one appertaining to sovereignty, and is not expressly conferred on congress. This is true. But all legislative powers appertain to sovereignty. The original power of giving the law on any subject whatever, is a sovereign power; and if the government of the Union is restrained from creating a corporation, as a means for performing its functions, on the single reason that the creation of a corporation is an act of sovereignty; if the sufficiency of this reason be acknowledged, there would be some difficulty in sustaining the authority of congress to pass other laws for the accomplishment of the same objects. . . .

The creation of a corporation, it is said, appertains to sovereignty. This is admitted. But to what portion of sovereignty does it appertain? Does it belong to one more than to another? In America, the powers of sovereignty are divided between the government of the Union, and those of the states. They are each sovereign, with respect to the objects committed to it, and neither sovereign, with respect to the objects committed to the other. . . . The power of creating a corporation, though appertaining to sovereignty, is not, like the power of making war, or levying taxes, or of regulating commerce, a great substantive and independent power, which cannot be implied as incidental to other powers, or used as a means of executing them. It is never the end for which other powers are exercised, but a means by which other objects are accomplished. . . . The power of creating a corporation is never used for its own sake, but for the purpose of effecting something else. No sufficient reason is, therefore, perceived, why it may not pass as incidental to those powers which are expressly given, if it be a direct mode of executing them.

But the constitution of the United States has not left the right of congress to employ the necessary means, for the execution of the powers conferred on the government, to general reasoning. To its enumeration of powers is added, that of making "all laws which shall be necessary and proper, for carrying into execution the foregoing powers, and all other powers vested by this constitution, in the government of the United States, or in any department thereof." The counsel for the state of Maryland has urged various arguments, to prove that this clause, though, in terms, a grant of power, is not so, in effect; but is really restrictive of the general right, which might otherwise be implied, of selecting means for executing the enumerated powers. . . .

[T]he argument on which most reliance is placed, is drawn from that peculiar language of this clause. Congress is not empowered by it to make all laws, which may have relation to the powers conferred on the government, but such only as may be *"necessary and proper"* for carrying them into execution. The word *"necessary"* is considered as controlling the whole sentence, and as limiting the right to pass laws for the execution of the granted powers, to such as are indispensable, and without which the power would be nugatory. That it excludes the choice of means, and leaves to congress, in each case, that only which is most direct and simple.

Is it true, that this is the sense in which the word "necessary" is always used? Does it always import an absolute physical necessity, so strong, that one thing to which another may be termed necessary, cannot exist without that other? We think it does not. If reference be had to its use, in the common affairs of the world, or in approved authors, we find that it frequently imports no more than that one thing is convenient, or useful, or essential to another. . . . Such is the character of human language, that no word conveys to the mind, in all situations, one single definite idea; and nothing is more common than to use words in a figurative sense. Almost all compositions contain words, which, taken in their rigorous sense, would convey a meaning different from that which is obviously intended. It is essential to just construction, that many words which import something excessive, should be understood in a more mitigated sense—in that sense which common usage justifies. The word "necessary" is of this description. It has not a fixed character, peculiar to itself. It admits of all degrees of comparison; and is often connected with other words, which increase or diminish the impression the mind receives of the urgency it imports. A thing may be necessary, very necessary, absolutely or indispensably necessary. To no mind would the same idea be conveyed by these several phrases. . . . This word, then, like others, is used in various senses; and, in its construction, the subject, the context, the intention of the person using them, are all to be taken into view.

Let this be done in the case under consideration. The subject is the execution of those great powers on which the welfare of a nation essentially depends. It must have been the intention of those who gave these powers, to insure, so far as human prudence could insure, their beneficial execution. This could not be done, by confiding the choice of means to such narrow limits as not to leave it in the power of congress to adopt any which might be appropriate, and which were conducive to the end. This provision is made in a constitution, intended to endure for ages to come, and consequently, to be adapted to the various *crises* of human affairs. To have prescribed the means by which government should, in all future time, execute its powers, would have been to change, entirely, the character of the instrument, and give it the properties of a legal code. It would have been an unwise attempt to provide, by immutable rules, for exigencies which, if foreseen at all, must have been seen dimly, and which can be best provided for as they occur. To have declared, that the best means shall not be used, but those alone, without which the power given would be nugatory, would have been to deprive the legislature of the capacity to avail itself of experience, to exercise its reason, and to accommodate its legislation to circumstances. . . .

But the argument which most conclusively demonstrates the error of the construction contended for by the counsel for the state of Maryland, is founded on the intention of the convention, as manifested in the whole clause. To waste time and argument in proving that, without it, congress might carry its powers into execution, would be not much less idle, than to hold a lighted taper to the sun. As little can it be required to prove, that in the absence of this clause, congress would have some choice of means. That it might employ those which, in its judgment, would most advantageously effect the object to be accomplished. That any means adapted to the end, any means which tended directly to the execution of the constitutional powers of the government, were in themselves constitutional. This clause, as construed by the state of Maryland, would abridge, and almost annihilate, this useful and necessary right of the legislature to select its means. That this could not be intended is, we should think, had it not been already controverted, too apparent for controversy.

We think so for the following reasons: 1st. The clause is

placed among the powers of congress, not among the limitations on those powers. 2d. Its terms purport to enlarge, not to diminish the powers vested in the government. It purports to be an additional power, not a restriction on those already granted. No reason has been, or can be assigned, for thus concealing an intention to narrow the discretion of the national legislature, under words which purport to enlarge it. The framers of the constitution wished its adoption, and well knew that it would be endangered by its strength, not by its weakness. Had they been capable of using language which would convey to the eye one idea, and, after deep reflection, impress on the mind, another, they would rather have disguised the grant of power than its limitation. If, then, their intention had been, by this clause, to restrain the free use of means which might otherwise have been implied, that intention would have been inserted in another place, and would have been expressed in terms resembling these. "In carrying into execution the foregoing powers, and all others," &c., "no laws shall be passed but such as are necessary and proper." Had the intention been to make this clause restrictive, it would unquestionably have been so in form as well as in effect.

The result of the most careful and attentive consideration bestowed upon this clause is, that if it does not enlarge, it cannot be construed to restrain the powers of congress, or to impair the right of the legislature to exercise its best judgment in the selection of measures to carry into execution the constitutional powers of the government. If no other motive for its insertion can be suggested, a sufficient one is found in the desire to remove all doubts respecting the right to legislate on that vast mass of incidental powers which must be involved in the constitution, if that instrument be not a splendid bauble.

We admit, as all must admit, that the powers of the government are limited, and that its limits are not to be transcended. But we think the sound construction of the constitution must allow to the national legislature that discretion, with respect to the means by which the powers it confers are to be carried into execution, which will enable that body to perform the high duties assigned to it, in the manner most beneficial to the people. Let the end be legitimate, let it be within the scope of the constitution, and all means which are appropriate, which are plainly adapted to that end, which are not prohibited, but consist with the letter and spirit of the constitution, are constitutional. . . .

If a corporation may be employed, indiscriminately with other means, to carry into execution the powers of the government, no particular reason can be assigned for excluding the use of a bank, if required for its fiscal operations. To use one, must be within the discretion of congress, if it be an appropriate mode of executing the powers of government. That it is a convenient, a useful, and essential instrument in the prosecution of its fiscal operations, is not now a subject of controversy. All those who have been concerned in the administration of our finances, have concurred in representing its importance and necessity; and so strongly have they been felt, that statesmen of the first class, whose previous opinions against it had been confirmed by every circumstance which can fix the human judgment, have yielded those opinions to the exigencies of the nation. . . . The time has passed away, when it can be necessary to enter into any discussion, in order to prove the importance of this instrument, as a means to effect the legitimate objects of the government.

But were its necessity less apparent, none can deny its being an appropriate measure; and if it is, the decree of its necessity, as has been very justly observed, is to be discussed in another place. Should congress, in the execution of its powers, adopt measures which are prohibited by the constitution; or should congress, under the pretext of executing its powers, pass laws for the accomplishment of objects not intrusted to the government; it would become the painful duty of this tribunal, should a case requiring such a decision come before it, to say, that such an act was not the law of the land. But where the law is not prohibited, and is really calculated to effect any of the objects intrusted to the government, to undertake here to inquire into the decree of its necessity, would be to pass the line which circumscribes the judicial department, and to tread on legislative ground. This court disclaims all pretensions to such a power. . . .

After the most deliberate consideration, it is the unanimous and decided opinion of this court, that the act to incorporate the Bank of the United States is a law made in pursuance of the constitution, and is a part of the supreme law of the land.

The branches, proceeding from the same stock, and being conducive to the complete accomplishment of the object, are equally constitutional. It would have been unwise, to locate them in the charter, and it would be unnecessarily inconvenient, to employ the legislative power in making those subordinate arrangements. The great duties of the bank are prescribed; those duties require branches; and the bank itself may, we think, be safely trusted with the selection of places where those branches shall be fixed; reserving always to the government the right to require that a branch shall be located where it may be deemed necessary.

It being the opinion of the court, that the act incorporating the bank is constitutional; and that the power of establishing a branch in the state of Maryland might be properly exercised by the bank itself, we proceed to inquire—

2. Whether the state of Maryland may, without violating the constitution, tax that branch? That the power of taxation is one of vital importance; that it is retained by the states; that it is not abridged by the grant of a similar power to the government of the Union; that it is to be concurrently exercised by the two governments—are truths which have never been denied. But such is the paramount character of the constitution, that its capacity to withdraw any subject from the action of even this power, is admitted. The states are expressly forbidden to lay

any duties on imports or exports, except what may be absolutely necessary for executing their inspection laws. If the obligation of this prohibition must be conceded—if it may restrain a state from the exercise of its taxing power on imports and exports—the same paramount character would seem to restrain, as it certainly may restrain, a state from such other exercise of this power, as is in its nature incompatible with, and repugnant to, the constitutional laws of the Union. . . .

On this ground, the counsel for the bank place its claim to be exempted from the power of a state to tax its operations. There is no express provision for the case, but the claim has been sustained on a principle which so entirely pervades the constitution, is so intermixed with the materials which compose it, so interwoven with its web, so blended with its texture, as to be incapable of being separated from it, without rending it into shreds. This great principle is, that the constitution and the laws made in pursuance thereof are supreme; that they control the constitution and laws of the respective states, and cannot be controlled by them. From this, which may be almost termed an axiom, other propositions are deduced as corollaries, on the truth or error of which, and on their application to this case, the cause has been supposed to depend. These are, 1st. That a power to create implies a power to preserve: 2d. That a power to destroy, if wielded by a different hand, is hostile to, and incompatible with these powers to create and to preserve: 3d. That where this repugnancy exists, that authority which is supreme must control, not yield to that over which it is supreme.

These propositions, as abstract truths, would, perhaps, never be controverted. Their application to this case, however, has been denied; and both in maintaining the affirmative and the negative, a splendor of eloquence, and strength of argument, seldom, if ever, surpassed, have been displayed. . . .

The argument on the part of the state of Maryland, is, not that the states may directly resist a law of congress, but that they may exercise their acknowledged powers upon it, and that the constitution leaves them this right, in the confidence that they will not abuse it. Before we proceed to examine this argument, and to subject it to test of the constitution, we must be permitted to bestow a few considerations on the nature and extent of this original right of taxation, which is acknowledged to remain with the states. It is admitted, that the power of taxing the people and their property, is essential to the very existence of government, and may be legitimately exercised on the objects to which it is applicable, to the utmost extent to which the government may choose to carry it. . . .

All subjects over which the sovereign power of a state extends, are objects of taxation; but those over which it does not extend, are, upon the soundest principles, exempt from taxation. This proposition may almost be pronounced self-evident.

The sovereignty of a state extends to everything which exists by its own authority, or is introduced by its permission; but does it extend to those means which are employed by congress to carry into execution powers conferred on that body by the people of the United States? We think it demonstrable, that it does not. Those powers are not given by the people of a single state. They are given by the people of the United States, to a government whose laws, made in pursuance of the constitution, are declared to be supreme. Consequently, the people of a single state cannot confer a sovereignty which will extend over them.

If we measure the power of taxation residing in a state, by the extent of sovereignty which the people of a single state possess, and can confer on its government, we have an intelligible standard, applicable to every case to which the power may be applied. We have a principle which leaves the power of taxing the people and property of a state unimpaired; which leaves to a state the command of all its resources; and which places beyond its reach, all those powers which are conferred by the people of the United States on the government of the Union, and all those means which are given for the purpose of carrying those powers into execution. We have a principle which is safe for the states, and safe for the Union. We are relieved, as we ought to be, from clashing sovereignty; from interfering powers; from a repugnancy between a right in one government to pull down, what there is an acknowledged right in another to build up; from the incompatibility of a right in one government to destroy, what there is a right in another to preserve. We are not driven to the perplexing inquiry, so unfit for the judicial department, what degree of taxation is the legitimate use, and what degree may amount to the abuse of the power. . . . We find, then, on just theory, a total failure of this original right to tax the means employed by the government of the Union, for the execution of its powers. The right never existed, and the question whether it has been surrendered, cannot arise.

If we apply the principle for which the state of Maryland contends, to the constitution, generally, we shall find it capable of changing totally the character of that instrument. We shall find it capable of arresting all the measures of the government, and of prostrating it at the foot of the states. The American people have declared their constitution and the laws made in pursuance thereof, to be supreme; but this principle would transfer the supremacy, in fact, to the states. If the states may tax one instrument, employed by the government in the execution of its powers, they may tax any and every other instrument. They may tax the mail; they may tax the mint; they may tax patent-rights; they may tax the papers of the custom-house; they may tax judicial process; they may tax all the means employed by the government, to an excess which would defeat all the ends of government. This was not intended by the American people. They did not design to make their government dependent on the states. . . .

In the course of the argument, the Federalist has been

quoted; and the opinions expressed by the authors of that work have been justly supposed to be entitled to great respect in expounding the constitution. No tribute can be paid to them which exceeds their merit; but in applying their opinions to the cases which may arise in the progress of our government, a right to judge of their correctness must be retained; and to understand the argument, we must examine the proposition it maintains, and the objections against which it is directed. The subject of those numbers, from which passages have been cited, is the unlimited power of taxation which is vested in the general government. . . .

The objections to the constitution which are noticed in these numbers, were to the undefined power of the government to tax, not to the incidental privilege of exempting its own measures from state taxation. The consequences apprehended from this undefined power were, that it would absorb all the objects of taxation, "to the exclusion and destruction of the state governments." The arguments of the Federalist are intended to prove the fallacy of these apprehensions; not to prove that the government was incapable of executing any of its powers, without exposing the means it employed to the embarrassments of state taxation. . . . Had the authors of those excellent essays been asked, whether they contended for that construction of the constitution, which would place within the reach of the states those measures which the government might adopt for the execution of its powers; no man, who has read their instructive pages, will hesitate to admit, that their answer must have been in the negative.

It has also been insisted, that, as the power of taxation in the general and state governments is acknowledged to be concurrent, every argument which would sustain the right of the general government to tax banks chartered by the states, will equally sustain the right of the states to tax banks chartered by the general government. But the two cases are not on the same reason. The people of all the states have created the general government, and have conferred upon it the general power of taxation. The people of all the states, and the states themselves, are represented in congress, and, by their representatives, exercise this power. When they tax the chartered institutions of the states, they tax their constituents; and these taxes must be uniform. But when a state taxes the operations of the government of the United States, it acts upon institutions created, not by their own constituents, but by people over whom they claim no control. It acts upon the measures of a government created by others as well as themselves, for the benefit of others in common with themselves. The difference is that which always exists, and always must exist, between the action of the whole on a part, and the action of a part on the whole—between the laws of a government declared to be supreme, and those of a government which, when in opposition to those laws, is not supreme. . . .

The court has bestowed on this subject its most deliberate consideration. The result is a conviction that the states have no power, by taxation or otherwise, to retard, impede, burden, or in any manner control, the operations of the constitutional laws enacted by congress to carry into execution the powers vested in the general government. This is, we think, the unavoidable consequence of that supremacy which the constitution has declared. We are unanimously of opinion, that the law passed by the legislature of Maryland, imposing a tax on the Bank of the United States, is unconstitutional and void. . . .

18. *Taxing Fiscal Instruments*

WESTON v. CHARLESTON (1829)

(2 Peters 449)

In this opinion Marshall extended the reach of the principles of *McCulloch v. Maryland*. Basically he held that the fiscal instrumentalities of the federal government were exempted from state and local taxation. In this case, the city of Charleston had levied a tax on stock (we today would say bonds) issued by the federal government. The Chief Justice defended his invalidation of the tax on the principled ground that the supremacy of the federal government demanded a totally unobstructed exercise of legitimate powers. Here, indeed, he finally revealed his commitment to protecting the Union from any and all local intrusions, no matter how slight or indirect.

Marshall based this doctrine of immunity on the spirit of the Constitution, buttressed by the specific congressional power ("to borrow money") which the municipal tax offended. The stock in question, therefore, was probative evidence of a debt created by the legitimate exercise of national power; the issuance of the stock itself constituted a contract between the United States and a citizen; and this contract had to carry tax exemption with it or the government would be seriously disadvantaged in borrowing money.

Mr. Chief Justice Marshall delivered the Opinion of the Court: . . .

[T]he main question[:] Is the stock issued for loans made to the government of the United States liable to be taxed by states and corporations?

Congress has power "to borrow money on the credit of the United States." The stock it issues is the evidence of a debt created by the exercise of this power. The tax in question is a tax upon the contract subsisting between the government and the individual. It bears directly upon that contract, while subsisting and in full force. The power operates upon the contract the instant it is framed, and must imply a right to affect that contract. . . .

No one can be selected which is of more vital interest to the community than this of borrowing money on the credit of the United States. No power has been conferred by the American people on their government, the free and unburdened exercise of which more deeply affects every member of our republic. . . . Can anything be more dangerous, or more injurious, than the admission of a principle which authorizes every state and every corporation in the union, which possesses the right of taxation, to burden the exercise of this power at their discretion?

If the right to impose the tax exists, it is a right which in its nature acknowledges no limits. It may be carried to any extent, within the jurisdiction of the state or corporation which imposes it, which the will of each state and corporation may prescribe. A power which is given by the whole American people for their common good, which is to be exercised at the most critical periods for the most important purposes, on the free exercise of which the interest certainly, perhaps the liberty, of the whole may depend, may be burdened, impeded, if not arrested, by any of the organized parts of the confederacy.

In a society formed like ours with one supreme government for national purposes and numerous state governments for other purposes, in many respects independent and in the uncontrolled exercise of many important powers, occasional interferences ought not to surprise us. The power of taxation is one of the most essential to a state and one of the most extensive in its operation. The attempt to maintain a rule which shall limit its exercise is, undoubtedly, among the most delicate and difficult duties which can devolve on those whose province it is to expound the supreme law of the land in its application to the cases of individuals. This duty has more than once devolved on this Court. In the performance of it we have considered it as a necessary consequence from the supremacy of the government of the whole, that its action in the exercise of its legitimate powers should be free and unembarrassed by any conflicting powers in the possession of its parts; that the powers of a state cannot rightfully be so exercised as to impede and obstruct the free course of those measures which the government of the states united may rightfully adopt. . . .

A contract made by the government, in the exercise of its

power, to borrow money on the credit of the United States, is, undoubtedly, independent of the will of any state in which the individual who lends may reside, and is, undoubtedly, an operation essential to the important objects for which the government was created. It ought, therefore, on the principles settled in the case of *M'Cullough* vs. *State of Maryland,* to be exempt from state taxation, and consequently from being taxed by corporations deriving their power from states. . . .

It is not the want of original power in an independent sovereign state, to prohibit loans to a foreign government, which restrains the legislature from direct opposition to those made by the United States. The restraint is imposed by our constitution. The American people have conferred the power of borrowing money on their government, and by making that government supreme, have shielded its action, in the exercise of this power, from the action of the local governments. The grant of the power is incompatible with a restraining or controlling power; and the declaration of supremacy is a declaration that no such restraining or controlling power shall be exercised. . . .

The tax on government stock is thought by this Court to be a tax on the contract, a tax on the power to borrow money on the credit of the United States, and, consequently, to be repugnant to the constitution.

We are, therefore, of opinion that the judgment of the constitutional court of the state of South Carolina, reversing the order made by the court of common pleas, awarding a prohibition to the city council of Charleston to restrain them from levying a tax imposed on six and seven per cent. stock of the United States, under an ordinance to raise supplies to the use of the city of Charleston for the year 1823, is erroneous in this; that the said constitutional court adjudged that the said ordinance was not repugnant to the constitution of the United States; whereas, this Court is of opinion that such repugnancy does exist. We are, therefore, of opinion that the said judgment ought to be reversed and annulled, and the cause remanded to the constitutional court for the state of South Carolina, that farther proceedings may be had therein according to law.

19. *State Currency*

CRAIG v. MISSOURI (1830)
(4 Peters 410)

Soon after *Weston v. Charleston*, Marshall again manifested his zealous concern for insuring the supremacy of federal finance. In this opinion he invalidated a Missouri statute that had essentially established a state currency: the law authorized state loan offices to issue interest-bearing certificates designed to meet the current shortage of paper money. Believing that only the federal government could maintain general stability, the Chief Justice regarded the Missouri practice as one of a class of pernicious threats to America's financial condition. So he defined the certificates as "bills of credit," which the Constitution prohibited the states from issuing. (It should be recalled that the United States had no paper currency—the latter was issued by individual banks.)

The opinion, coming as it did late in Marshall's tenure of office, carried with only a majority of one. Three members of the Court refused to support his rather heavy-handed restraints upon state remedies for financial distress. In turn, Marshall regarded the published dissents of his "brethren" as little short of treason. He lamented in a letter to Story that opinions like the *Craig* dissents would effectively cause "the 25th Section . . . to be nullified by the Supreme Court of the United States . . . at no distant period" in the future. Marshall was unduly pessimistic as to the Court's imminent abdication of judicial review over state action, but his own opinion in this case was surely a short-lived precedent.

In 1837, the "reconstructed" Taney Court proceeded to chip away at Marshall's ruling along the very lines of the *Craig* dissents, providing in *Briscoe v. the Bank of Kentucky* a narrow definition of "bills of credit." But Marshall's voice was heard from the grave: Justice Story filed a posthumous dissent in his behalf.

Mr. Chief Justice MARSHALL delivered the opinion of the Court: Justices Thompson, Johnson, and M'Lean dissenting. . . .

The clause in the constitution which [the Missouri statute at issue] is supposed to violate is in these words: "No state shall" "emit bills of credit."

What is a bill of credit? What did the constitution mean to forbid?

In its enlarged and, perhaps, its literal sense, the term "bill of credit" may comprehend any instrument by which a state engages to pay money at a future day; thus including a certificate given for money borrowed. But the language of the constitution itself, and the mischief to be prevented, which we know from the history of our country, equally limit the interpretation of the terms. . . .

At a very early period of our colonial history the attempt to supply the want of the precious metals by a paper medium was made to a considerable extent; and the bills emitted for this purpose have been frequently denominated "bills of credit." During the war of our revolution we were driven to this expedient, and necessity compelled us to use it to a most fearful extent. The term has acquired an appropriate meaning, and "bills of credit" signify a paper medium, intended to circulate between individuals, and between government and individuals, for the ordinary purposes of society. Such a medium has been always liable to considerable fluctuation. Its value is continually changing; and these changes, often great and sudden, expose individuals to immense loss, are the sources of ruinous speculations, and destroy all confidence between man and man. To cut up this mischief by the roots, a mischief which was felt through the United States and which deeply affected the interest and prosperity of all, the people declared, in their constitution, that no state should emit bills of credit. If the prohibition means anything, if the words are not empty sounds, it must comprehend the emission of any paper medium, by a state government, for the purpose of common circulation.

What is the character of the certificates issued by authority of the act under consideration? What office are they to perform? Certificates, signed by the auditor and treasurer of the state, are to be issued by those officers to the amount of two hundred thousand dollars, of denominations not exceeding ten dollars, nor less than fifty cents. The paper purports on its face to be receivable at the treasury, or at any loan office of the state of Missouri, in discharge of taxes or debts due to the state.

The law makes them receivable in discharge of all taxes, or debts due to the state, or any county or town therein; and of all salaries and fees of office to all officers civil and military within the state, and for salt sold by the lessees of the public salt works. It also pledges the faith and funds of the state for their redemption.

It seems impossible to doubt the intention of the legislature in passing this act, or to mistake the character of these certificates, or the office they were to perform. The denominations of the bills, from ten dollars to fifty cents, fitted them for the purpose of ordinary circulation; and their reception in payment of taxes, and debts to the government and to corporations, and of salaries and fees, would give them currency. They were to be put into circulation, that is, emitted, by the government. In addition to all these evidences of an intention to make these certificates the ordinary circulating medium of the country, the law speaks of them in this character; and directs the auditor and treasurer to withdraw annually one-tenth of them from circulation. Had they been termed "bills of credit," instead of "certificates," nothing would have been wanting to bring them within the prohibitory words of the constitution.

And can this make any real difference? . . . We cannot think so. We think the certificates emitted under the authority of this act are as entirely bills of credit as if they had been so denominated in the act itself.

But it is contended, that though these certificates should be deemed bills of credit according to the common acceptation of the term, they are not so in the sense of the constitution; because they are not made a legal tender.

The constitution itself furnishes no countenance to this distinction. The prohibition is general. It extends to all bills of credit, not to bills of a particular description. That tribunal must be bold indeed, which, without the aid of other explanatory words, could venture on this construction. It is the less admissible in this case because the same clause of the constitution contains a substantive prohibition to the enactment of tender laws. The constitution, therefore, considers the emission of bills of credit, and the enactment of tender laws as distinct operations, independent of each other, which may be separately performed. Both are forbidden. To sustain the one because it is not also the other; to say that bills of credit may be emitted if they be not made a tender in payment of debts; is, in effect, to expunge that distinct, independent prohibition and to read the clause as if it had been entirely omitted. We are not at liberty to do this.

The history of paper money has been referred to for the purpose of showing that its great mischief consists in being made a tender; and that, therefore, the general words of the constitution may be restrained to a particular intent.

Was it even true that the evils of paper money resulted solely from the quality of its being made a tender, this court would not feel itself authorized to disregard the plain meaning of words, in search of a conjectural intent to which we are not conducted by the language of any part of the instrument. But we do not think that the history of our country proves either that being made a tender in payment of debts is an essential quality of bills of credit or the only mischief resulting from them. It may, indeed, be the most pernicious; but that will not authorise a court to convert a general into a particular prohibition. . . .

The certificates for which this note was given being in truth "bills of credit" in the sense of the constitution, we are brought to the inquiry:

Is the note valid of which they form the consideration?

It has been long settled, that a promise made in consideration of an act which is forbidden by law is void. It will not be questioned that an act forbidden by the constitution of the United States, which is the supreme law, is against law. Now the constitution forbids a state to "emit bills of credit." The loan of these certificates is the very act which is forbidden. It is not the making of them, while they lie in the loan offices, but the issuing of them, the putting them into circulation, which is the act of emission; the act that is forbidden by the constitution. The consideration of this note is the emission of bills of credit by the state. The very act which constitutes the consideration is the act of emitting bills of credit, in the mode prescribed by the law of Missouri; which act is prohibited by the constitution of the United States. . . .

A majority of the court feels constrained to say that the consideration on which the note in this case was given is against the highest law of the land, and that the note itself is utterly void. In rendering judgment for the plaintiff, the court for the state of Missouri decided in favor of the validity of a law which is repugnant to the constitution of the United States. . . .

The judgment of the supreme court of the state of Missouri for the first judicial district is reversed; and the cause remanded, with directions to enter judgment for the defendants.

Part Five

COMMERCE

AND STATE AUTHORITY

20. *Navigation as Commerce, I*

BRIG WILSON v. U. S. (1820)

(1 Brockenbrough 423, C.C. Va.)

Marshall examined the scope of congressional power over commerce for the first time in 1820 when on circuit duty in Virginia. In the following case he declared that commerce comprehends navigation, fully anticipating by four years his announcement of that doctrine on the Supreme Court level in *Gibbons v. Ogden*. Of further interest was the joining of the commerce clause with the slavery issue in this particular case, which arose under a punitive statute that Congress had passed to enforce the southern policy of excluding free Negroes from slave states. (The presence and activities of free Negroes were believed to contribute to slave insurrections.) The entry of free Negroes through the ports was to be blocked by penalizing ship owners with forfeiture of their vessels for bringing these subversives to shore. The congressional legislation took the form of enforcing whatever pattern of exclusion a state set for itself. Marshall claimed the constitutional basis for this statute was the commerce clause since "navigation" was the subject under control.

Marshall avoided ruling the Virginia statute an unconstitutional impingement upon the domain of commerce. In the instant case, "coloured" crew members of a privateer, commissioned by the government of "Buenos Ayres," disembarked in Norfolk, and for that offense the vessel was seized. But Marshall decided on the basis of devious statutory construction that the forfeiture was not justified. The Brig Wilson had to be returned, but Virginia was advised, in effect, to redraft its law and revise its categories of excluded persons so that next time the forfeiture would be valid. Unlike Marshall, Justice Johnson ruled a similar statute in South Carolina to be flatly unconstitutional. Johnson was damned for apostasy—he was a native son—and his ruling was flouted. (He then entered a bitter newspaper controversy, using a *nom de plume*, and in the best polemical style defended the ruling.)

Marshall took a different attitude. In a letter to Justice Story, Marshall wrote:

> . . . (A) case has been brought before me in which I might have considered its constitutionality, had I chosen to do so; but it was not absolutely necessary, and as I am not fond of butting against a wall in sport, I escaped on the construction of the act.

The following opinion was delivered by Marshall, C. J.: . . .
I proceed, now, to the fifth count in the libel.

The first question which will be considered in this part of the case, will be the constitutionality of the act of congress, under which this condemnation has been made.

It will readily be admitted, that the power of the legislature of the Union, on this subject, is derived entirely from the 3d clause of the 8th section of the 1st article of the Constitution. That clause enables congress, "to regulate commerce with foreign nations, and among the several States, and with the Indian Tribes."

What is the extent of this power to regulate commerce? Does it not comprehend the navigation of the country? May not the vessels, as well as the articles they bring, be regulated? Upon what principle is it, that the ships of any foreign nation have been forbidden, under pain of forfeiture, to enter our ports? The authority to make such laws has never been questioned; and yet, it can be sustained by no other clause in the Constitution, than that which enables congress to regulate commerce. If this power over vessels is not in congress, where does it reside? Certainly it is not annihilated; and if not, it must reside somewhere. Does it reside in the states? No American politician has ever been so extravagant as to contend for this. No man has been wild enough to maintain, that, although the power to regulate commerce, gives congress an unlimited power over the cargoes, it does not enable that body to control the vehicle in which they are imported: that, while the whole power of commerce is vested in congress, the state legislatures may confiscate every vessel which enters their ports, and congress is unable to prevent their entry. Let it be admitted, for the sake of argument, that a law, forbidding a free man of any colour, to come into the United States, would be void, and that no penalty, imposed on him by Congress, could be enforced: still, the vessel, which should bring him into the United States, might be forfeited, and that forfeiture enforced; since even an empty vessel, or a packet, employed solely in the conveyance of passengers and letters, may be regulated and forfeited. There is not in the Constitution, one syllable on the subject of navigation. And yet, every power that pertains to navigation has been uniformly exercised, and, in the opinion of all, been rightfully exercised, by congress. From the adoption of the Constitution, till this time, the universal sense of America has been, that the word commerce, as used in that instrument, is to be considered a generic term, comprehending navigation, or, that a control over navigation is necessarily incidental to the power to regulate commerce.

I could feel no difficulty in saying, that the power to regulate commerce, clearly comprehended the case, were there no other clauses in the Constitution, showing the sense of the convention on that subject. But there is a clause which would remove the doubt, if any could exist.

The first clause of the ninth section, declares, that "the migration, or importation of such persons as any of the states, now existing, shall think proper to admit, shall not be prohibited by the congress, prior to the year 1808." This has been truly said to be a limitation of the power of congress to regulate commerce, and it will not be pretended, that a limitation of a power is to be construed into a grant of power. . . .

Suppose the grant and the limitation be brought together, the clause would read thus: "Congress shall have power to regulate commerce, &c., but this power shall not be so exercised, as to prohibit the migration, or importation of such persons, as any of the states now existing, may think proper to admit, prior to the year 1808." Would it be possible to doubt, that the power to regulate commerce, in the sense in which those words were used in the Constitution, included the power to prohibit the migration, or importation, of any persons whatever, into the states, except so far as this power might be restrained by other clauses of the Constitution? I think it would be impossible. It appears to me, then, that the power of congress over vessels, which might bring in persons of any description, whatever, was complete before the year 1808, except that it could not be so exercised, as to prohibit the importation or migration of any persons, whom any state, in existence at the formation of the Constitution, might think proper to admit. The act of congress, then, is to be construed with a view to this restriction, on the power of the legislature; and the only question will be, whether it comprehends this case?

The case is, that the brig *Wilson,* a private armed cruizer, commissioned by the government of Buenos Ayres, came into Norfolk, navigated by a crew some of whom were people of colour. They were however, all free men, and all of them sailors, composing a part of the crew. While in port some of them were discharged, and came on shore.

The libel charges that three persons of colour were landed from the vessel, whose admission or importation was prohibited by the laws of Virginia, contrary to the act of congress, by which the vessel was forfeited.

Is this case within the act of congress, passed the 28th of February 1803?

The first section, which is the prohibiting part of the act, is in these words: "From and after the first day of April next, no master or captain of any ship or vessel, or any other person, shall import or bring, or cause to be imported or brought, any negro, mulatto, or any person of colour, &c." There are nice shades or gradations in language, which are more readily perceived than described, and the mind impressed with a particular idea, readily employs those words which express it most appropriately. Words which have a direct and common meaning, may also be used in a less common sense, but we do not understand them in the less common sense, unless the context, or the clear design of the person using them, requires them to be so understood. Now the verbs, "to import," or "to bring in," seem to me to indicate, and are most commonly employed as indicating, the action of a person on any thing, animate or inanimate, which is itself passive. The agent, or those who are concerned in the agency or importation, are not, in common language, said to be imported or brought in. It is true that a vessel coming into port, is the vehicle which brings in her crew, but we do not in common language say, that the mariners are "imported," or brought in by a particular vessel; we rather say they bring in the vessel. So, too, if the legislature intended to punish the captain of a vessel, for employing seamen of a particular description, or for allowing these seamen to come on shore, we should expect that this intention would be expressed by more appropriate words, than "to import" or "bring in." These words are peculiarly applicable to persons not concerned in navigating the vessel. It is not probable, then, that in making this provision, a regulation respecting the crew of a vessel was in the mind of congress. But it is contended, on the part of the prosecution, that the succeeding words of the sentence, exempting certain descriptions of persons from the general prohibition, show that the prohibition itself was intended to comprehend the crew, as well as those who did not belong to the vessel. Those words are, "not being a native, a citizen, or registered seaman of the United States, or seamen natives of countries beyond the Cape of Good Hope."

That this limitation, proves the prohibition to have been intended to comprehend freemen, as well as slaves, must, I think, be admitted. But it does not follow, that it was, also, intended to comprehend the crew of a vessel, actually employed in her navigation, and not put on board, in fraud of the law. A person of colour, who is a registered seaman of the United States, may be imported, or brought into the United States, in a vessel in which he is not employed as a mariner. The construction, therefore, which would extend the prohibitory part of the sentence, to the crew of the vessel, in consequence of the language of the exception, is not a necessary construction, though I must admit, that it derives much strength from that language.

The forfeiture of the vessel is not, in this section of the act, but I have noticed its construction, because it is not reasonable to suppose, that it was intended to forfeit a vessel for an act which was not prohibited. The second section enacts, "that no ship or vessel, arriving in any of the said ports or places of the United States, and *having on board* any negro, mulatto, or other person of colour, not being a native, a citizen, or registered seaman of the United States; or seamen, natives of countries beyond the Cape of Good Hope, as aforesaid, shall be admitted to an entry."

It is obvious, that this clause was intended to refuse an entry to every vessel, which had violated the prohibition contained in the first section; and that the words, "having on board" were used, as co-extensive with the words "import," or "bring." We had, at that time, a treaty with the Emperor of Morocco, and with several other Barbary powers. Their subjects are all people of colour. It is true, they are not so engaged in commerce, as to send ships abroad. But the arrival of a Moorish vessel in our ports, is not an impossibility; and can it be believed, that this law was intended to refuse an entry to such a vessel? It may be said, that an occurrence which has never taken place, and which, in all probability, never will take place, was not in the mind of congress; and, consequently the omission to provide for it, ought not to influence the construction of their acts. But there are many nations, with whom we have regular commerce, who employ coloured seamen. Could it be intended by congress, to refuse an entry to a French, a Spanish, an English, or a Portuguese merchant vessel, in whose crew there was a man of colour? I think this construction could never be given to the act. The words, *"having on board* a negro, mulatto, or other person of colour" would not, I think, be, applied to a vessel, one of whose crew was a person of colour.

The section then proceeds: "And if any such negro, &c., shall be landed from on board any ship or vessel, &c., the said ship or vessel, &c., shall be forfeited."

"The words, "shall be landed," seem peculiarly applicable to a person, or thing, which is imported, or *brought in,* and which is landed, not by its own act, but by the authority of the importer, not to a mariner, going on shore voluntarily, or on the business of the ship. The words, *"such* negro," &c., refer to the preceding passages, describing those whom a captain of a vessel is forbidden to import, and whose being on board a vessel excludes such vessel from an entry, and no others. If, then, the commentary, which has been made on those passages, is correct, the forfeiture is not incurred by a person of colour, coming in as part of a ship's crew, and going on shore.

Although the powers of Barbary, do not send merchant ships across the Atlantic, yet their treaties with us, contemplate the possibility of their cruizers entering our ports. Would the cruizer be forfeited, should one of the crew come on shore?

I have contended, that the power of congress to regulate commerce, comprehends, necessarily, a power over navigation, and warrants every act of national sovereignty, which any other sovereign nation may exercise over vessels, foreign or domestic, which enter our ports. But there is a portion of this power, so far as respects foreign vessels, which it is unusual for any nation to exercise, and the exercise of which would be deemed an unfriendly interference with the just rights of foreign powers. An example of this would be, an attempt to regulate the manner in which a foreign vessel should be navigated in order to be admitted into our ports; and to subject such vessel to forfeiture, if not so navigated. I will not say, that this is beyond the power of a government, but I will say, that no act ought to have this effect given to it, unless the words be such as to admit of no other rational construction.

I will now take some notice of that part of the act which has a reference to the state law.

The language, both of the Constitution and of the act of congress, shows, that the forfeiture was not intended to be inflicted in any case but where the state law was violated. In addition to the words, in the first and second sections of the act, which confine its operation to importations, into "a state which, by law, has prohibited, or shall prohibit, the importation of such negro," &c.; the third section enjoins it on the officers of the United States, in the states having laws containing such prohibition, "to notice and be governed by the provisions of the laws, now existing, of the several states, prohibiting the admission or importation of any negro, mulatto, or any person of colour, as aforesaid." This is not inflicting a penalty for the violation of a state law, but is limiting the operation of the penal law of the United States, by a temporary demarcation given in the Constitution. The power of congress to prevent migration or importation, was not to be exercised prior to the year 1808, on any person whom any of the states might think proper to admit. All were admissible who were not prohibited.

It was proper, therefore, that the act of congress should make the prohibitory act of the state, the limit of its own operation. The act of congress does not, necessarily, extend to every object comprehended in the state law, but neither its terms, nor the Constitution, will permit it to be extended farther than the state law.

The first section of the act "to prevent the migration of free negroes and mulattoes" into [Virginia], prohibits their coming voluntarily or being imported. The second section imposes a penalty on any master of a vessel, who shall bring any free negro or mulatto. The third section provides, that "the act shall not extend to any masters of vessels, who shall bring into this state any free negro or mulatto, employed on board, and belonging to such vessel, and who shall therewith depart." The act, then, does not prohibit the master of a vessel, navigated by free negroes or mulattos, from coming into port, and setting only part of the crew on shore, provided they depart with the vessel. The state prohibition, then, does not commence, until the vessel departs without the negro or mulatto seaman. No probability, however strong, that the vessel will depart without the seaman, can extend the act to such a case, until the vessel has actually departed. If this be true, neither does the act of congress extend to such a case.

But this is not all. The act of assembly prohibits the admission of free negroes and mulattos only, not of other persons of colour. Other persons of colour were admissible into Virginia. The act of congress makes a clear distinction between free negroes, and mulattos, and other persons of colour. But so much of the act of congress, as respects other persons of colour, does not apply to Virginia, because such persons were admissible into this state.

The libel charges the sailors landed, to have been persons of colour, not negroes or mulattos. If, under this libel it were allowable to prove, that the sailors landed, were, in fact, negroes or mulattos, it is not proved. Mr. Bush does not prove, that any were landed, but says, that those discharged were "of different colours and nations." Andrew Johnson says, "that on the 29th of October, *the people of colour* received their prize tickets, went on shore, and, of course, took their own discharge."

There is, then, no evidence, that these people were negroes or mulattos. Upon these grounds, I am of opinion, that no forfeiture of the vessel has been incurred, and that so much of the sentence as condemns the brig *Wilson,* ought to be reversed and restitution awarded.

21. *Navigation as Commerce, II*

GIBBONS v. OGDEN (1824)

(9 Wheaton 1)

The following opinion is generally regarded as one of Marshall's greatest state papers. (Indeed, when the Supreme Court sustained the Civil Rights Act of 1964, it cited *Gibbons v. Ogden* as the controlling precedent!) Its immediate popularity, however, depended far more upon the holding (which struck down a notorious monopoly) than upon the incidental doctrines. The case originated as a challenge to a New York statute under which Gibbons was enjoined from operating a steamboat line on the Hudson River. The state had granted monopoly control over that type of transportation in state waters to Messrs. Fulton and Livingston as a reward for designing and producing an efficient steamboat, and Ogden had been granted a license by the monopolists to conduct the Hudson River traffic. In response to the New York law, neighboring states passed vindictive legislation, e.g., boats licensed by the New York monopolists could not enter New Jersey and Connecticut waters. It was precisely to prevent such disruption of commercial enterprise, however, that control over commerce had been allocated to Congress by the Constitution. Under the Confederation, retaliatory state laws almost brought interstate commerce to a standstill.

The terse wording of the commerce clause provided no definition of commerce and conferred no jurisdiction over commerce to the states. Were the states, then, excluded from legislating on all kinds of commercial subjects? Or could the states legislate on subjects, properly under congressional control, when Congress failed to act? In the instant case, the New York judiciary—in a notable opinion by Chancellor James Kent—had defended the steamboat monopoly as an exercise of state authority over a "local" subject *and/or* over a "federal" subject where Congress was silent. Marshall rejected New York's statement of the legal facts: Congress, he argued, had legislated over the "federal" subject of navigation in the Coasting Act of 1789.

Before announcing the supremacy of the federal statute over the state statute upon which the narrow holding was actually based, Marshall casually took his famous exploratory soundings of the commerce clause. He refused, however, to canvass the question of the validity of state commercial legislation on subjects to which Congress had *not* addressed itself. That question was hypothetical because his esoteric construction of the Coasting Act purported to demonstrate that Congress had already spoken. Although he was unwilling to explore the metaphysics of concurrent jurisdiction, the Chief Justice did consent to delineate the type of subjects which lay within state authority. Almost off-handedly he conceded that states could legislate on "completely internal commerce" that does not "affect other states, and with which it is not necessary to interfere, for the purpose of executing some of the general powers of the government." An open-ended definition of this sort, when invoked in future cases, brought the opinion its justified reputation as a victory for the federal government. In one sense, the opinion was better rhetoric than precedent, for most of the memorable phrases were *obiter dicta* (and Justice Johnson's concurring opinions set forth the really hard line, that the commerce clause *ex proprio vigore* terminated state authority in the area—even if Congress had not legislated).

Marshall, in short, was unwilling to announce a definitive interpretation of the commerce clause in all its ramifications, but the drift of all his arguments pointed to quite comprehensive federal control. In the way of concrete results, he did manage to destroy an unpopular monopoly (albeit in his own fashion) by invalidating an act of state interference in the congressional domain. The New York statute, as it were, provided Marshall with an opportunity to establish congressional hegemony over a rather broadly undefined sector of commercial activity.

MARSHALL, Ch. J., delivered the opinion of the court, and, after stating the case, proceeded as follows:—The appellant contends, that this decree is erroneous, because the laws which purport to give the exclusive privilege it sustains, are repugnant to the constitution and laws of the United States. They are said to be repugnant—1st. To that clause in the constitution which authorizes congress to regulate commerce. . . .

The state of New York maintains the constitutionality of these laws; and their legislature, their council of revision, and their judges, have repeatedly concurred in this opinion. It is supported by great names—by names which have all the titles to consideration that virtue, intelligence and office can bestow. No tribunal can approach the decision of this question, without feeling a just and real respect for that opinion which is sustained by such authority; but it is the province of this court, while it respects, not to bow to it implicitly; and the judges must exercise, in the examination of the subject, that understanding which Providence has bestowed upon them, with that independence which the people of the United States expect from this department of the government.

As preliminary to the very able discussions of the constitution, which we have heard from the bar, and as having some influence on its construction, reference has been made to the political situation of these states, anterior to its formation. It has been said, that they were sovereign, were completely independent, and were connected with each other only by a league. This is true. But when these allied sovereigns converted their league into a government, when they converted their congress of ambassadors, deputed to deliberate on their common concerns, and to recommend measures of general utility, into a legislature, empowered to enact laws on the most interesting subjects, the whole character in which the states appear, underwent a change, the extent of which must be determined by a fair consideration of the instrument by which that change was effected.

This instrument contains an enumeration of powers expressly granted by the people to their government. It has been said, that these powers ought to be construed strictly. But why ought they to be so construed? Is there one sentence in the constitution which gives countenance to this rule? In the last of the enumerated powers, that which grants, expressly, the means for carrying all others into execution, congress is authorized "to make all laws which shall be necessary and proper" for the purpose. But this limitation on the means which may be used, is not extended to the powers which are conferred; nor is there one sentence in the constitution, which has been pointed out by the gentlemen of the bar, or which we have been able to discern, that prescribes this rule. We do not, therefore, think ourselves justified in adopting it. . . . If, from the imperfection of human language, there should be serious doubts respecting the extent of any given power, it is a well-settled rule, that the objects for which it was given, especially, when those objects are expressed in the instrument itself, should have great influence in the construction. We know of no reason for excluding this rule from the present case. The grant does not convey power which might be beneficial to the grantor, if retained by himself, or which can inure solely to the benefit of the grantee; but is an investment of power for the general advantage, in the hands of agents selected for that purpose; which power can never be exercised by the people themselves, but must be placed in the hands of agents, or lie dormant. We know of no rule for construing the extent of such powers, other than is given by the language of the instrument which confers them, taken in connection with the purposes for which they were conferred.

The words are, "congress shall have power to regulate commerce with foreign nations, and among the several states, and with the Indian tribes." The subject to be regulated is commerce; and our constitution being, as was aptly said at the bar, one of enumeration, and not of definition, to ascertain the extent of the power, it becomes necessary to settle the meaning of the word. The counsel for the appellee would limit it to traffic, to buying and selling, or the interchange of commodities, and do not admit that it comprehends navigation. This would restrict a general term, applicable to many objects, to one of its significations. Commerce, undoubtedly, is traffic, but it is something more—it is intercourse. It describes the commercial intercourse between nations, and parts of nations, in all its branches, and is regulated by prescribing rules for carrying on that intercourse. The mind can scarcely conceive a system for regulating commerce between nations, which shall exclude all laws concerning navigation, which shall be silent on the admission of the vessels of the one nation into the ports of the other, and be confined to prescribing rules for the conduct of individuals, in the actual employment of buying and selling, or of barter. If commerce does not include navigation, the government of the Union has no direct power over that subject, and can make no law prescribing what shall constitute American vessels, or requiring that they shall be navigated by American seamen. Yet this power has been exercised from the commencement of the government, has been exercised with the consent of all, and has been understood by all to be a commercial regulation. All America understands, and has uniformly understood, the word "commerce," to comprehend navigation. It was so understood, and must have been so understood, when the constitution was framed. The power over commerce, including navigation, was one of the primary objects for which the people of America adopted their government, and must have been contemplated in forming it. The convention must have used the word in that sense, because all have understood it in that sense; and the attempt to restrict it comes too late. . . .

The universally acknowledged power of the government to impose embargoes, must also be considered as showing, that all America is united in that construction which comprehends navigation in the word commerce. Gentlemen have said, in argument, that this is a branch of the war-making power, and that an embargo is an instrument of war, not a regulation of trade. That it may be, and often is, used as an instrument of war, cannot be denied. . . . But all embargoes are not of this description. They are sometimes resorted to, without a view to war, and with a single view to commerce. In such case, an embargo is no more a war measure, than a merchantman is a ship of war, because both are vessels which navigate the ocean with sails and seamen. When congress imposed that embargo which, for a time, engaged the attention of every man in the United States, the avowed object of the law was, the protection of commerce, and the avoiding of war. By its friends and its enemies, it was treated as a commercial, not as a war measure. The persevering earnestness and zeal with which it was opposed, in a part of our country which supposed its interests to be vitally affected by the act, cannot be forgotten. A want of acuteness in discovering objections to a measure to which they felt the most deep-rooted hostility, will not be imputed to those who were arrayed in opposition to this. Yet they never suspected that navigation was no branch of trade, and was, therefore, not comprehended in the power to regulate commerce. They did, indeed, contest the constitutionality of the act, but, on a principle which admits the construction for which the appellant contends. They denied that the particular law in question was made in pursuance of the constitution, not because the power could not act directly on vessels, but because a perpetual embargo was the annihilation, and not the regulation of commerce. In terms, they admitted the applicability of the words used in the constitution to vessels; and that, in a case which produced a degree and an extent of excitement, calculated to draw forth every principle on which legitimate resistance could be sustained. No example could more strongly illustrate the universal understanding of the American people on this subject.

The word used in the constitution, then, comprehends, and has been always understood to comprehend, navigation within its meaning; and a power to regulate navigation, is as expressly granted, as if that term had been added to the word "commerce." To what commerce does this power extend? The constitution informs us, to commerce "with foreign nations, and among the several states, and with the Indian tribes." It has, we believe, been universally admitted, that these words comprehend every species of commercial intercourse between the United States and foreign nations. No sort of trade can be carried on between this country and any other, to which this power does not extend. It has been truly said, that commerce, as the word is used in the constitution, is a unit, every part of which is indicated by the term.

If this be the admitted meaning of the word, in its application to foreign nations, it must carry the same meaning throughout the sentence, and remain a unit, unless there be some plain intelligible cause which alters it. The subject to which the power is next applied, is to commerce, "among the several states." The word "among" means intermingled with. A thing which is among others, is intermingled with them. Commerce among the states, cannot stop at the external boundary line of each state, but may be introduced into the interior. It is not intended to say, that these words comprehend that commerce, which is completely internal, which is carried on between man and man in a state, or between different parts of the same state, and which does not extend to or affect other states. Such a power would be inconvenient, and is certainly unnecessary. Comprehensive as the word "among" is, it may very properly be restricted to that commerce which concerns more states than one. The phrase is not one which would probably have been selected to indicate the completely interior traffic of a state, because it is not an apt phrase for that purpose; and the enumeration of the particular classes of commerce to which the power was to be extended, would not have been made, had the intention been to extend the power to every description. The enumeration presupposes something not enumerated; and that something, if we regard the language or the subject of the sentence, must be the exclusively internal commerce of a state. The genius and character of the whole government seem to be, that its action is to be applied to all the external concerns of the nation, and to those internal concerns which affect the states generally; but not to those which are completely within a particular state, which do not affect other states, and with which it is not necessary to interfere, for the purpose of executing some of the general powers of the government. The completely internal commerce of a state, then, may be considered as reserved for the state itself.

But in regulating commerce with foreign nations, the power of congress does not stop at the jurisdictional lines of the several states. It would be a very useless power, if it could not pass those lines. The commerce of the United States with foreign nations, is that of the whole United States; every district has a right to participate in it. The deep streams which penetrate our country in every direction, pass through the interior of almost every state in the Union, and furnish the means of exercising this right. If congress has the power to regulate it, that power must be exercised whenever the subject exists. If it exists within the states, if a foreign voyage may commence or terminate at a port within a state, then the power of congress may be exercised within a state.

This principle is, if possible, still more clear, when applied to commerce "among the several states." . . . Commerce among the states must, of necessity, be commerce with the states. In regulation of trade with the Indian tribes, the action of the law, especially, when the constitution was made, was chiefly within a state. The power of congress, then, whatever it may be, must be exercised within the territorial jurisdiction of the several states. . . .

We are now arrived at the inquiry—what is this power? It is the power to regulate; that is, to prescribe the rule by which commerce is to be governed. This power, like all others vested in congress, is complete in itself, may be exercised to its utmost extent, and acknowledges no limitations, other than are prescribed in the constitution. These are expressed in plain terms, and do not affect the questions which arise in this case, or which have been discussed at the bar. . . . The power of congress, then, comprehends navigation, within the limits of every state in the Union; so far as that navigation may be, in any manner, connected with "commerce with foreign nations, or among the several states, or with the Indian tribes." It may, of consequence, pass the jurisdictional line of New York, and act upon the very waters to which the prohibition now under consideration applies.

But it has been urged, with great earnestness, that although the power of congress to regulate commerce with foreign nations, and among the several states, be co-extensive with the subject itself, and have no other limits than are prescribed in the constitution, yet the states may severally exercise the same power, within their respective jurisdictions. . . . The sole question is, can a state regulate commerce with foreign nations and among states, while congress is regulating it?

The counsel for the respondent answer this question in the affirmative, and rely very much on the restrictions in the 10th section, as supporting their opinion. They say, very truly, that limitations of a power furnish a strong argument in favor of the existence of that power, and that the section which prohibits the states from laying duties on imports or exports, proves that this power might have been exercised, had it not been expressly forbidden; and, consequently, that any other commercial regulation, not expressly forbidden, to which the original power of the state was competent, may still be made. That this restriction shows the opinion of the convention, that a state might impose duties on exports and imports, if not expressly forbidden, will be conceded; but that it follows, as a consequence, from this concession, that a state may regulate commerce with foreign nations and among the states, cannot be admitted.

We must first determine, whether the act of laying "duties or imposts on imports or exports," is considered, in the constitution, as a branch of the taxing power, or of the power to regulate commerce. We think it very clear, that it is considered as a branch of the taxing power. It is so treated in the first clause of the 8th section: "Congress shall have power to lay and collect taxes, duties, imposts and excises;" and before commerce is mentioned, the rule by which the exercise of this power must be governed, is declared. It is, that all duties, imposts and excises shall be uniform. In a separate clause of the enumeration, the power to regulate commerce is given, as being entirely distinct from the right to levy taxes and imposts, and as being a new power, not before conferred. The constitution, then, considers these powers as substantive, and distinct from each other; and so places them in the enumeration it contains. The power of imposing duties on imports is classed with the power to levy taxes, and that seems to be its natural place. But the power to levy taxes could never be considered as abridging the right of the states on that subject; and they might, consequently, have exercised it, by levying duties on imports or exports, had the constitution contained no prohibition on this subject. This prohibition, then, is an exception from the acknowledged power of the states to levy taxes, not from the questionable power to regulate commerce.

"A duty of tonnage" is as much a tax, as a duty on imports or exports; and the reason which induced the prohibition of those taxes, extends to this also. This tax may be imposed by a state, with the consent of congress; and it may be admitted, that congress cannot give a right to a state, in virtue of its own powers. But a duty of tonnage, being part of the power of imposing taxes, its prohibition may certainly be made to depend on congress, without affording any implication respecting a power to regulate commerce. . . . These restrictions, then, are on the taxing power, not on that to regulate commerce; and presuppose the existence of that which they restrain, not of that which they do not purport to restrain.

But the inspection laws are said to be regulations of commerce, and are certainly recognised in the constitution, as being passed in the exercise of a power remaining with the states. That inspection laws may have a remote and considerable influence on commerce, will not be denied; but that a power to regulate commerce is the source from which the right to pass them is derived, cannot be admitted. The object of inspection laws, is to improve the quality of articles produced by the labor of a country; to fit them for exportation; or, it may be, for domestic use. They act upon the subject, before it becomes an article of foreign commerce, or of commerce among the states, and prepare it for that purpose. They form a portion of that immense mass of legislation, which embraces everything within the territory of a state, not surrendered to the general government; all which can be most advantageously exercised by the states themselves. Inspection laws, quarantine laws, health laws of every description, as well as laws for regulating the internal commerce of a state, and those which respect turnpike-roads, ferries, &c., are component parts of this mass.

No direct general power over these objects is granted to congress; and, consequently, they remain subject to state legislation. If the legislative power of the Union can reach them, it must be for national purposes; it must be, where the power is expressly given for a special purpose, or is clearly incidental to some power which is expressly given. It is obvious, that the government of the Union, in the exercise of its express powers, that, for example, of regulating commerce with foreign nations and among the states, may use means that may also be employed by a state, in the exercise of its acknowledged powers; that, for example, of regulating commerce within the state. . . . All experience shows, that the same measures, or measures scarcely distinguishable from each other, may flow from distinct powers; but this does not prove that the powers themselves are identical. Although the means used in their execution may sometimes approach each other so nearly as to be confounded, there are other situations in which they are sufficiently distinct, to establish their individuality. . . .

It has been said, that the act of August 7th, 1789, acknowledges a concurrent power in the states to regulate the conduct of pilots, and hence is inferred an admission of their concurrent right with congress to regulate commerce with foreign nations, and amongst the states. But this inference is not, we think, justified by the fact. Although congress cannot enable a state to legislate, congress may adopt the provisions of a state on any subject. When the government of the Union was brought into existence, it found a system for the regulation of its pilots in full force in every state. The act which has been mentioned, adopts this system, and gives it the same validity as if its provisions had been specially made by congress. But the act, it may be said, is prospective also, and the adoption of laws to be made in future, presupposes the right in the maker to legislate on the subject. The act unquestionably manifests an intention to leave this subject entirely to the states, until congress should think proper to interpose; but the very enactment of such a law indicates an opinion that it was necessary; that the existing system would not be applicable to the new state of things, unless expressly applied to it by congress. But this section is confined to pilots within the "bays, inlets, rivers, harbors and ports of the United States," which are, of course, in whole or in part, also within the limits of some particular state. The acknowledged power of a state to regulate its police, its domestic trade, and to govern its own citizens, may enable it to legislate on this subject, to a considerable extent; and the adoption of its system by congress, and the application of it to the whole subject of commerce, does not seem to the court to imply a right in the states so to apply it of their own authority. But the adoption of the state system being temporary, being only "until further legislative provision shall be made by congress," shows, conclusively, an opinion, that congress could control the whole subject, and might adopt the system of the states, or provide one of its own. . . .

These acts were cited at the bar for the purpose of showing an opinion in congress, that the states possess, concurrently with the legislature of the Union, the power to regulate commerce with foreign nations and among the states. Upon reviewing them, we think, they do not establish the proposition they were intended to prove. They show the opinion, that the states retain powers enabling them to pass the laws to which allusion has been made, not that those laws proceed from the particular power which has been delegated to congress.

It has been contended by the counsel for the appellant, that, as the word "to regulate" implies in its nature, full power over the thing to be regulated, it excludes, necessarily, the action of all others that would perform the same operation on the same thing. That regulation is designed for the entire result, applying to those parts which remain as they were, as well as to those which are altered. It produces a uniform whole, which is as much disturbed and deranged by changing what the regulating power designs to leave untouched, as that on which it has operated. There is great force in this argument, and the court is not satisfied that it has been refuted.

Since, however, in exercising the power of regulating their own purely internal affairs, whether of trading or police, the states may sometimes enact laws, the validity of which depends on their interfering with, and being contrary to, an act of congress passed in pursuance of the constitution, the court will enter upon the inquiry, whether the laws of New York, as expounded by the highest tribunal of that state, have, in their application to this case, come into collision with an act of congress, and deprived a citizen of a right to which that act entitles him. Should this collision exist, it will be immaterial, whether those laws were passed in virtue of a concurrent power "to regulate commerce with foreign nations and among the several states," or, in virtue of a power to regulate their domestic trade and police. In one case and the other, the acts of New York must yield to the law of congress; and the decision sustaining the privilege they confer, against a right given by a law of the Union, must be erroneous. . . .

It will at once occur, that, when a legislature attaches certain privileges and exemptions to the exercise of a right over which its control is absolute, the law must imply a power to exercise the right. The privileges are gone, if the right itself be annihilated. It would be contrary to all reason, and to the course of human affairs, to say that a state is unable to strip a vessel of the particular privileges attendant on the exercise of a right, and yet may annul the right itself; that the state of New York cannot prevent an enrolled and licensed vessel, proceeding from Elizabethtown, in New Jersey, to New York, from enjoying, in her course, and on her entrance into port, all the privileges conferred by the act of congress; but can shut her up in her own port, and prohibit altogether her entering the waters and ports of another state. To the court, it seems very clear, that the whole act on the subject of the coasting trade, according to those principles which govern the construction of statutes, implies, unequivocally, an authority to licensed vessels to carry on the coasting trade.

But we will proceed briefly to notice those sections which bear more directly on the subject. The first section declares, that vessels enrolled by virtue of a previous law, and certain other vessels, enrolled as described in that act, and having a license in force, as is by the act required, "and no others, shall be deemed ships or vessels of the United States, entitled to the privileges of ships or vessels employed in the coasting trade." This section seems to the court to contain a positive enactment, that the vessels it describes shall be entitled to the privileges of ships or vessels employed in the coasting trade. These privileges cannot be separated from the trade, and cannot be enjoyed, unless the trade may be prosecuted. The grant of the privilege is an idle, empty form, conveying nothing, unless it convey the right to which the privilege is attached, and in the exercise of which its whole value consists. To construe these words otherwise than as entitling the ships or vessels described, to carry on the coasting trade, would be, we think, to disregard the apparent intent of the act.

The fourth section directs the proper officer to grant to a vessel qualified to receive it, "a license for carrying on the coasting trade," and prescribes its form. After reciting the compliance of the applicant with the previous requisites of the law, the operative words of the instrument are, "license is hereby granted for the said steam-boat Bellona, to be employed in carrying on the coasting trade for one year from the date hereof, and no longer." These are not the words of the officer; they are the words of the legislature; and convey as explicitly the authority the act intended to give, and operate as effectually, as if they had been inserted in any other part of the act, than in the license itself. . . . The license must be understood to be what it purports to be, a legislative authority to the steam-boat Bellona, "to be employed in carrying on the coasting trade, for one year from this date." . . .

But if the license be a permit to carry on the coasting trade, the respondent denies that these boats were engaged in that trade, or that the decree under consideration has restrained them from prosecuting it. The boats of the appellant were, we are told, employed in the transportation of passengers; and this is no part of that commerce which congress may regulate. . . . The argument urged at the bar, rests on the foundation, that the power of congress does not extend to navigation, as a branch of commerce, and can only be applied to that subject, incidentally and occasionally. But if that foundation be removed, we must show some plain, intelligible distinction, supported by the constitution or by reason, for discriminating between the power of congress over vessels employed in navigating the same seas. We can perceive no such distinction. . . .

If the power reside in congress, as a portion of the general grant to regulate commerce, then, acts applying that power to vessels generally, must be construed as comprehending all vessels. If none appear to be excluded by the language of the act, none can be excluded by construction. Vessels have always been employed to a greater or less extent in the transportation of passengers, and have never been supposed to be, on that account, withdrawn from the control or protection of congress. Packets which ply along the coast, as well as those which make voyages between Europe and America, consider the transportation of passengers as an important part of their business. Yet it has never been suspected, that the general laws of navigation did not apply to them. The duty act, contains provisions respecting passengers, and shows, that vessels which transport them, have the same rights, and must perform the same duties, with other vessels. They are governed by the general laws of navigation. In the progress of things, this seems to have grown into a particular employment, and to have attracted the particular attention of government. Congress was no longer satisfied with comprehending vessels engaged specially in this business, within those provisions which were intended for vessels generally; and on the 2d of March 1819, passed "an act regulating passenger ships and vessels." This wise and humane law provides for the safety and comfort of passengers, and for the communication of everything concerning them which may interest the government, to the department of state, but makes no provision concerning the entry of the vessel, or her conduct in the waters of the United States. This, we think, shows conclusively the sense of congress (if, indeed, any evidence to that point could be required), that the pre-existing regulations comprehended passenger ships among others; and in prescribing the same duties, the legislature must have considered them as possessing the same rights.

If, then, it were even true, that the Bellona and the Stoudinger were employed exclusively in the conveyance of passengers between New York and New Jersey, it would not follow, that this occupation did not constitute a part of the coasting trade of the United States, and was not protected by the license annexed to the answer. But we cannot perceive how the occupation of these vessels can be drawn into question, in the case before the court. The laws of New York, which grant the exclusive privilege set up by the respondent, take no notice of the employment of vessels, and relate only to the principle by which they are propelled. Those laws do not inquire whether vessels are engaged in transporting men or merchandise, but whether they are moved by steam or wind. If by the former, the waters of New York are closed against them, though their cargoes be dutiable goods, which the laws of the United States permit them to enter and deliver in New York. If by the latter, those waters are free to them, though they should carry passengers only. In conformity with the law, is the bill of the plaintiff in the state court. The bill does not complain that the Bellona and the Stoudinger carry passengers, but that they are moved by steam. This is the injury of which he complains, and is the sole injury against the continuance of which he asks relief. . . . The questions, then, whether the conveyance of passengers be a part of the coasting trade, and whether a vessel can be protected in that occupation by a coasting license, are not, and cannot be raised in this case. The real and sole question seems to be, whether a steam-machine, in actual use, deprives a vessel of the privileges conferred by a license.

In considering this question, the first idea which presents itself is, that the laws of congress for the regulation of commerce, do not look to the principle by which vessels are moved. That subject is left entirely to individual discretion; and in that vast and complex system of legislative enactment concerning it, which embraces everything that the legislature thought it necessary to notice, there is not, we believe, one word respecting the peculiar principle by which vessels are propelled through the water, except what may be found in a single act, granting a particular privilege to steam-boats. With this exception, every act, either prescribing duties, or granting privileges, applies to every vessel, whether navigated by the instrumentality of wind or fire, of sails or machinery. The whole weight of proof, then, is thrown upon him who would introduce a distinction to which the words of the law give no countenance. If a real difference could be admitted to exist between vessels carrying passengers and others, it has already been observed, that there is no fact in this case which can bring up that question. And if the occupation of steam-boats be a matter of such general notoriety, that the court may be presumed to know it, although not specially informed by the record, then we deny that the transportation of passengers is their exclusive occupation. It is a matter of general history, that, in our western waters, their principal employment is the transportation of merchandise; and all know, that in the waters of the Atlantic, they are frequently so employed.

But all inquiry into this subject seems to the court to be put completely at rest, by the act already mentioned, entitled, "an act for the enrolling and licensing of steam-boats." This act authorizes a steam boat employed, or intended to be employed, only in a river or bay of the United States, owned wholly or in part by an alien, resident within the United States, to be en-rolled and licensed as if the same belonged to a citizen of the United States. This act demonstrates the opinion of congress, that steam-boats may be enrolled and licensed, in common with vessels using sails. They are, of course, entitled to the same privileges, and can no more be restrained from navigat-ing waters, and entering ports which are free to such vessels, than if they were wafted on their voyage by the winds, instead of being propelled by the agency of fire. The one element may be as legitimately used as the other, for every commercial pur-pose authorized by the laws of the Union; and the act of a state inhibiting the use of either, to any vessel having a license un-der the act of congress, comes, we think, in direct collision with that act. . . .

The court is aware that, in stating the train of reasoning by which we have been conducted to this result, much time has been consumed in the attempt to demonstrate propositions which may have been thought axioms. It is felt, that the tedi-ousness inseparable from the endeavor to prove that which is already clear, is imputable to a considerable part of this opin-ion. But it was unavoidable. The conclusion to which we have come, depends on a chain of principles which it was necessary to preserve unbroken; and although some of them were thought nearly self-evident, the magnitude of the question, the weight of character belonging to those from whose judgment we dissent, and the argument at the bar, demanded that we should assume nothing.

Powerful and ingenious minds, taking, as postulates, that the powers expressly granted to the government of the Union, are to be contracted, by construction, into the narrowest possible compass, and that the original powers of the states are retained, if any possible construction will retain them, may, by a course of well-digested, but refined and metaphysical reasoning, founded on these premises, explain away the constitution of our country, and leave it, a magnificent structure, indeed, to look at, but totally unfit for use. They may so entangle and perplex the understanding, as to obscure principles, which were before thought quite plain, and induce doubts where, if the mind were to pursue its own course, none would be perceived. In such a case, it is peculiarly necessary to recur to safe and fundamental principles, to sustain those principles, and, when sustained, to make them the tests of the arguments to be examined.

22. *Commerce in Original Packages*

BROWN v. MARYLAND (1827)

(12 Wheaton 419)

Marshall revealed the astounding potential scope of the *Gibbons v. Ogden* doctrines in the following opinion. The instant case involved a state license fee upon wholesalers of imported goods, which was authorized by Maryland as a patriotic measure to curtail the sale of foreign merchandise. (According to "informed sources" of the day, the statute was also an inventive effort by the rurally dominated state assembly to extract the bulk of state revenue from Baltimore, where the importing firms were located.) But the statute in taxing these wholesalers could be construed to affect foreign commerce and impose a duty on imports, subjects both under congressional regulatory jurisdiction.

Once again, then, Marshall had the chance to strike down a state statute solely on the ground that it invaded the national preserve, but this time he refused to rule on that basis. He had already encountered considerable opposition in his efforts to maintain judicial review over the states without adding on the further burden of defending the doctrine we now label "dormant exclusion." (This doctrine maintains that Congress does not have to exercise its jurisdiction in order to bar certain types of state action; the mere existence of jurisdiction preempts the field.) Thus, Marshall went to work to discover Congress' views as expressed in a statute on the subject, and happily he came upon the Federal Tariff Act.

In Marshall's formative hands, the act yielded a prohibition of the Maryland license fee as an illegal tax upon imported goods in their original package. The Chief Justice, however, let it be inferred that states were permitted to tax imported goods removed from their "original package." This was hardly an unqualified concession, for he added that he "supposed" that the original package principle applied as well to goods imported from "sister states," i.e., he attempted to keep a substantial share of both foreign and interstate commerce free from state regulation. When Chief Justice Roger B. Taney delivered an opinion in an early prohibition case (*The License Cases* of 1847), he reasoned away Marshall's "supposition" on the ground that no federal statute applied to interstate commerce: Taney, who had been counsel for the state in *Brown v. Maryland*, thus attempted to regain some lost ground, but his logic on this point was not supported by a majority of his brethren. Marshall's "supposition" continued, therefore, to disrupt the cause of prohibition: state authorities could not pursue every "original package" of alcohol to its destination and wait for its contents to be "mixed with the commerce" of the state.

Mr. Chief Justice MARSHALL delivered the opinion of the court:
    This is a writ of error to a judgment rendered in the Court of Appeals of Maryland, affirming a judgment of the City Court of Baltimore, on an indictment found in that Court against the plaintiffs in error, for violating an act of the legislature of Maryland. . . .
    The cause depends entirely on the question whether the leg-

islature of a State can constitutionally require the importer of foreign articles to take out a license from the State before he shall be permitted to sell a bale or package so imported. . . .

1. The first inquiry is into the extent of the prohibition upon States "to lay any imposts, or duties on imports or exports." The counsel for the State of Maryland would confine this prohibition to laws imposing duties on the act of importation or exportation. The counsel for the plaintiffs in error give it a much wider scope.

In performing the delicate and important duty of construing clauses in the constitution of our country, which involve conflicting powers of the government of the Union and the respective States, it is proper to take a view of the literal meaning of the words to be expounded, of their connexion with other words, and of the general objects to be accomplished by the prohibitory clause, or by the grant of power.

What, then, is the meaning of the words, "imposts, or duties on imports or exports?"

An impost, or duty on imports, is a custom or a tax levied on articles brought into a country, and is most usually secured before the importer is allowed to exercise his rights of ownership over them, because evasions of the law can be prevented more certainly by executing it while the articles are in its custody. It would not, however, be less an impost or duty on the articles, if it were to be levied on them after they were landed. The policy, and consequent practice, of levying or securing the duty before or on entering the port, does not limit the power to that state of things, nor, consequently, the prohibition, unless the true meaning of the clause so confines it. What, then, are "imports"? The lexicons inform us, they are "things imported." If we appeal to usage for the meaning of the word, we shall receive the same answer. They are the articles themselves which are brought into the country. "A duty on imports," then, is not merely a duty on the act of importation, but is a duty on the thing imported. It is not, taken in its literal sense, confined to a duty levied while the article is entering the country, but extends to a duty levied after it has entered the country. . . .

If we quit this narrow view of the subject, and, passing from the literal interpretation of the words, look to the objects of the prohibition, we find no reason for withdrawing the act under consideration from its operation.

From the vast inequality between the different States of the confederacy, as to commercial advantages, few subjects were viewed with deeper interest, or excited more irritation, than the manner in which the several States exercised, or seemed disposed to exercise, the power of laying duties on imports. From motives which were deemed sufficient by the statesmen of that day, the general power of taxation, indispensably necessary as it was, and jealous as the States were of any encroachment on it, was so far abridged as to forbid them to touch imports or exports, with the single exception which has been noticed. Why are they restrained from imposing these duties? Plainly, because, in the general opinion, the interest of all would be best promoted by placing that whole subject under the control of Congress. Whether the prohibition to "lay imposts, or duties on imports or exports" proceeded from an apprehension that the power might be so exercised as to disturb that equality among the States which was generally advantageous, or that harmony between them which it was desirable to preserve, or to maintain unimpaired our commercial connections with foreign nations, or to confer this source of revenue on the government of the Union, or whatever other motive might have induced the prohibition, it is plain that the object would be as completely defeated by a power to tax the article in the hands of the importer the instant it was landed as by a power to tax it while entering the port. There is no difference, in effect, between a power to prohibit the sale of an article and a power to prohibit its introduction into the country. The one would be a necessary consequence of the other. No goods would be imported if none could be sold. No object of any description can be accomplished by laying a duty on importation which may not be accomplished with equal certainty by laying a duty on the thing imported in the hands of the importer. It is obvious that the same power which imposes a light duty can impose a very heavy one, one which amounts to a prohibition. Questions of power do not depend on the degree to which it may be exercised. If it may be exercised at all, it must be exercised at the will of those in whose hands it is placed. If the tax may be levied in this form by a State, it may be levied to an extent which will defeat the revenue by impost, so far as it is drawn from importations into the particular State. . . .

The counsel for the State of Maryland insist, with great reason, that, if the words of the prohibition be taken in their utmost latitude they will abridge the power of taxation, which all admit to be essential to the States, to an extent which has never yet been suspected, and will deprive them of resources which are necessary to supply revenue, and which they have heretofore been admitted to possess. These words must, therefore, be construed with some limitation; and, if this be admitted, they insist, that entering the country is the point of time when the prohibition ceases, and the power of the State to tax commences.

It may be conceded, that the words of the prohibition ought not to be pressed to their utmost extent; that, in our complex system, the object of the powers conferred on the government of the Union, and the nature of the often conflicting powers which remain in the States, must always be taken into view, and may aid in expounding the words of any particular clause. But while we admit that sound principles of construction ought to restrain all Courts from carrying the words of the prohibition beyond the object the constitution is intended to secure, that there must be a point of time when the prohibition ceases and the power of the State to tax commences; we cannot admit that this point of time is the instant that the articles enter the country. It is, we think, obvious, that this construction would defeat the prohibition.

The constitutional prohibition on the States to lay a duty on imports, a prohibition which a vast majority of them must feel an interest in preserving, may certainly come in conflict with their acknowledged power to tax persons and property within their territory. The power, and the restriction on it, though quite distinguishable when they do not approach each other, may yet, like the intervening colours between white and black, approach so nearly as to perplex the understanding, as colours perplex the vision in marking the distinction between them. Yet the distinction exists, and must be marked as the cases arise. Till they do arise, it might be premature to state any rule as being universal in its application. It is sufficient for the present, to say, generally, that, when the importer has so acted upon the thing imported that it has become incorporated and mixed up with the mass of property in the country, it has, perhaps, lost its distinctive character as an import, and has become subject to the taxing power of the State; but while remaining the property of the importer, in his warehouse, in the original form or package in which it was imported, a tax upon it is too plainly a duty on imports to escape the prohibition in the constitution.

The counsel for the plaintiffs in error contend, that the importer purchases, by payment of the duty to the United States, a right to dispose of his merchandise, as well as to bring it into the country; and certainly the argument is supported by strong reason, as well as by the practice of nations, including our own. The object of importation is sale; it constitutes the motive for paying the duties; and if the United States possess the power of conferring the right to sell, as the consideration for which the duty is paid, every principle of fair dealing requires that they should be understood to confer it. The practice of the most commercial nations conforms to this idea. Duties, according to that practice, are charged on those articles only which are intended for sale or consumption in the country. . . .

But if it should be proved that a duty on the article itself would be repugnant to the constitution, it is still argued that this is not a tax upon the article, but on the person. The State, it is said, may tax occupations, and this is nothing more.

It is impossible to conceal from ourselves that this is varying the form without varying the substance. It is treating a prohibition which is general as if it were confined to a particular mode of doing the forbidden thing. All must perceive, that a tax on the sale of an article, imported only for sale, is a tax on the article itself. It is true, the State may tax occupations generally, but this tax must be paid by those who employ the individual, or is a tax on his business. The lawyer, the physician, or the mechanic, must either charge more on the article in which he deals, or the thing itself is taxed through his person. This the State has a right to do, because no constitutional prohibition extends to it. So, a tax on the occupation of an importer is, in like manner, a tax on importation. It must add to the price of the article, and be paid by the consumer, or by the importer himself, in like manner as a direct duty on the article itself would be made. This the State has not a right to do, because it is prohibited by the constitution. . . .

We think, then, that the act under which the plaintiffs in error were indicted, is repugnant to that article of the constitution which declares that "no State shall lay any imposts, or duties on imports or exports."

2. Is it also repugnant to that clause in the constitution which empowers "Congress to regulate commerce with foreign nations, and among the several States, and with the Indian tribes?"

The oppressed and degraded state of commerce previous to the adoption of the constitution can scarcely be forgotten. It was regulated by foreign nations with a single view to their own interests; and our disunited efforts to counteract their restrictions were rendered impotent by want of combination. Congress, indeed, possessed the power of making treaties; but the inability of the federal government to enforce them had become so apparent as to render that power in a great degree useless. Those who felt the injury arising from this state of things, and those who were capable of estimating the influence of commerce on the prosperity of nations, perceived the necessity of giving the control over this important subject to a single government. It may be doubted whether any of the evils proceeding from the feebleness of the federal government contributed more to that great revolution which introduced the present system, than the deep and general conviction that commerce ought to be regulated by Congress. It is not, therefore, matter of surprise that the grant should be as extensive as the mischief, and should comprehend all foreign commerce, and all commerce among the States. To construe the power so as to impair its efficacy would tend to defeat an object in the attainment of which the American public took, and justly took, that strong interest which arose from a full conviction of its necessity.

What, then, is the just extent of a power to regulate commerce with foreign nations and among the several States?

This question was considered in the case of *Gibbons* v. *Ogden* (9 Wheaton I.), in which it was declared to be complete in itself, and to acknowledge no limitations other than are prescribed by the constitution. The power is co-extensive with the subject on which it acts and cannot be stopped at the external boundary of a State, but must enter its interior.

We deem it unnecessary now to reason in support of these propositions. Their truth is proved by facts continually before our eyes, and was, we think, demonstrated, if they could require demonstration, in the case already mentioned.

If this power reaches the interior of a State, and may be

there exercised, it must be capable of authorizing the sale of those articles which it introduces. Commerce is intercourse; one of its most ordinary ingredients is traffic. It is inconceivable, that the power to authorize this traffic, when given in the most comprehensive terms, with the intent that its efficacy should be complete, should cease at the point when its continuance is indispensable to its value. To what purpose should the power to allow importation be given, unaccompanied with the power to authorize a sale of the thing imported? Sale is the object of importation, and is an essential ingredient of that intercourse of which importation constitutes a part. It is as essential an ingredient, as indispensable to the existence of the entire thing, then, as importation itself. It must be considered as a component part of the power to regulate commerce. Congress has a right, not only to authorize importation, but to authorize the importer to sell. . . .

If the principles we have stated be correct, the result to which they conduct us cannot be mistaken. Any penalty inflicted on the importer for selling the article in his character of importer, must be in opposition to the act of Congress which authorizes importation. Any charge on the introduction and incorporation of the articles into and with the mass of property in the country, must be hostile to the power given to Congress to regulate commerce, since an essential part of that regulation, and principal object of it, is to prescribe the regular means for accomplishing that introduction and incorporation. . . .

It may be proper to add that we suppose the principles laid down in this case to apply equally to importations from a sister State. We do not mean to give any opinion on a tax discriminating between foreign and domestic articles.

We think there is error in the judgment of the Court of Appeals of the State of Maryland in affirming the judgment of the Baltimore City Court, because the act of the legislature of Maryland, imposing the penalty for which the said judgment is rendered, is repugnant to the constitution of the United States, and, consequently, void. The judgment is to be reversed, and the cause remanded to that Court, with instructions to enter judgment in favour of the appellants.

23. *Commerce on Small Streams*

WILLSON v.
BLACKBIRD CREEK MARSH CO. (1829)
(2 Peters 245)

The following opinion is probably the slightest of Marshall's judicial writings, because the Chief Justice doubtless considered the case hardly worth the Court's concern. The brief opinion duly reflects this evaluation, for it reads as though he was rather annoyed at being bothered with such trivia. The case concerned a shipowner, operating with a federal coasting license (as in *Gibbons v. Ogden*), who had crashed through a dam on a small but navigable creek. The state of Delaware had authorized the construction of the dam. In light of the circumstances, Marshall upheld the validity of the fine that the state had imposed upon the destructive shipowner. In effect, the Chief Justice suggested that the guilty party find a damless creek to navigate.

But the opinion is also probably the most assiduously criticized of Marshall's judicial corpus. The Chief Justice in his holding haphazardly sanctioned the assumption by a state of jurisdiction to regulate commerce under the guise of its police power. Did not Marshall thus contradict the principles of *Gibbons v. Ogden*? Generations of lawyers were prepared to answer in the affirmative when desperate for precedents in support of state limitations on interstate commerce. Needless to say, that called for some rather unmerciful squeezing of the phrases in the following case as Marshall had clearly applied the maxim *de minimis non curet lex* with little concern for the "great principles" involved.

Mr. Chief Justice Marshall delivered the opinion of the court: . . .

The plaintiffs sustain their right to build a dam across the creek by the Act of the Assembly. Their declaration is founded upon that Act. The injury of which they complain is to a right given by it. They do not claim for themselves any right independent of it. They rely entirely upon the Act of Assembly.

The plea does not controvert the existence of the Act, but denies its capacity to authorize the construction of a dam across a navigable stream, in which the tide ebbs and flows; and in which there was, and of right ought to have been a certain common and public way in the nature of a highway. This plea draws nothing into question but the validity of the Act; and the judgment of the court must have been in favor of its validity. Its consistency with, or repugnancy to the Constitution of the United States, necessarily arises upon these pleadings and must have been determined. This court has repeatedly decided in favor of its jurisdiction in such a case. . . .

The jurisdiction of the court being established, the more doubtful question is to be considered, whether the Act incorporating the Black Bird Creek Marsh Company is repugnant to the Constitution, so far as it authorizes a dam across the creek. . . . The Act of Assembly by which the plaintiffs were authorized to construct their dam shows plainly that this is one of those many creeks, passing through a deep, level marsh adjoining the Delaware, up which the tide flows for some distance. The value of the property on its banks must be enhanced by excluding the water from the marsh, and the health of the inhabitants probably improved. Measures calculated to produce, these objects, provided that they do not come in collision with the powers of the general government, are undoubtedly within those which are reserved to the States. But the measure authorized by this Act stops a navigable creek, and must be supposed to abridge the rights of those who have been accustomed to use it. But this abridgment, unless it comes in conflict with the Constitution or a law of the United States is an affair between the government of Delaware and its citizens, of which the court can take no cognizance.

The counsel for the plaintiffs in error insist that it comes in conflict with the power of the United States "to regulate commerce with foreign nations and among the several States."

If Congress had passed any Act which bore upon the case; any Act in execution of the power to regulate commerce, the object of which was to control State legislation over those small navigable creeks into which the tide flows, and which abound throughout the lower country of the Middle and Southern States, we should not feel much difficulty in saying that a State law coming in conflict with such an Act would be void. But Congress has passed no such Act. The repugnancy of the law of Delaware to the Constitution is placed entirely on its repugnancy to the power to regulate commerce with foreign nations and among the several States; a power which has not been so exercised as to affect the question.

We do not think that the Act empowering the Black Bird Creek Marsh Company to place a dam across the creek, can, under all the circumstances of the case, be considered as repugnant to the power to regulate commerce in its dormant state, or as being in conflict with any law passed on the subject.

There is no error and the judgment is affirmed.

Part Six

TREATIES
AND TERRITORIES

24. *Legislative Courts in the Territories*

AMERICAN INSURANCE CO. v. CANTER (1828)

(1 Peters 511)

In the process of deciding an apparently minor and technical point of jurisdiction, Marshall inventively sanctioned the structure of territorial government. The following case escalated from a dispute over the competence of a Key West court to order an auction to a challenge to the competence of the United States Government to acquire additional territory. Once Marshall had rather offhandedly settled the right of the government to acquire territory—a question which had greatly vexed Jefferson at the time of the Louisiana Purchase—he continued to defend the Key West court order as part of Congress' power to regulate the territories.

This power derived (Marshall seemed not quite sure himself) either from the general right of sovereignty or from the relevant constitutional provision. But the intriguing implication of the whole opinion was the plenary authority that Congress was assigned to fashion the structure of territorial government. Although retrospectively this wide jurisdiction can be extrapolated from Marshall's decision in this narrow instance, the full implication of the holding was not drawn until later when the debate over congressional control of slavery in the territories led both sides to comb early court opinions for authoritative pronouncements and new angles.

The Key West court, "consisting of a notary and five jurors," had exercised admiralty jurisdiction, although it obviously did not resemble the courts established by the Judiciary Act of 1789. Was this court then improperly exercising judicial power? In short, was this body constitutionally speaking, a "court" at all? This was an interesting question, but Marshall was prepared for it. He differentiated two types of courts: "constitutional," i.e., those created under Article III of the Constitution, and "legislative," i.e., those established by Congress to exercise authority granted in Article I (in this instance, the power to legislate for the territories).

In the states of the Union, he concluded, admiralty jurisdiction could only be exercised by "constitutional" courts, but in the territories Congress could establish, in its wisdom, such institutions as it deemed necessary and proper. The concept of "legislative" courts was a useful innovation, one which gave Congress great flexibility in dealing with a variety of special problems—a number of these courts (e.g. Court of Customs and Patent Approvals, Tax Court of the United States, Customs Court) are still in operation, largely distinguished from "constitutional" courts by the fact that their judges do not sit for life but for stipulated terms.

Mr. Chief Justice Marshall delivered the opinion of the Court:—

The plaintiffs filed their libel in this cause in the District Court of South Carolina, to obtain restitution of three hundred and fifty-six bales of cotton, part of the cargo of the ship Point à Petre, which had been insured by them on a voyage from New Orleans to Havre de Grâce, in France. The Point à Petre was wrecked on the coast of Florida, the cargo saved by the inhabitants, and carried into Key West, where it was sold for the purpose of satisfying the salvors, by virtue of a decree of a

Court, consisting of a notary and five jurors, which was erected by an Act of the territorial legislature of Florida. The owners abandoned to the underwriters, who, having accepted the same, proceeded against the property; alleging that the sale was not made by order of a court competent to change the property.

David Canter claimed the cotton as a *bona fide* purchaser, under the decree of a competent Court, which awarded seventy-six per cent to the salvors on the value of the property saved. . . .

The cause depends mainly on the question whether the property in the cargo saved was changed by the sale at Key West. The conformity of that sale to the order under which it was made has not been controverted. Its validity has been denied on the ground that it was ordered by an incompetent tribunal.

The tribunal was constituted by an Act of the territorial legislature of Florida, passed on the 4th July, 1823, which is inserted in the record. That Act purports to give the power which has been exercised; consequently, the sale is valid, if the territorial legislature was competent to enact the law.

The course which the argument has taken, will require that, in deciding this question, the Court should take into view the relation in which Florida stands to the United States.

The Constitution confers absolutely on the government of the Union the powers of making war and of making treaties; consequently that government possesses the power of acquiring territory, either by conquest or by treaty. . . .

On the 2d of February, 1819, Spain ceded Florida to the United States. . . . This treaty is the law of the land, and admits the inhabitants of Florida to the enjoyment of the privileges, rights and immunities of the citizens of the United States. . . . They do not, however, participate in political power; they do not share in the government till Florida shall become a state. In the meantime Florida continues to be a Territory of the

United States, governed by virtue of that clause in the Constitution which empowers Congress "to make all needful rules and regulations respecting the territory or other property belonging to the United States." . . .

Congress, in 1822, passed "an Act for the establishment of a territorial government in Florida"; and on the 3d of March, 1823, passed another Act to amend the Act of 1822. Under this Act, the territorial legislature enacted the law now under consideration. . . .

The powers of the territorial legislature extend to all rightful objects of legislation, subject to the restriction that their laws shall not be "inconsistent with the laws and Constitution of the United States." As salvage is admitted to come within this description, the act is valid, unless it can be brought within the restriction.

The counsel for the libelants contend that it is inconsistent with both the law and the Constitution; that it is inconsistent with the provisions of the law by which the territorial government was created, and with the amendatory Act of March, 1823. It vests, they say, in an inferior tribunal a jurisdiction which is by those acts vested exclusively in the Superior Courts of the territory.

This argument requires an attentive consideration of the sections which define the jurisdiction of the Superior Courts.

The 7th section of the Act of 1823 vests the whole judicial power of the territory "in two Superior Courts, and in such inferior Courts, and justices of the peace, as the legislative council of the territory may from time to time establish." This general grant is common to the superior and inferior Courts, and their jurisdiction is concurrent, except so far as it may be made exclusive, in either, by other provisions of the statute. The jurisdiction of the Superior Courts is declared to be exclusive over capital offences; on every other question on which those Courts may take cognizance by virtue of this section, concurrent jurisdiction may be given to the inferior Courts.

Among these subjects are "all civil cases arising under and cognizable by the laws of the territory, now in force therein, or which may at any time be enacted by the legislative council thereof."

[All] the laws which were in force in Florida while a province of Spain, those excepted which were political in their character, which concerned the relations between the people and their sovereign, remained in force until altered by the government of the United States. Congress recognizes this principle by using the words "laws of the Territory now in force therein." No laws could then have been in force but those enacted by the Spanish government. If among these a law existed on the subject of salvage, and it is scarcely possible there should not have been such a law, jurisdiction over cases arising under it was conferred on the Superior Courts, but that jurisdiction was not exclusive. A territorial Act, conferring jurisdiction over the same cases on an inferior Court, would not have been inconsistent with this section.

The 8th section extends the jurisdiction of the Superior Courts, in terms which admit of more doubt. The words are, "That each of the said Superior Courts shall, moreover, have and exercise the same jurisdiction, within its limits, in all cases arising under the laws and Constitution of the United States, which, by an Act to establish the judicial Courts of the United States, was vested in the Court of the Kentucky district."

The 11th section of the Act declares, "That the laws of the United States relating to the revenue and its collection, and all other public Acts of the United States not inconsistent or repugnant to this Act, shall extend to, and have full force and effect in, the territory aforesaid."

The laws which are extended to the territory, by this section, were either for the punishment of crime or for civil purposes. Jurisdiction is given in all criminal cases by the seventh section; but in civil cases, that section gives jurisdiction only in those which arise under and are cognizable by the laws of the territory; consequently, all civil cases, arising under the laws which are extended to the territory by the 11th section, are cognizable in the territorial Courts by virtue of the eighth section; and in those cases the superior Courts may exercise the same jurisdiction as is exercised by the Court for the Kentucky district.

The question suggested by this view of the subject, on which the case under consideration must depend, is this:

Is the admiralty jurisdiction of the District Courts of the United States vested in the Superior Courts of Florida under the words of the eighth section declaring that each of the said courts "shall, moreover, have and exercise the same jurisdiction within its limits, in all cases arising under the laws and Constitution of the United States," which was vested in the Courts of the Kentucky district?

It is observable that this clause does not confer on the territorial Courts all the jurisdiction which is vested in the Court of the Kentucky district, but that part of it only which applies to "cases arising under the laws and Constitution of the United States." Is a case of admiralty of this description?

The Constitution and laws of the United States give jurisdiction to the District Courts over all cases in admiralty; but jurisdiction over the case does not constitute the case itself. We are, therefore, to inquire whether cases in admiralty, and cases arising under the laws and Constitution of the United States, are identical.

If we have recourse to that pure fountain from which all the jurisdiction of the Federal Courts is derived, we find language employed which cannot well be misunderstood. The Constitution declares that "the judicial power shall extend to all cases in law and equity, arising under this Constitution, the laws of the United States, and treaties made, or which shall be made, under their authority; to all cases affecting ambassadors, or other public ministers and consuls; to all cases of admiralty and maritime jurisdiction."

The Constitution certainly contemplates these as three distinct classes of cases; and if they are distinct, the grant of jurisdiction over one of them does not confer jurisdiction over either of the other two. The discrimination made between them, in the Constitution, is, we think, conclusive against their identity. If it were not so, if this were a point open to inquiry, it would be difficult to maintain the proposition that they are the same. A case in admiralty does not, in fact, arise under the Constitution or laws of the United States. These cases are as old as navigation itself; and the law, admiralty and maritime, as it has existed for ages, is applied by our Courts to the cases as they arise. It is not, then, to the eighth section of the territorial law that we are to look for the grant of admiralty and maritime jurisdiction to the territorial Courts. Consequently, if that jurisdiction is exclusive, it is not made so by the reference to the District Court of Kentucky.

It has been contended that, by the Constitution, the judicial power of the United States extends to all cases of admiralty and maritime jurisdiction; and that the whole of this judicial power must be vested "in one Supreme Court, and in such inferior Courts as Congress shall from time to time ordain and establish." Hence it has been argued that Congress cannot vest admiralty jurisdiction in Courts created by the territorial legislature.

We have only to pursue this subject one step further to perceive that this provision of the Constitution does not apply to it. The next sentence declares that "the Judges both of the Supreme and inferior Courts shall hold their offices during good behavior." The Judges of the Superior Courts of Florida hold their offices for four years. These Courts, then, are not Constitutional Courts, in which the judicial power conferred by the Constitution on the general government can be deposited. They are incapable of receiving it. They are legislative Courts, created in virtue of the general right of sovereignty which exists in the government, or in virtue of that clause which enables Congress to make all needful rules and regulations respecting the territory belonging to the United States. The jurisdiction with which they are invested is not a part of that judicial power which is defined in the third article of the Constitution; but is conferred by Congress in the execution of those general powers which that body possesses over the Territories of the United States. Although admiralty jurisdiction can be exercised, in the States, in those Courts only which are established in pursuance of the third article of the Constitution, the same limitation does not extend to the Territories. In legislating for them. Congress exercises the combined powers of the general and of a state government.

We think, then, that the Act of the territorial legislature, erecting the Court by whose decree the cargo of the Point à Petre was sold, is not "inconsistent with the laws and Constitution of the United States," and is valid. Consequently, the sale made in pursuance of it changed the property, and the decree of the Circuit Court, awarding restitution of the property to the claimant, ought to be affirmed with costs.

25. *Land Claims Under Treaties*

FOSTER v. NEILSON (1829)

(2 Peters 253)

This opinion provides another instance of Marshall's reluctance to render or sanction independent judicial determination of matters generally related to foreign affairs. Involved here was the validity of a land title which in turn depended upon the prior interpretation of the claims and boundary provisions of a treaty. The Chief Justice invoked the doctrine of "political questions" to justify judicial acquiescence in the decisions made by Congress in international disputes. Legal questions arising under treaties were to be generally decided in line with the interpretations of the political departments of the federal government.

Unfortunately, Congress had not expressed any views on the contested title in this case, a fact which might have suggested that in the view of Congress, legislation was unnecessary because the relevant articles of the treaty were self-executing. If that were the case (and Marshall seemed ambivalent on the point) then the history of congressional actions prior to the ratification could supply the Court's guidelines. Somewhat hesitantly, then, Marshall seems to have held that the articles were self-executing. (A few years later he had second thoughts on this matter and reversed himself in *U.S. v. Percheman* [1833].) Nevertheless, he did find reassuring support for his holding in the overall pattern of congressional policy. Machinery had been set up to implement all sections of the treaty grant except the one which conveyed the land disputed in this case. He interpreted that exception to mean that Congress regarded the treaty as having settled all questions about land claims for that single, specific area.

Mr. Chief Justice MARSHALL delivered the opinion of the Court:

This suit was brought by the plaintiffs in error in the court of the United States for the eastern district of Louisiana, to recover a tract of land lying in that district, about thirty miles east of the Mississippi, and in the possession of the defendant. The plaintiffs claimed under a grant for 40,000 arpents of land, made by the Spanish Governor, on the 2d of January, 1804, to Jayme Joydra, and ratified by the king of Spain on the 29th of May, 1804. The petition and order of survey are dated in September, 1803, and the return of the survey itself was made on the 27th of October in the same year. The defendant excepted to the petition of the plaintiffs, alleging that it does not show a title on which they can recover; that the territory within which the land claimed is situated, had been ceded, before the grant, to France, and by France to the United States; and that the grant is void, being made by persons who had no authority to make it. The court sustained the exception, and dismissed the petition. The cause is brought before this Court by a writ of error.

The case presents this very intricate, and at one time very interesting question: To whom did the country between the Iberville and the Perdido rightfully belong, when the title now asserted by the plaintiffs was acquired?

This question has been repeatedly discussed with great talent and research, by the government of the United States and that of Spain. The United States have perseveringly and earnestly insisted, that by the treaty of St. Ildefonso, made on the 1st of October in the year 1800, Spain ceded the disputed territory as part of Louisiana to France; and that France, by the treaty of Paris, signed on the 30th of April, 1803, and ratified on the 21st of October in the same year, ceded it to the United States. Spain has with equal perseverance and earnestness maintained, that her cession to France comprehended that territory only which was at that time denominated Louisiana, consisting of the island of New Orleans, and the country she received from France west of the Mississippi. . . .

[O]n the 26th of March, 1804, congress passed an act erecting Louisiana into two territories. . . . The 14th section enacts "that all grants for lands within the territories ceded by the French republic to the United States by the treaty of the 30th of April 1803, the title whereof was at the date of the treaty of St. Ildefonso in the crown, government, or nation of Spain, and every act and proceeding subsequent thereto of whatsoever nature towards the obtaining any grant, title or claim to such lands, and under whatsoever authority transacted or pretended, be, and the same are hereby declared to be, and to have been from the beginning, null, void, and of no effect in law or equity." A proviso excepts the titles of actual settlers acquired before the 20th of December, 1803, from the operation of this section. It was obviously intended to act on all grants made by Spain after her retrocession of Louisiana to France, and without deciding on the extent of that retrocession, to put the titles which might be thus acquired through the whole territory, whatever might be its extent, completely under the control of the American government.

The president was authorized to appoint registers or recorders of lands acquired under the Spanish and French governments, and boards of commissioners who should receive all claims to lands, and hear and determine in a summary way all matters respecting such claims. Their proceedings were to be reported to the secretary of the treasury, to be laid before congress for the final decision of that body. . . .

The phrase on which the controversy mainly depends, that Spain retrocedes Louisiana with the same extent that it had when France possessed it, might so readily have been expressed in plain language, that it is difficult to resist the persuasion that the ambiguity was intentional. Had Louisiana been retroceded with the same extent that it had when France ceded it to Spain, or with the same extent that it had before the cession of any part of it to England, no controversy respecting its limits could have arisen. Had the parties concurred in their intention, a plain mode of expressing that intention would have presented itself to them. But Spain has always manifested infinite repugnance to the surrender of territory, and was probably unwilling to give back more than she had received. The introduction of ambiguous phrases into the treaty, which power might afterwards construe according to circumstances, was a measure which the strong and the politic might not be disinclined to employ.

However this may be, it is, we think, incontestable, that the American construction of the article, if not entirely free from question, is supported by arguments of great strength which cannot be easily confuted.

In a controversy between two nations concerning national boundary, it is scarcely possible that the courts of either should refuse to abide by the measures adopted by its own government. There being no common tribunal to decide between them, each determines for itself on its own rights, and if they cannot adjust their differences peaceably, the right remains with the strongest. The judiciary is not that department of the government to which the assertion of its interests against foreign powers is confided; and its duty commonly is to decide upon individual rights, according to those principles which the political departments of the nation have established. If the course of the nation has been a plain one, its courts would hesitate to pronounce it erroneous.

We think, then, however individual judges might construe the treaty of St. Ildefonso, it is the province of the Court to conform its decisions to the will of the legislature, if that will has been clearly expressed.

The convulsed state of European Spain affected her influence over her colonies; and a degree of disorder prevailed in the Floridas, at which the United States could not look with indifference. In October, 1810, the president issued his proclamation, directing the governor of the Orleans territory to take possession of the country as far east as the Perdido, and to hold it for the United States. This measure was avowedly intended as an assertion of the title of the United States; but as an assertion which was rendered necessary in order to avoid evils which might contravene the wishes of both parties, and which would still leave the territory "a subject of fair and friendly negotiation and adjustment."

In April 1812, congress passed "an act to enlarge the limits of the state of Louisiana." This act describes lines which comprehend the land in controversy, and declares that the country included within them shall become and form a part of the state of Louisiana.

In May of the same year, another act was passed, annexing

the residue of the country west of the Perdido to the Mississippi territory.

And in February 1813, the president was authorized "to occupy and hold all that tract of country called West Florida, which lies west of the river Perdido, not now in possession of the United States."

On the third of March 1817, congress erected that part of Florida which had been annexed to the Mississippi territory, into a separate territory, called Alabama.

The powers of government were extended to, and exercised in those parts of West Florida which composed a part of Louisiana and Mississippi, respectively; and a separate government was erected in Alabama. (U. S. L., c. 4, 409.)

In March 1819, "congress passed an act to enable the people of Alabama to form a constitution and state government." And in December, 1819, she was admitted into the Union, and declared one of the United States of America. The treaty of amity, settlement and limits, between the United States and Spain, was signed at Washington on the 22d day of February, 1819, but was not ratified by Spain till the 24th day of October, 1820; nor by the United States until the 22d day of February, 1821. So that Alabama was admitted into the union as an independent state, in virtue of the title acquired by the United States to her territory under the treaty of April 1803.

After these acts of sovereign power over the territory in dispute, asserting the American construction of the treaty by which the government claims it, to maintain the opposite construction in its own courts would certainly be an anomaly in the history and practice of nations. If those departments which are entrusted with the foreign intercourse of the nation, which assert and maintain its interests against foreign powers, have unequivocally asserted its rights of dominion over a country of which it is in possession, and which it claims under a treaty; if the legislature has acted on the construction thus asserted, it is not in its own courts that this construction is to be denied.

A question like this respecting the boundaries of nations, is, as has been truly said, more a political than a legal question; and in its discussion, the courts of every country must respect the pronounced will of the legislature. . . . If the rights of the parties are in any degree changed, that change must be produced by the subsequent arrangements made between the two governments.

A "treaty of amity, settlement, and limits, between the United States of America and the king of Spain," was signed at Washington on the 22d day of February, 1819. By the 2d article "his catholic majesty cedes to the United States in full property and sovereignty, all the territories which belong to him, situated to the eastward of the Mississippi, known by the name of East and West Florida."

The 8th article stipulates, that "all the grants of land made before the 24th of January, 1818, by his catholic majesty, or by his lawful authorities, in the said territories ceded by his majesty to the United States, shall be ratified and confirmed to the persons in possession of the lands, to the same extent that the same grants would be valid if the territories had remained under the dominion of his catholic majesty."

The Court will not attempt to conceal the difficulty which is created by these articles.

It is well known that Spain had uniformly maintained her construction of the treaty of St. Ildefonso. His catholic majesty had perseveringly insisted that no part of West Florida had been ceded by that treaty, and that the whole country which had been known by that name still belonged to him. It is then a fair inference from the language of the treaty, that he did not mean to retrace his steps, and relinquish his pretensions; but to cede on a sufficient consideration all that he had claimed as his; and consequently, by the 8th article, to stipulate for the confirmation of all those grants which he had made while the title remained in him.

But the United States had uniformly denied the title set up by the crown of Spain; had insisted that a part of West Florida had been transferred to France by the treaty of St. Ildefonso, and ceded to the United States by the treaty of April, 1803; had asserted this construction by taking actual possession of the country; and had extended its legislation over it. The United States therefore cannot be understood to have admitted that this country belonged to his catholic majesty, or that it passed from him to them by this article. Had his catholic majesty ceded to the United States "all the territories situated to the eastward of the Mississippi known by the name of East and West Florida," omitting the words "which belong to him," the United States, in receiving this cession, might have sanctioned the right to make it, and might have been bound to consider the 8th article as co-extensive with the second. The stipulation of the 8th article might have been construed to be an admission that West Florida to its full extent was ceded by this treaty.

But the insertion of these words materially affects the construction of the article. They cannot be rejected as surplusage. They have a plain meaning, and that meaning can be no other than to limit the extent of the cession. We cannot say they were inserted carelessly or unadvisedly, and must understand them according to their obvious import.

It is not improbable that terms were selected which might not compromise the dignity of either government, and which each might understand, consistently with its former pretensions. But if a court of the United States would have been bound under the state of things existing at the signature of the treaty, to consider the territory then composing a part of the state of Louisiana as rightfully belonging to the United States, it would be difficult to construe this article into an admission that it belonged rightfully to his catholic majesty.

The 6th article of the treaty may be considered in connection with the second. The 6th stipulates "that the inhabitants of the territories which his catholic majesty cedes to the United States by this treaty, shall be incorporated in the union of the United States, as soon as may be consistent with the principles of the federal constitution."

This article, according to its obvious import, extends to the whole territory which was ceded. The stipulation for the incorporation of the inhabitants of the ceded territory into the union, is co-extensive with the cession. But the country in which the land in controversy lies, was already incorporated into the union. It composed a part of the state of Louisiana, which was already a member of the American confederacy.

A part of West Florida lay east of the Perdido; and to that the right of his catholic majesty was acknowledged. There was, then, an ample subject on which the words of the cession might operate, without discarding those which limit its general expressions.

Such is the construction which the Court would put on the treaties by which the United States have acquired the country east of New Orleans. . . . Whatever difference may exist respecting the effect of the ratification, in whatever sense it may be understood, we think the sound construction of the eighth article will not enable this Court to apply its provisions to the present case. . . . Do [the] words [of the article] act directly on the grants, so as to give validity to those not otherwise valid; or do they pledge the faith of the United States to pass acts which shall ratify and confirm them?

A treaty is in its nature a contract between two nations, not a legislative act. It does not generally effect, of itself, the object to be accomplished, especially so far as its operation is infra-territorial; but is carried into execution by the sovereign power of the respective parties to this instrument.

In the United States a different principle is established. Our constitution declares a treaty to be the law of the land. It is, consequently, to be regarded in courts of justice as equivalent to an act of the legislature, whenever it operates of itself without the aid of any legislative provision. But when the terms of the stipulation import a contract—when either of the parties engages to perform a particular act—the treaty addresses itself to the political, not the judicial department; and the legislature must execute the contract before it can become a rule for the Court.

The article under consideration does not declare that all the grants made by his catholic majesty before the 24th of January, 1818, shall be valid to the same extent as if the ceded territories had remained under his dominion. It does not say that those grants are hereby confirmed. Had such been its language, it would have acted directly on the subject, and would have repealed those acts of congress which were repugnant to it; but its language is that those grants shall be ratified and confirmed to the persons in possession, &c. By whom shall they be ratified and confirmed? This seems to be the language of contract; and if it is, the ratification and confirmation which are promised must be the act of the legislature. Until such act shall be passed, the Court is not at liberty to disregard the existing laws on the subject. Congress appears to have understood this article as it is understood by the Court. Boards of commissioners have been appointed for East and West Florida, to receive claims for lands; and on their reports titles to lands not exceeding —— acres have been confirmed, and to a very large amount. . . .

Congress has reserved to itself the supervision of the titles reported by its commissioners, and has confirmed those which the commissioners have approved, but has passed no law withdrawing grants generally for lands west of the Perdido from the operation . . . of the act of 1804, or repealing that section.

We are of opinion, then, that the court committed no error in dismissing the petition of the plaintiff, and that the judgment ought to be affirmed with costs.

26. *The Constitutional Status of Indian Nations*

CHEROKEE NATION v. GEORGIA (1831)

(5 Peters 1)

This case arose from Georgia's irate refusal to tolerate Cherokee self-determination. Congress had authorized the Cherokees to establish a semi-autonomous regime upon some four million acres of treaty-protected land within the state boundaries of Georgia. However, with the blessings of that famed Indian fighter, now President, Andrew Jackson, the state legislature annulled all the Cherokee "laws, usages, and customs" and divided their lands into counties under state jurisdiction. Moreover, to prove that the Cherokees were wholly subject to Georgia criminal law, a state superior court convicted one George Tassels for a homicide committed against another Cherokee on the reservation. Nor was Georgia prepared to admit that the federal courts had any more jurisdiction over the Cherokees than had the outlawed courts of the reservation. When a writ of habeas corpus was issued by the Supreme Court in Tassels' case, the Governor defiantly responded by ordering the Indian's immediate execution. To press the point in the present case, Georgia preferred to argue the lack of federal jurisdiction by silence—the state refused to send counsel.

Against this background, it was not surprising that the Court failed to rescue the Cherokee nation from Georgia's imperialistic designs. It was, in practical terms, hopeless for the judiciary to relieve the enormous political animus against the Indians. Marshall, clearly distressed, rationalized judicial nonintervention on jurisdictional grounds: The Cherokee nation failed to qualify as a foreign state—seemingly the only jurisdictional door through which it could, under Article III of the Constitution, be admitted to federal court. Never backward about devising *ad hoc* legal categories, Marshall defined the Cherokees as a "domestic dependent nation" and advised them to return with a better case. Their lawyers did so in *Worcester v. Georgia*.

Mr. Chief Justice MARSHALL delivered the opinion of the Court.

This bill is brought by the Cherokee Nation, praying an injunction to restrain the state of Georgia from the execution of certain laws of that state, which, as is alleged, go directly to annihilate the Cherokees as a political society, and to seize, for the use of Georgia, the lands of the nation, which have been assured to them by the United States in solemn treaties repeatedly made and still in force. . . .

Before we can look into the merits of the case a preliminary inquiry presents itself: Has this court jurisdiction of the cause?

The third article of the constitution describes the extent of the judicial power. The second section closes an enumeration of the cases to which it is extended, with "controversies" "between a state, or the citizens thereof, and foreign states, citizens, or subjects." . . . Do the Cherokees constitute a foreign state in the sense of the constitution? . . .

Though the Indians are acknowledged to have an unquestionable, and heretofore unquestioned, right to the lands they occupy, until that right shall be extinguished by a voluntary cession to our government, yet it may well be doubted whether those tribes which reside within the acknowledged boundaries of the United States can, with strict accuracy, be denominated foreign nations. They may, more correctly, perhaps, be denominated domestic dependent nations. They occupy a territory to which we assert a title independent of their will, which must take effect in point of possession when their right of possession ceases. Meanwhile they are in a state of pupilage. Their relation to the United States resembles that of a ward to his guardian.

They look to our government for protection; rely upon its kindness and its power; appeal to it for relief to their wants, and address the president as their great father. They and their country are considered by foreign nations, as well as by ourselves, as being so completely under the sovereignty and dominion of the United States that any attempt to acquire their lands, or to form a political connexion with them, would be considered by all as an invasion of our territory, and an act of hostility.

These considerations go far to support the opinion that the framers of our constitution had not the Indian tribes in view when they opened the courts of the union to controversies between a state, or the citizens thereof, and foreign states. . . .

[The] peculiar relations between the United States and the Indians occupying our territory are such that we should feel much difficulty in considering them as designated by the term "foreign state," were there no other part in the constitution which might shed light on the meaning of these words. But we think that, in construing them, considerable aid is furnished by that clause, in the eighth section of the third article, which empowers congress to "regulate commerce with foreign nations, and among the several states, and with the Indian tribes."

In this clause they are as clearly contradistinguished, by a name appropriate to themselves, from foreign nations, as from the several states composing the union. They are designated by a distinct appellation; and as this appellation can be applied to neither of the others, neither can the appellation distinguishing either of the others be, in fair construction, applied to them. The objects to which the power of regulating commerce might be directed are divided into three distinct classes—foreign nations, the several states, and Indian tribes. When forming this article the convention considered them as entirely distinct. We cannot assume that the distinction was lost in framing a subsequent article, unless there be something in its language to authorize the assumption. . . .

"Foreign nations" is a general term, the application of which to Indian tribes, when used in the American constitution, is, at best, extremely questionable. In one article, in which a power is given to be exercised in regard to foreign nations generally, and to the Indian tribes particularly, they are mentioned as separate in terms clearly contradistinguishing them from each other. We perceive plainly that the constitution in this article does not comprehend Indian tribes in the general term "foreign nations," not, we presume, because a tribe may not be a nation, but because it is not foreign to the United States. When, afterwards, the term "foreign state" is introduced, we cannot impute to the convention the intention to desert its former meaning, and to comprehend Indian tribes within it, unless the context force that construction on us. We find nothing in the context, and nothing in the subject of the article, which leads to it.

The court has bestowed its best attention on this question, and, after mature deliberation, the majority is of opinion that an Indian tribe or nation within the United States is not a foreign state in the sense of the constitution, and cannot maintain an action in the courts of the United States.

A serious additional objection exists to the jurisdiction of the court. Is the matter of the bill the proper subject for judicial inquiry and decision? It seeks to restrain a state from the forcible exercise of legislative power over a neighboring people asserting their independence; their right to which the state denies. On several of the matters alleged in the bill, for example, on the laws making it criminal to exercise the usual powers of self-government in their own country by the Cherokee nation, this court cannot interpose; at least in the form in which those matters are presented.

That part of the bill which respects the land occupied by the Indians, and prays the aid of the court to protect their possession, may be more doubtful. The mere question of right might, perhaps, be decided by this court in a proper case with proper parties. But the court is asked to do more than decide

on the title. The bill requires us to control the legislature of
Georgia, and to restrain the exertion of its physical force. The
propriety of such an interposition by the court may be well
questioned. It savors too much of the exercise of political
power to be within the proper province of the judicial department. But the opinion on the point respecting parties makes it
unnecessary to decide this question.

If it be true that the Cherokee nation have rights, this is
not the tribunal in which those rights are to be asserted. If it
be true that wrongs have been inflicted, and that still greater
are to be apprehended, this is not the tribunal which can redress the past or prevent the future.

The motion for an injunction is denied.

27. *Treaty Law Over State Law*

WORCESTER v. GEORGIA (1832)

(6 Peters 515)

Counsel for the Cherokees soon returned with an aggrieved party
who had standing in Court to challenge the Georgia statutes regulating Indian affairs. One of these laws required that all white
persons be licensed to reside in Indian territory. The plaintiff, a
missionary on the reservation, was sentenced to four years at hard
labor for unauthorized residency—he had refused to apply for a
license. Marshall held that the conviction ought to be reversed and
annulled. Before so holding, however, he fully explored the determi-
nants of Indian rights. The Cherokees, he asserted, were guaranteed
the right of self–government by federal treaties. Consequently, the
Georgia statutes generally invaded the exclusive jurisdiction of the
federal government.

Marshall's sweeping indictment immediately gave way, in his
typical fashion, to a narrow holding, which he based on a statutory
conflict. To overrule the conviction of the missionary, he employed

a congressional statute of 1819 which authorized the President to appoint, in effect, the first peace corpsmen to work among the American Indians. The convicted missionary was such a presidential appointee whose presence on the Cherokee reservation, then, had been authorized by the federal government; Georgia's action thus fell afoul of the Supremacy Clause. But Marshall launched a comprehensive assault upon *all* the Georgia statutes regulating Indian affairs, despite the fact that the actual law of the case was definitely quite limited in impact. Only one statute pertaining to white persons fell, but in theory the rights of Indians were vindicated and a severe condemnation given to Georgia.

Marshall cleverly categorized the invalidated statute as an unconstitutional challenge to presidential authority. The Chief Justice was doubtless delighted to thus outwit President Jackson, who had unmercifully barracked the Court for taking the case. That maneuver neatly provided a vehicle for an exercise of review in which the Court defended the full scope of *presidential* authority over the states, and once again (as in *Marbury v. Madison*) the Chief Justice lectured a President on his proper duties. If Jackson were to continue supporting Georgian imperialism, he could, therefore, be accused of failing to defend his own prerogatives.

Jackson, as might be predicted, did not appreciate Marshall's unsurpassed mastery of jurisdictional irony, and the Chief Justice himself was acutely aware of his exposed position since, by a default in the Court's enabling statutes, the latter had no authority to invoke appropriate sanctions if Georgia refused to release the missionary. Even without this defect, Jackson would not have enforced judicial orders against Georgia; but because of the defect, Marshall could not force the President's hand. Georgia did, however, release the missionary, once it had demonstrated its impunity.

Mr. Chief Justice Marshall delivered the opinion of the Court. . . .

The indictment and plea in this case draw in question, we think, the validity of the treaties made by the United States with the Cherokee Indians; if not so, their construction is certainly drawn in question; and the decision has been, if not against their validity, "against the right, privilege, or exemption, specially set up and claimed under them." They also draw into question the validity of a statute of the state of Georgia, "on the ground of its being repugnant to the constitution, treaties, and laws of the United States, and the decision is in favor of its validity."

We must examine the defense set up in this plea. We must inquire and decide whether the act of the legislature of Georgia, under which the plaintiff in error has been prosecuted and condemned, be consistent with, or repugnant to, the constitution, laws, and treaties of the United States.

It has been said at the bar that the acts of the legislature of Georgia seize on the whole Cherokee country, parcel it out among the neighboring counties of the state, extend her code over the whole country, abolish its institutions and its laws, and annihilate its political existence.

If this be the general effect of the system, let us inquire into the effect of the particular statute and section on which the indictment is founded.

It enacts that "all white persons, residing within the limits of the Cherokee nation on the 1st day of March next, or at any time thereafter, without a license or permit from his excellency the governor, or from such agent as his excellency the governor shall authorize to grant such permit or license, and who shall not have taken the oath hereinafter required, shall be guilty of a high misdemeanor, and, upon conviction thereof, shall be punished by confinement to the penitentiary at hard labor, for a term not less than four years."

The eleventh section authorizes the governor, should he deem it necessary for the protection of the mines, or the enforcement of the laws in force within the Cherokee nation, to raise and organize a guard, &c.

The thirteenth section enacts "that the said guard, or any

member of them, shall be, and they are hereby, authorized and empowered to arrest any person legally charged with, or detected in, a violation of the laws of this state, and to convey, as soon as practicable, the person so arrested before a justice of the peace, judge of the superior, or justice of an inferior court of this state, to be dealt with according to law."

The extra-territorial power of every legislature being limited in its action to its own citizens or subjects, the very passage of this act is an assertion of jurisdiction over the Cherokee nation, and of the rights and powers consequent on jurisdiction.

The first step, then, in the inquiry, which the constitution and laws impose on this court, is an examination of the rightfulness of this claim. . . .

From the commencement of our Government Congress has passed acts to regulate trade and intercourse with the Indians, which treat them as nations, respect their rights, and manifest a firm purpose to afford that protection which treaties stipulate. All these acts, and especially that of 1802, which is still in force, manifestly consider the several Indian nations as distinct political communities, having territorial boundaries, within which their authority is exclusive, and having a right to all the lands within those boundaries, which is not only acknowledged, but guaranteed by the United States.

In 1819 congress passed an act promoting those humane designs of civilizing the neighboring Indians which had long been cherished by the executive. It enacts "that, for the purpose of providing against the further decline and final extinction of the Indian tribes adjoining to the frontier settlements of the United States, and for introducing among them the habits and arts of civilization, the president of the United States shall be, and he is hereby authorized, in every case where he shall judge improvement in the habits and condition of such Indians practicable, and that the means of instruction can be introduced *with their own consent,* to employ capable persons, of good moral character, to instruct them in the mode of agriculture suited to their situation, and for teaching their children in reading, writing and arithmetic, and for performing such other duties as may be enjoined, according to such instructions and rules as the president may give and prescribe for the regulation of their conduct in the discharge of their duties."

This act avowedly contemplates the preservation of the Indian nations as an object sought by the United States, and proposes to effect this object by civilizing and converting them from hunters into agriculturists. Though the Cherokees had already made considerable progress in this improvement, it cannot be doubted that the general words of the act comprehend them. Their advance in "the habits and arts of civilization" rather encouraged perseverance in the laudable exertions still further to meliorate their condition. This act furnishes strong additional evidence of a settled purpose to fix the Indians in their country by giving them security at home.

The treaties and laws of the United States contemplate the Indian territory as completely separated from that of the states; and provide that all intercourse with them shall be carried on exclusively by the government of the union. . . .

[The constitution] confers on congress the powers of war and peace, of making treaties, and of regulating commerce with foreign nations, and among the several states, and *with the Indian tribes*. These powers comprehend all that is required for the regulation of our intercourse with the Indians. They are not limited by any restrictions on their free actions. The shackles imposed on this power in the confederation are discarded.

The Indian nations had always been considered as distinct, independent political communities, retaining their original natural rights, as the undisputed possessors of the soil from time immemorial, with the single exception of that imposed by irresistible power, which excluded them from intercourse with any other European potentate than the first discoverer of the coast of the particular region claimed; and this was a restriction which those European potentates imposed on themselves, as well as on the Indians. The very term "nation," so generally applied to them, means "a people distinct from others." The constitution, by declaring treaties already made, as well as those to be made, to be the supreme law of the land, has adopted and sanctioned the previous treaties with the Indian nations, and, consequently, admits their rank among those powers who are capable of making treaties. The words "treaty" and "nation" are words of our own language, selected in our diplomatic and legislative proceedings by ourselves, having each a definite and well understood meaning. We have applied them to Indians, as we have applied them to the other nations of the earth. They are applied to all in the same sense.

Georgia herself has furnished conclusive evidence that her former opinions on this subject concurred with those entertained by her sister states, and by the government of the United States. . . . Her new series of laws, manifesting her abandonment of these opinions, appears to have commenced in December, 1828. . . .

If the objection to the system of legislation lately adopted by the legislature of Georgia, in relation to the Cherokee nation, was confined to its extra-territorial operation, the objection, though complete so far as respected mere right, would give this court no power over the subject. But it goes much further. If the review which has been taken be correct, and we think it is, the acts of Georgia are repugnant to the constitution, laws and treaties of the United States.

They interfere forcibly with the relations established between the United States and the Cherokee nation, the regulation of which, according to the settled principles of our constitution, is committed exclusively to the government of the union.

They are in direct hostility with treaties, repeated in a succession of years, which mark out the boundary that separates the Cherokee country from Georgia, guaranty to them all the land within their boundary, solemnly pledge the faith of the United States to restrain their citizens from trespassing on it, and recognize the pre-existing power of the nation to govern itself.

They are in equal hostility with the acts of congress for regulating this intercourse and giving effect to the treaties.

The forcible seizure and abduction of the plaintiff in error, who was residing in the nation with its permission and by authority of the president of the United States, is also a violation of the acts which authorize the chief magistrate to exercise this authority.

Will those powerful considerations avail the plaintiff in error? We think they will. He was seized and forcibly carried away while under guardianship of treaties guarantying the country in which he resided and taking it under the protection of the United States. He was seized while performing, under the sanction of the chief magistrate of the union, those duties which the humane policy adopted by congress had recommended. He was apprehended, tried and condemned under color of a law which has been shown to be repugnant to the constitution, laws and treaties of the United States. Had a judgment, liable to the same objections, been rendered for property, none would question the jurisdiction of this court. It cannot be less clear when the judgment affects personal liberty, and inflicts disgraceful punishment, if punishment could disgrace when inflicted on innocence. The plaintiff in error is not less interested in the operation of this unconstitutional law than if it affected his property. He is not less entitled to the protection of the constitution, laws and treaties of his country. . . .

It is the opinion of this court that the judgment of the superior court for the county of Gwinnett, in the state of Georgia, condemning Samuel A. Worcester to hard labor in the penitentiary of the state of Georgia for four years, was pronounced by that court under color of a law which is void, as being repugnant to the constitution, treaties, and laws of the United States, and ought, therefore, to be reversed and annulled.

Part Seven

CIVIL RIGHTS

28. *The Law of Treason, I*

EX PARTE BOLLMAN (1807)

(4 Cranch 75)

The legal result of the Burr conspiracy consisted of a definitive statement of the American law of treason. Marshall declared that in a trial for treason, courts could only admit evidence purporting to establish one fact: namely, that men had actually assembled for a treasonous purpose. He seemed to rule out as proper grounds for conviction mere participation in an abstract conspiracy to levy war against the country. But then he qualified his ruling, conceding that once men had been assembled for a treasonous purpose the dragnet could fall upon persons who "perform any part, however minute, or however remote from the scene of action, and who are actually leagued in the general conspiracy." To propitiate zealous prosecutors—e.g., President Jefferson—Marshall remarked that legislation could be passed to meet the lesser crime of subversion. For all its circumlocution the *Bollman* opinion is considered a libertarian performance because Marshall clearly limited any approaches to doctrines of constructive treason. He appreciated the possibilities of political repression which would be encouraged by permissive definitions of treason.

Bollman and Swartwout were, at best, messengers for Aaron Burr. As Marshall recounts the facts, it is plain that Burr was an empire-builder with the least specific of plans. The vagueness of Burr's goals weakened the evidence against Bollman and Swartwout: indeed, to this day no one is certain in which direction Burr's ambitions were directed, and it is possible that he did not know himself. Levying a private war against Spain was hardly treason against the United States, and in the view of his supporters, at least, this was Burr's objective.

After his case was dismissed, Bollman—whose earlier adventures included helping General Lafayette escape from prison in Austria—returned to Europe where he wrote treatises on economics. Swartwout turned to more lucrative endeavors: as Collector of Customs in the Port of New York in the 1830's he defalcated with more than one and a quarter million dollars. Later the government seized some of his land holdings to recoup its losses, leading to a famous decision that administrative adjudication did not contravene the Fifth Amendment guarantee of due process of law! (See *Murray v. Hoboken Land Co.*, 1855.)

Marshall, Ch. J. delivered the opinion of the court.

The prisoners having been brought before this court on a writ of habeas corpus, . . . the question to be determined is, whether the accused shall be discharged or held to trial; and if the latter, in what place they are to be tried, and whether they shall be confined or admitted to bail. . . .

The specific charge brought against the prisoners is treason in levying war against the United States. . . .

To constitute that specific crime for which the prisoners now before the court have been committed, war must be actually levied against the United States. However flagitious may be the crime of conspiring to subvert by force the government of our country, such conspiracy is not treason. To conspire to levy war, and actually to levy war, are distinct offenses. The first must be brought into open action by the assemblage of men for a purpose treasonable in itself, or the fact of levying war cannot have been committed. . . .

It is not the intention of the court to say that no individual can be guilty of this crime who has not appeared in arms against his country. On the contrary, if war be actually levied, that is, if a body of men be actually assembled for the purpose of effecting by force a treasonable purpose, all those who perform any part, however minute, or however remote from the scene of action, and who are actually leagued in the general conspiracy, are to be considered as traitors. But there must be an actual assembling of men for the treasonable purpose, to constitute a levying of war.

Crimes so atrocious as those which have for their object the subversion by violence of those laws and those institutions which have been ordained in order to secure the peace and happiness of society, are not to escape punishment because they have not ripened into treason. The wisdom of the legislature is competent to provide for the case; and the framers of our constitution, who not only defined and limited the crime, but with jealous circumspection attempted to protect their limitation by providing that no person should be convicted of it, unless on the testimony of two witnesses to the same overt act, or on confession in open court, must have conceived it more safe that punishment in such cases should be ordained by general laws, formed upon deliberation, under the influence of no resentments, and without knowing on whom they were to operate, than that it should be inflicted under the influence of those passions which the occasion seldom fails to excite, and which a flexible definition of the crime, or a construction which would render it flexible, might bring into operation. It is, therefore, more safe as well as more consonant to the principles of our constitution, that the crime of treason should not be extended by construction to doubtful cases; and that crimes not clearly within the constitutional definition, should receive such punishment as the legislature in its wisdom may provide. . . .

The application of these general principles to the particular case before the court will depend on the testimony which has been exhibited against the accused.

The first deposition to be considered is that of General Eaton. This gentleman connects in one statement the purport of numerous conversations held with Col. Burr throughout the last winter. In the course of these conversations were communicated various criminal projects which seem to have been revolving in the mind of the projector. An expedition against Mexico seems to have been the first and most matured part of his plan, if indeed it did not constitute a distinct and separate plan, upon the success of which other schemes still more culpable, but not yet well digested, might depend. Maps and other information preparatory to its execution, and which would rather indicate that it was the immediate object, had been procured, and for a considerable time, in repeated conversations, the whole efforts of Col. Burr were directed to prove to the witness, who was to have held a high command under him, the practicability of the enterprise, and in explaining to him the means by which it was to be effected.

This deposition exhibits the various schemes of Col. Burr, and its materiality depends on connecting the prisoners at the bar in such of those schemes as were treasonable. For this purpose the affidavit of General Wilkinson, comprehending in its body the substance of a letter from Col. Burr, has been offered, and was received by the circuit court. . . .

[It is] deemed necessary to look into the affidavit for the purpose of discovering whether, if admitted, it contains matter which would justify the commitment of the prisoners at the bar on the charge of treason.

That the letter from Col. Burr to General Wilkinson relates to a military enterprise meditated by the former, has not been questioned. If this enterprise was against Mexico, it would amount to a high misdemeanor; if against any of the territories of the United States, or if in its progress the subversion of the government of the United States in any of their territories was a mean clearly and necessarily to be employed, if such mean formed a substantive part of the plan, the assemblage of a body of men to effect it would be levying war against the United States.

The letter is in language which furnishes no distinct view of the design of the writer. The co-operation, however, which is stated to have been secured, points strongly to some expedition against the territories of Spain. . . .

There certainly is not in the letter delivered to General Wilkinson, so far as the letter is laid before the court, one syllable which has a necessary or a natural reference to an enterprise against any territory of the United States.

That the bearer of this letter must be considered as acquainted with its contents is not to be controverted. The letter and his own declarations evince the fact.

After stating himself to have passed through New York, and the western states and territories, without insinuating that he had performed on his route any act whatever which was connected with the enterprise, he states their object to be, "to carry an expedition to the Mexican provinces."

This statement may be considered as explanatory of the letter of Col. Burr, if the expressions of that letter could be thought ambiguous.

But there are other declarations made by Mr. Swartwout, which constitute the difficulty of this case. On an inquiry from General Wilkinson, he said, "this territory would be revolutionized where the people were ready to join them, and that there would be some seizing, he supposed at New Orleans."

If these words import that the government established by the United States in any of its territories, was to be revolutionized by force, although merely as a step to, or a means of executing some greater projects, the design was unquestionably treasonable, and any assemblage of men for that purpose would amount to a levying of war. . . .

But whether this treasonable intention be really imputable to the plan or not, it is admitted that it must have been carried into execution by an open assemblage of men for that purpose, previous to the arrest of the prisoner, in order to consummate the crime as to him; and a majority of the court is of opinion that the conversation of Mr. Swartwout affords no sufficient proof of such assembling.

The prisoner stated that "Col. Burr, with the support of a powerful association extending from New York to New Orleans, was levying an armed body of 7,000 men from the state of New York and the western states and territories, with a view to carry an expedition to the Mexican territories." . . . The question, then, is, whether this evidence proves Col. Burr to have advanced so far in levying an army as actually to have assembled them. . . .

The particular words used by Mr. Swartwout are, that Col. Burr "was levying an armed body of 7,000 men." If the term levying in this place, imports that they were assembled, then such fact would amount, if the intention be against the United States, to levying war. If it barely imports that he was enlisting or engaging them in his service, the fact would not amount to levying war. It is thought sufficiently apparent that the latter is the sense in which the term was used. The fact alluded to, if taken in the former sense, is of a nature so to force itself upon the public view, that if the army had then actually assembled, either together or in detachments, some evidence of such assembling would have been laid before the court.

The words used by the prisoner in reference to seizing at New Orleans, and borrowing perhaps by force from the bank, though indicating a design to rob, and consequently importing a high offense, do not designate the specific crime of levying war against the United States.

It is, therefore, the opinion of a majority of the court, that in the case of Samuel Swartwout there is not sufficient evidence of his levying war against the United States to justify his commitment on the charge of treason.

Against Erick Bollman there is still less testimony. Nothing has been said by him to support the charge that the enterprise in which he was engaged had any other object than was stated in the letter of Col. Burr. Against him, therefore, there is no evidence to support a charge of treason. . . .

The act of Congress, which the prisoners are supposed to have violated, describes as offenders those who begin, or set on foot, or provide, or prepare, the means for any military expedition or enterprise to be carried on from thence against the dominions of a foreign prince or state with whom the United States are at peace.

There is a want of precision in the description of the offense which might produce some difficulty in deciding what cases would come within it. But several other questions arise, which a court consisting of four judges finds itself unable to decide, and, therefore, as the crime with which the prisoners stand charged has not been committed, the court can only direct them to be discharged. This is done with the less reluctance because the discharge does not acquit them from the offense which there is probable cause for supposing they have committed, and if those whose duty it is to protect the nation, by prosecuting offenders against the laws, shall suppose those who have been charged with treason to be proper objects for punishment, they will, when possessed of less exceptionable testimony, and when able to say at what place the offense has been committed, institute fresh proceedings against them.

29. *The Law of Treason, II*

UNITED STATES v. AARON BURR (1807)
(25 Fed. Cas. 55, C.C. Va.)

In the preceding case, Marshall for the Supreme Court, disposed of the treason indictments of two of Aaron Burr's minor flunkies. In this decision, Marshall—in his capacity as Circuit Justice in the Virginia Circuit Court of the United States—had the far more difficult responsibility of evaluating the sufficiency of the evidence adduced against the former Vice–President himself. The issue again was the meaning of the constitutional definition of treason.

The Burr case was a political trial of the first magnitude. President Jefferson was savagely determined that Burr should hang and—as Leonard W. Levy has documented in *Jefferson and Civil Liberties*—threw the whole weight and prestige of the administration behind the prosecution. He was quite prepared to circumvent the Constitution to this end. Burr, for instance, had been seized and held for trial in the Mississippi Territory, but a grand jury there had released him (virtually conferring a citation in the process) and denounced the anti-Burr actions of General James Wilkinson, Jefferson's commander in New Orleans, as "destructive of personal liberty." The Legislature of the Orleans Territory similarly attacked Wilkinson's "measures and motives" soundly (Wilkinson had been deeply involved with Burr until he decided it was too risky and double-crossed his mentor. Interestingly enough, more than a century later documents were unearthed in Spain which showed the American general to have been a secret agent of the Spanish Crown!).

Despite these initial defeats, Wilkinson captured Burr and sent him under arrest to Richmond, Virginia. And the United States Attorney, George Hay, under Jefferson's sharp eye, brought an indictment for treason. Hay later observed with a good deal of justice that "there never was such a trial from the beginning of the world to this day." Just about everything happened: Bollman, supposed to turn state's evidence in return for a presidential pardon, rejected the pardon and refused to testify, touching off an immediate dispute on whether it was mandatory to accept a pardon; Burr, and his clever attorney Luther Martin, demanded that President Jefferson be subpoened to testify and Marshall issued the subpoena; Jefferson denied the jurisdiction and the Chief Justice let it pass; and to top it all, General Wilkinson, the prosecution's star witness, himself barely escaped indictment by the grand jury.

Once Burr was indicted, the second stage of the trial began. The government's problem was that the "overt act" required by the Constitution was somewhat nebulous. It was alleged to be the gathering of a conspiracy to levy war against the United States at Blennerhasset's Island. (This island lay in Virginia, thus providing putative jurisdiction over the accused to the U.S. Circuit Court of that state.) But Burr had not been there at the time of the meeting! Thus Burr had to be implicated constructively in the conspiracy.

Here Marshall had snared himself in *Ex parte Bollman* by noting that "if war be actually levied . . . all those who perform any part, however minute or however remote from the scene of action, and who are actually leagued in the general conspiracy, are to be considered as traitors." In other words, it would seem that if the gathering on Blennerhasset's Island had been in fact an overt act of treason, the physical absence of Burr was irrelevant.

Conspiracy in an overt act of war against the United States—once such an act had been committed—was thus seemingly equated with treason, *i.e.*, conspiracy to betray was apparently made a crime of the same magnitude as betrayal itself. For Burr, the differentiation, which seems esoteric, was crucial: his position was that the Constitution barred "constructive treason" when it provided (Art. III, Section 3) that "Treason against the United States shall consist only in levying War against them, or in adhering to their Enemies, giving them Aid and Comfort." Of course, he also denied that the gathering at Blennerhasset's Island had been an overt act of war against the United States—the sole purpose of his actions in the West, he asserted, was to wage war on Spain.

Burr's counsel were, at this stage in the trial, more interested in undermining the Bollman doctrine than in arguing the merits. Luther Martin let go a characteristic broadside in which he asserted that Marshall's statement (quoted above) was pure *dictum* which had "no more [precedental] weight than the ballad of Chevy Chase."

On August 31, 1807, the Chief Justice delivered his opinion on the sufficiency of the evidence to sustain the indictment: that is, he charged the jury with the law that should be applied to Burr's activities. Even as abridged here, Marshall's statement is long and sprawling; the full text is enormous. It is interesting to note how he qualifies his Bollman ruling, even going so far as to suggest that it might not have represented the views of a majority of the court.

The upshot was that the jury retired only briefly, and shortly the foreman (Colonel Edward Carrington, Marshall's brother-in-law!) announced that "Aaron Burr is not proved to be guilty under this indictment by any evidence submitted to us. We therefore find him not guilty." This was an odd formulation, approximating the Scottish verdict of "Not Proven" (which has been interpreted as "not guilty, but don't do it again").

This did not end the case. Burr was subsequently tried in the same court for the misdemeanor of violating the neutrality acts by conspiring to invade Mexico and was again acquitted. Jefferson then tried to get a new indictment in Ohio, but authorities there dropped the matter. But for one concerned with Marshall's views, the significant aspect of the whole embroglio was his interpretation of the meaning of treason. Although Justice Joseph Story in his *Commentaries* later asserted that *Bollman* was better law than *Burr*, the limitations Marshall imposed in the latter case have, in essence, remained valid to this day.

OPINION ON THE MOTION TO INTRODUCE CERTAIN EVIDENCE IN THE TRIAL OF AARON BURR FOR TREASON. PRONOUNCED MONDAY, AUGUST 31, [1807]

The question now to be decided has been argued in a manner worthy of its importance, and with an earnestness evincing the strong conviction felt by the counsel on each side that the law is with them.

A degree of eloquence seldom displayed on any occasion has

embellished a solidity of argument, and a depth of research, by which the court has been greatly aided in forming the opinion it is about to deliver.

The testimony adduced on the part of the United States, to prove the overt act laid in the indictment, having shown, and the attorney for the United States having admitted, that the prisoner was not present when the act, whatever may be its character, was committed, and there being no reason to doubt but that he was at a great distance and in a different state, it is objected to the testimony offered on the part of the United States to connect him with those who committed the overt act, that such testimony is totally irrelevant, and must, therefore, be rejected.

The arguments in support of this motion respect in part the merits of the case as it may be supposed to stand independent of the pleadings, and in part as exhibited by the pleadings.

On the first division of the subject two points are made.

1st. That conformably to the constitution of the United States, no man can be convicted of treason who was not present when the war was levied.

2d. That if this construction be erroneous, no testimony can be received to charge one man with the overt acts of others, until those overt acts, as laid in the indictment, be proved to the satisfaction of the court.

The question which arises on the construction of the constitution, in every point of view in which it can be contemplated, is of infinite moment to the people of this country and to their government, and requires the most temperate and the most deliberate consideration.

"Treason against the United States shall consist only in levying war against them."

What is the natural import of the words "levying war"? And who may be said to levy it? Had their first application to treason been made by our constitution, they would certainly have admitted of some latitude of construction. Taken most literally, they are, perhaps, of the same import with the words raising or creating war, but as those who join after the commencement are equally the object of punishment, there would probably be a general admission, that the term also comprehended making war, or carrying on war. In the construction which courts would be required to give these words, it is not improbable that those who should raise, create, make, or carry on war, might be comprehended. The various acts which would be considered as coming within the term, would be settled by a course of decisions, and it would be affirming boldly, to say that those only who actually constituted a portion of the military force appearing in arms could be considered as levying war. There is no difficulty in affirming that there must be a war, or the crime of levying it cannot exist; but there would often be considerable difficulty in affirming that a particular act did or did not involve the person committing it in the guilt, and in the fact of levying war. If, for example, an army should be actually raised for the avowed purpose of carrying on open war against the United States and subverting their government, the point must be weighed very deliberately before a judge would venture to decide that an overt act of levying war had not been committed by a commissary of purchases, who never saw the army, but who, knowing its object, and leaguing himself with the rebels, supplied that army with provisions, or by a recruiting officer holding a commission in the rebel service, who, though never in camp, executed the particular duty assigned to him.

But the term is not for the first time applied to treason by the constitution of the United States. It is a technical term. It is used in a very old statute of that country, whose language is our language, and whose laws form the substratum of our laws. It is scarcely conceivable that the term was not employed by the framers of our constitution in the sense which had been affixed to it by those from whom we borrowed it. So far as the meaning of any terms, particularly terms of art, is completely ascertained, those by whom they are employed must be considered as employing them in that ascertained meaning, unless the contrary be proved by the context. It is, therefore, reasonable to suppose, unless it be incompatible with other expressions of the constitution, that the term "levying war," is used in that instrument in the same sense in which it was understood in England, and in this country, to have been used in the statute of the 25th of Edward III, from which it was borrowed.

It is said that this meaning is to be collected only from adjudged cases. But this position cannot be conceded to the extent in which it is laid down. The superior authority of adjudged cases will never be controverted. But those celebrated elementary writers who have stated the principles of the law, whose statements have received the common approbation of legal men, are not to be disregarded. Principles laid down by such writers as Coke, Hale, Foster and Blackstone, are not lightly to be rejected. These books are in the hands of every student. Legal opinions are formed upon them, and those opinions are afterwards carried to the bar, the bench, and the legislature. In the exposition of terms, therefore, used in instruments of the present day, the definitions and the dicta of those authors, if not contradicted by adjudications, and if compatible with the words of the statute, are entitled to respect. It is to be regretted that they do not shed as much light on this part of the subject as is to be wished. . . .

Although we may find among the commentators upon treason enough to satisfy the inquiry, what is a state of internal war, yet no precise information can be acquired from them, which would enable us to decide, with clearness, whether persons not in arms, but taking part in a rebellion, could be said to levy war independent of that doctrine which attaches to the accessory the guilt of his principal. . . .

It is not deemed necessary to trace the doctrine that in treason all are principals, to its source. Its origin is most probably stated correctly by Judge Tucker, in a work, the merit of which is with pleasure acknowledged. But if a spurious doctrine has been introduced into the common law, and has for centuries been admitted as genuine, it would require great hardihood in a judge to reject it. Accordingly, we find those of the English jurists, who seem to disapprove the principle, declaring that it is now too firmly settled to be shaken.

It is unnecessary to trace this doctrine to its source for another reason. The terms of the constitution comprise no question respecting principal and accessory, so far as either may be truly and in fact said to levy war. Whether in England a person would be indicted in express terms for levying war, or for assisting others in levying war, yet if, in correct and legal language, he can be said to have levied war, and if it has never been decided that the act would not amount to levying war, his case may, without violent construction, be brought within the letter and the plain meaning of the constitution.

In examining these words, the argument which may be drawn from felonies, as for example, from murder, is not more conclusive. Murder is the single act of killing with malice aforethought. But war is a complex operation composed of many parts, cooperating with each other. No one man, or body of men, can perform them all, if the war be of any continuance. Although, then, in correct and in law language, he alone is said to have murdered another who has perpetrated the fact of killing, or has been present aiding that fact, it does not follow that he alone can have levied war who has borne arms. All those who perform the various and essential military parts of prosecuting the war which must be assigned to different persons, may with correctness and accuracy be said to levy war.

Taking this view of the subject, it appears to the court, that those who perform a part in the prosecution of the war may correctly be said to levy war, and to commit treason under the constitution. It will be observed that this opinion does not extend to the case of a person who performs no act in the prosecution of the war, who counsels and advises it, or who, being engaged in the conspiracy, fails to perform his part. Whether such persons may be implicated by the doctrine, that whatever would make a man an accessory in felony makes him a principal in treason, or are excluded, because that doctrine is inapplicable to the United States, the constitution having declared that treason shall consist only in levying war, and having made the proof of overt acts necessary to conviction, is a question of vast importance, which it would be proper for the Supreme Court to take a fit occasion to decide, but which an inferior tribunal would not willingly determine, unless the case before them should require it.

It may now be proper to notice the opinion of the Supreme Court of the *United States against Bollman and Swartwout.* It is said that this opinion, in declaring that those who do not bear arms may yet be guilty of treason, is contrary to law, and is not obligatory, because it is extrajudicial, and was delivered on a point not argued. This court is, therefore, required to depart from the principle there laid down.

It is true, that in that case, after forming the opinion that no treason could be committed, because no treasonable assemblage had taken place, the court might have dispensed with proceeding further in the doctrines of treason. But it is to be remembered, that the judges might act separately, and, perhaps, at the same time, on the various prosecutions which might be instituted, and that no appeal lay from their decisions. Opposite judgments on the point would have presented a state of things infinitely to be deplored by all. It was not surprising, then, that they should have made some attempt to settle principles which would probably occur, and which were in some degree connected with the point before them.

The court had employed some reasoning to show that without the actual embodying of men, war could not be levied. It might have been inferred from this, that those only who were so embodied could be guilty of treason. Not only to exclude this inference, but also to affirm the contrary, the court proceeded to observe, "It is not the intention of the court to say that no individual can be guilty of this crime who has not appeared in arms against his country. On the contrary, if war be actually levied; that is, if a body of men be actually assembled for the purpose of effecting by force a treasonable object, all those who perform any part, however minute, or however remote from the scene of action, and who are actually leagued in the general conspiracy, are to be considered as traitors."

This court is told that if this opinion be incorrect it ought not to be obeyed, because it was extrajudicial. For myself, I can say that I could not lightly be prevailed on to disobey it, were I even convinced that it was erroneous, but I would certainly use any means which the law placed in my power to carry the question again before the supreme court, for reconsideration, in a case in which it would directly occur and be fully argued.

The court which gave this opinion was composed of four judges. At the time I thought them unanimous, but I have since had reason to suspect that one of them, whose opinion is entitled to great respect, and whose indisposition prevented his entering into the discussions, on some of those points which were not essential to the decision of the very case under consideration, did not concur in this particular point with his brethren. Had the opinion been unanimous it would have been given by a majority of the judges. But should the three who were absent concur with that judge who was present, and who, perhaps, dissents from what was then the opinion of the court, a majority of the judges may overrule this decision. I should, therefore, feel no objection, although I then thought, and still think, the opinion perfectly correct, to carry the point, if possible, again before the supreme court, if the case should depend upon it.

In saying that I still think the opinion perfectly correct, I do not consider myself as going further than the preceding reasoning goes. Some gentlemen have argued as if the Supreme Court had adopted the whole doctrine of the English books on the subject of accessories to treason. But certainly such is not the fact. Those only who perform a part and who are leagued in the conspiracy, are declared to be traitors. To complete the definition both circumstances must concur. They must "perform a part," which will furnish the overt act, and they must be "leagued in the conspiracy." The person who comes within this description, in the opinion of the court, levies war. The present motion, however, does not rest upon this point; for, if under this indictment the United States might be let in to prove the part performed by the prisoner, if he did perform any part, the court could not stop the testimony in its present stage.

2d. The second point involves the character of the overt act which has been given in evidence, and calls upon the court to declare whether that act can amount to levying war. Although the court ought now to avoid any analysis of the testimony which has been offered in this case, provided the decision of the motion should not rest upon it, yet many reasons concur in giving peculiar propriety to a delivery, in the course of these trials, of a detailed opinion on the question, what is levying war? As this question has been argued at great length, it may probably save much trouble to the counsel now to give that opinion.

In opening the case it was contended by the attorney for the United States, and has since been maintained on the part of the prosecution, that neither arms, nor the application of force or violence, are indispensably necessary to constitute the fact of levying war. To illustrate these positions, several cases have been stated, many of which would clearly amount to treason. In all of them, except that which was probably intended to be this case, and on which no observation will be made, the object of the assemblage was clearly treasonable; its character was unequivocal, and was demonstrated by evidence furnished by the assemblage itself; there was no necessity to rely upon information drawn from extrinsic sources, or in order to understand the fact, to pursue a course of intricate reasoning, and to conjecture motives. A force is supposed to be collected for an avowed treasonable object, in a condition to attempt that object, and to have commenced the attempt by moving towards it. I state these particulars, because, although the cases put may establish the doctrine they are intended to support, may prove that the absence of arms, or the failure to apply force to sensible objects by the actual commission of violence on those objects, may be supplied by other circumstances, yet, they also serve to show that the mind requires those circumstances to be satisfied that war is levied.

Their construction of the opinion of the Supreme Court is, I think, thus far correct. It is certainly the opinion which was at the time entertained by myself, and which is still entertained. If a rebel army, avowing its hostility to the sovereign power, should front that of the government, should march and countermarch before it, should manœuvre in its face, and should then disperse, from any cause whatever, without firing a gun, I confess I could not, without some surprise, hear gentlemen seriously contend that this could not amount to an act of levying war. A case equally strong may be put with respect to the absence of military weapons. If the party be in a condition to execute the purposed treason without the usual implements of war, I can perceive no reason for requiring those implements in order to constitute the crime.

It is argued that no adjudged case can be produced from the English books where actual violence has not been committed. Suppose this were true. No adjudged case has, or, it is believed, can be, produced from those books in which it has been laid down, that war cannot be levied without the actual application of violence to external objects. The silence of the reporters on this point may be readily accounted for. In cases of actual rebellion against the government, the most active and influential leaders are generally most actively engaged in the war, and as the object can never be to extend punishment to extermination, a sufficient number are found among those who have committed actual hostilities, to satisfy the avenging arm of justice. In cases of constructive treason, such as pulling down meeting-houses, where the direct and avowed object is not the destruction of the sovereign power, some act of violence might be generally required to give the crime a sufficient degree of malignity to convert it into treason, to render the guilt of an individual unequivocal. . . .

[The Supreme Court's opinion in *Ex parte Bollman*] I am informed, has been construed to mean that any assemblage whatever for a treasonable purpose, whether in force, or not in force, whether in a condition to use violence, or not in that condition, is a levying of war. It is this construction, which has not, indeed, been expressly advanced at the bar, but which is said to have been adopted elsewhere, that the court deems it necessary to examine.

Independent of authority, trusting only to the dictates of reason, and expounding terms according to their ordinary signification, we should probably all concur in the declaration that war could not be levied without the employment and exhibition of force. War is an appeal from reason to the sword, and he who makes the appeal evidences the fact by the use of the means. His intention to go to war may be proved by words, but the actual going to war is a fact which is to be proved by open deed. The end is to be effected by force, and it would seem that in cases where no declaration is to be made, the state of actual war could only be created by the employment of force, or being in a condition to employ it.

But the term having been adopted by our constitution, must be understood in that sense in which it was universally received in this country, when the constitution was framed. The sense in which it was received is to be collected from the most approved authorities of that nation from which we have borrowed the term. . . .

It would seem . . . from the English authorities, that the words "levying war," have not received a technical, different from their natural meaning, so far as respects the character of the assemblage of men which may constitute the fact. It must be a warlike assemblage, carrying the appearance of force, and in a situation to practice hostility.

Several judges of the United States have given opinions at their circuits on this subject, all of which deserve and will receive the particular attention of this court. . . . [These opinions indicate that the] judges of the United States . . . seem to have required still more to constitute the fact of levying war, than has been required by the English books. Our judges seem to have required the actual exercise of force, the actual employment of some degree of violence. This, however, may be, and probably is, because in the cases in which their opinions were given, the design not having been to overturn the government, but to resist the execution of a law, such an assemblage would be sufficient for the purpose, as to require the actual employment of force to render the object unequivocal.

But it is said, all these authorities have been overruled by the decision of the Supreme Court in the case of the *United States against Swartwout and Bollman.*

If the Supreme Court have indeed extended the doctrine of treason further than it has heretofore been carried by the judges of England, or of this country, their decision would be submitted to. At least, this court could go no further than to endeavor again to bring the point directly before them. It would, however, be expected that an opinion which is to overrule all former precedents, and to establish a principle never before recognized, should be expressed in plain and explicit terms. A mere implication ought not to prostrate a principle which seems to have been so well established. Had the intention been entertained to make so material a change in this respect, the court ought to have expressly declared, that any assemblage of men whatever, who had formed a treasonable design, whether in force or not, whether in a condition to attempt the design or not, whether attended with warlike appearances or not, constitutes the fact of levying war. Yet no declaration to this amount is made. Not an expression of the kind is to be found in the opinion of the Supreme Court. The foundation on which this argument rests is the omission of the court to state, that the assemblage which constitutes the fact of levying war ought to be in force, and some passages which show that the question respecting the nature of the assemblage was not in the mind of the court when the opinion was drawn, which passages are mingled with others, which at least show that there was no intention to depart from the course of the precedents in cases of treason by levying war.

Every opinion, to be correctly understood, ought to be considered with a view to the case in which it was delivered. In the case of the *United States against Bollman and Swartwout,* there was no evidence that even two men had ever met for the purpose of executing the plan, in which those persons were charged with having participated. It was, therefore, sufficient for the court to say, that unless men were assembled, war could not be levied. That case was decided by this declaration. The court might, indeed, have defined the species of assemblage which would amount to levying of war; but, as this opinion was not a treatise on treason, but a decision of a particular case, expressions of doubtful import should be construed in reference to the case itself; and the mere omission to state that a particular circumstance was necessary to the consummation of the crime, ought not to be construed into a declaration that the circumstance was unimportant. General expressions ought not to be considered as overruling settled principles, without a direct declaration to that effect. After these preliminary observations the court will proceed to examine the opinion which has occasioned them.

The first expression in it bearing on the present question is, "To constitute that specific crime for which the prisoner now before the court has been committed, war must be actually levied against the United States. However flagitious may be the crime of conspiracy to subvert by force the government of our country, such conspiracy is not treason. To conspire to levy war, and actually to levy war, are distinct offences. The first must be brought into operation by the assemblage of men for a purpose treasonable in itself, or the fact of levying war cannot have been committed."

Although it is not expressly stated that the assemblage of men for the purpose of carrying into operation the treasonable intent, which will amount to levying war, must be an assemblage in force, yet it is fairly to be inferred from the context, and nothing like dispensing with force appears in this paragraph. The expressions are, "To constitute the crime, war must be actually levied." A conspiracy to levy war is spoken of as "a conspiracy to subvert by force the government of our country." Speaking in general terms of an assemblage of men for this, or for any other purpose, a person would naturally be understood as speaking of an assemblage in some degree adapted to the purpose. An assemblage to subvert by force the government of our country, and amounting to a levying of war, should be an assemblage in force.

In a subsequent paragraph, the court says, "It is not the intention of the court to say, that no individual can be guilty of this crime who has not appeared in arms against his country. On the contrary, if war be actually levied, that is, if a body of men be actually assembled in order to effect by force a treasonable purpose, all those who perform any part, however minute, etc., and who are actually, leagued in the general conspiracy, are traitors. But there must be an actual assembling of men for the treasonable purpose, to constitute a levying of war.

The observations made on the preceding paragraph apply to this. "A body of men actually assembled, in order to effect by force a treasonable purpose," must be a body assembled with such appearance of force as would warrant the opinion that they were assembled for the particular purpose; an assemblage to constitute an actual levying of war, should be an assemblage with such appearance of force as would justify the opinion that they met for the purpose.

This explanation, which is believed to be the natural, certainly not a strained, explanation of the words, derives some additional aid from the terms in which the paragraph last quoted commences. "It is not the intention of the court to say that no individual can be guilty of treason who has not appeared in arms against his country." These words seem to obviate an inference which might otherwise have been drawn from the preceding paragraph. They indicate that in the mind of the court the assemblage stated in that paragraph was an assemblage in arms. That the individuals who composed it had appeared in arms against their country. That is, in other words, that the assemblage was a military, a warlike assemblage.

The succeeding paragraph in the opinion relates to a conspiracy, and serves to show that force and violence were in the mind of the court, and that there was no idea of extending the crime of treason by construction beyond the constitutional definition which had been given of it. . . .

[A detailed and extended analysis of the Court's opinion in the Swartwout and Bollman case indicates] that the direct question whether an assemblage of men which might be construed to amount to a levying of war, must appear in force or in military form, was not in argument or in fact before the court, and does not appear to have been in terms decided. The opinion seems to have been drawn without particularly adverting to this question, and, therefore, upon a transient view of particular expressions, might inspire the idea that a display of force, that appearances of war, were not necessary ingredients to constitute the fact of levying war. But upon a more intent and more accurate investigation of this opinion, although the terms force and violence are not employed as descriptive of the assemblage, such requisites are declared to be indispensable as can scarcely exist without the appearance of war, and the existence of real force. It is said that war must be levied in fact; that the object must be one which is to be effected by force; that the assemblage must be such as to prove that this is its object; that it must not be an equivocal act, without a warlike appearance; that it must be an open assemblage for the purpose of force. In the course of this opinion, decisions are quoted and approved, which require the employment of force to constitute the crime. It seems extremely difficult, if not impossible, to reconcile these various declarations with the idea that the Supreme Court considered a secret, unarmed meeting, although that meeting be of conspirators, and although it met with a treasonable intent, as an actual levying of war. Without saying that the assemblage must be in force or in warlike form, they express themselves so as to show that this idea was never discarded, and they use terms which cannot be otherwise satisfied.

The opinion of a single judge certainly weighs as nothing if opposed to that of the Supreme Court; but if he was one of the judges who assisted in framing that opinion, if while the impression under which it was framed was yet fresh upon his mind, he delivered an opinion on the same testimony, not contradictory to that which had been given by all the judges together, but showing the sense in which he understood terms that might be differently expounded, it may fairly be said to be in some measure explanatory of the opinion itself.

To the judge before whom the charge against the prisoner at the bar was first brought [John Marshall], the same testimony was offered with that which had been exhibited before the Supreme Court, and he was required to give an opinion in almost the same case. Upon this occasion, he said, "War can only be levied by the employment of actual force. Troops must be embodied; men must be assembled in order to levy war."

Again, he observed, "The fact to be proved in this case, is an act of public notoriety. It must exist in the view of the world, or it cannot exist at all. The assembling of forces to levy war is a visible transaction, and numbers must witness it."

It is not easy to doubt what kind of assemblage was in the mind of the judge who used these expressions, and it is to be recollected that he had just returned from the Supreme Court, and was speaking on the very facts on which the opinion of that court was delivered.

The same judge, in his charge to the grand jury who found this bill, observed, "To constitute the fact of levying war, it is not necessary that hostilities shall have actually commenced by engaging the military force of the United States, or that measures of violence against the government shall have been carried into execution. But levying war is a fact, in the constitution of which force is an indispensable ingredient. Any combination to subvert, by force, the government of the United States, violently to dismember the union, to compel a change in the administration, to coerce the repeal or adoption of a general law, is a conspiracy to levy war, and if the conspiracy be carried into effect by the actual employment of force, by the embodying and assembling of men for the purpose of executing the treasonable design which was previously conceived, it amounts to levying of war. It has been held that arms are not essential to levying war provided the force assembled be sufficient to attain, or perhaps to justify attempting, the object without them." This paragraph is immediately followed by a reference to the opinion of the Supreme Court.

It requires no commentary upon these words to show that, in the opinion of the judge who uttered them, an assemblage of men which should constitute the fact of levying war must be an assemblage in force, and that he so understood the opinion of the Supreme Court. If in that opinion there may be found in some passages, a want of precision, and indefiniteness of expression, which has occasioned it to be differently understood by different persons, that may well be accounted for, when it is recollected that in the particular case there was no assemblage whatever. In expounding that opinion the whole should be taken together, and in reference to the particular case in which it was delivered. It is, however, not improbable that the misunderstanding has arisen from this circumstance. The court, unquestionably, did not consider arms as an indispensable requisite to levying war; an assemblage adapted to the object might be in a condition to effect or to attempt it without them. Nor did the court consider the actual application of the force to the object, at all times, an indispensable requisite; for an assemblage might be in a condition to apply force, might be in a state adapted to real war, without having made the actual application of that force. From these positions, which are to be found in the opinion, it may have been inferred, it is thought too hastily, that the nature of the assemblage was unimportant, and that war might be considered as actually levied by any meeting of men, if a criminal intention can be imputed to them by testimony of any kind whatever. . . .

On that division of the subject which respects the merits of the case connected with the pleadings, two points are also made.

1st. That this indictment, having charged the prisoner with levying war on Blennerhassett's island, and containing no other overt act, cannot be supported by proof that war was levied at that place by other persons, in the absence of the prisoner, even admitting those persons to be connected with him in one common treasonable conspiracy.

2d. That admitting such an indictment could be supported by such evidence, the previous conviction of some person who committed the act which is said to amount to levying war, is indispensable to the conviction of a person who advised or procured that act.

As to the first point, the indictment contains two counts, one of which charges that the prisoner, with a number of persons unknown, levied war on Blennerhassett's island, in the county of Wood, in the district of Virginia; and the other adds the circumstance of their proceeding from that island down the river, for the purpose of seizing New Orleans by force.

In point of fact, the prisoner was not on Blennerhassett's island, nor in the county of Wood, nor in the district of Virginia.

In considering this point the court is led first to inquire whether an indictment for levying war must specify an overt act, or would be sufficient if it merely charged the prisoner in general terms with having levied war, omitting the expression of place or circumstance.

The place in which a crime was committed is essential to an indictment, were it only to show the jurisdiction of the court. It is also essential for the purpose of enabling the prisoner to make his defense. That, at common law, an indictment would have been defective which did not mention the place in which the crime was committed, can scarcely be doubted. . . . This necessity is rendered the stronger by the constitutional provision that the offender "shall be tried in the state and district wherein the crime shall have been committed," and by the act of Congress which requires that twelve petty jurors at least shall be summoned from the county where the offense was committed.

A description of the particular manner in which the war was levied seems also essential to enable the accused to make his defense. The law does not expect a man to be prepared to defend every act of his life which may be suddenly and without notice alleged against him. In common justice, the particular fact with which he is charged ought to be stated, and stated in such a manner as to afford a reasonable certainty of the nature of the accusation, and the circumstances which will be adduced against him. The general doctrine on the subject of indictments is full to this point. . . . That clause in the constitution, too, which says that in all criminal prosecutions the accused shall enjoy the right "to be informed of the nature and cause of the accusation," is considered as having a direct bearing on this point. It secures to him such information as will enable him to prepare for his defense.

It seems, then, to be perfectly clear, that it would not be sufficient for an indictment to allege generally that the accused had levied war against the United States. The charge must be more particularly specified by laying what is termed an overt act of levying war. . . . All the authorities which require an overt act, require also that this overt act should be proved. . . .

But it is contended on the part of the prosecution that, although the accused had never been with the party which assembled at Blennerhassett's island, and was, at the time, at a great distance, and in a different state, he was yet legally present, and, therefore, may properly be charged in the indictment as being present in fact.

It is, therefore, necessary to inquire whether in this case the doctrine of constructive presence can apply.

It is conceived by the court to be possible that a person may be concerned in a treasonable conspiracy, and yet be legally, as well as actually absent, while some one act of the treason is perpetrated. If a rebellion should be so extensive as to spread through every state in the union, it will scarcely be contended that every individual concerned in it is legally present at every overt act committed in the course of that rebellion. It would be a very violent presumption indeed, too violent to be made without clear authority, to presume that even the chief of the rebel army was legally present at every such overt act. If the main rebel army with the chief at its head, should be prosecuting war at one extremity of our territory, say in New Hampshire, if this chief should be there captured and sent to the other extremity for the purpose of trial, if his indictment, instead of alleging an overt act which was true in point of fact, should allege that he had assembled some small party, which, in truth, he had not seen, and had levied war by engaging in a

skirmish in Georgia at a time when in reality he was fighting
a battle in New Hampshire, if such evidence would support
such an indictment, by the fiction that he was legally present
though really absent, all would ask to what purpose are those
provisions in the constitution which direct the place of trial,
and ordain that the accused shall be informed of the nature
and cause of the accusation?

But that a man may be legally absent who has counselled or
procured a treasonable act, is proved by all those books which
treat upon the subject, and which concur in declaring that such
a person is a principal traitor, not because he was legally present, but because in treason all are principals. Yet the indictment, upon general principles, would charge him according to
the truth of the case. Lord Coke says: "If many conspire to
levy war, and some of them do levy the same according to the
conspiracy, this is high treason in all." Why? Because all were
legally present when the war was levied? No. "For in treason,"
continues Lord Coke, "all be principals, and war is levied." In
this case the indictment, reasoning from analogy, would not
charge that the absent conspirators were present, but would
state the truth of the case. If the conspirator had done nothing
which amounted to levying of war, and if, by our constitution,
the doctrine that an accessory becomes a principal be not
adopted, in consequence of which the conspirator could not be
condemned under an indictment stating the truth of the case,
it would be going very far to say that this defect, if it be
termed one, may be cured by an indictment stating the case
untruly.

This doctrine of Lord Coke has been adopted by all subsequent writers; and it is generally laid down in the English
books, that whatever will make a man an accessory in felony,
will make him a principal in treason; but it is nowhere suggested that he is by construction to be considered as present
when in point of fact he was absent. . . .

The whole treason laid in this indictment is the levying of

war in Blennerhassett's island, and the whole question to which the inquiry of the court is now directed is, whether the prisoner was legally present at that fact.

I say this is the whole question, because the prisoner can only be convicted on the overt act laid in the indictment. With respect to this prosecution, it is as if no other overt act existed. If other overt acts can be inquired into, it is for the sole purpose of proving the particular fact charged; it is as evidence of the crime consisting of this particular fact, not as establishing the general crime by a distinct fact.

The counsel for the prosecution have charged those engaged in the defense with considering the overt act as the treason, whereas it ought to be considered solely as the evidence of the treason; but the counsel for the prosecution seem themselves not to have sufficiently adverted to this clear principle, that though the overt act may not be itself the treason, it is the sole act of that treason which can produce conviction. It is the sole point in issue between the parties. And the only division of that point, if the expression be allowed, which the court is now examining, is the constructive presence of the prisoner at the fact charged.

To return, then, to the application of the cases.

Had the prisoner set out with the party from Beaver for Blennerhassett's island, or, perhaps, had he set out for that place, though not from Beaver, and had arrived in the island, he would have been present at the fact; had he not arrived in the island, but had taken a position near enough to co-operate with those on the island, to assist them in any act of hostility, or to aid them if attacked, the question whether he was constructively present would be a question compounded of law and fact, which would be decided by the jury, with the aid of the court, so far as respected the law. In this case the accused would have been of the particular party assembled on the island, and would have been associated with them in the particular act of levying war said to have been committed on the island.

But if he was not with the party at any time before they reached the island; if he did not join them there, or intend to join them there; if his personal co-operation in the general plan was to be afforded elsewhere, at a great distance, in a different state; if the overt acts of treason to be performed by him were to be distinct overt acts, then he was not of the particular party assembled at Blennerhassett's island, and was not constructively present, aiding and assisting in the particular act which was there committed.

The testimony on this point, so far as it has been delivered, is not equivocal. There is not only no evidence that the accused was of the particular party which assembled on Blennerhassett's island, but the whole evidence shows he was not of that party. . . .

In conformity with principle and with authority, then, the prisoner at the bar was neither legally nor actually present at Blennerhassett's island; and the court is strongly inclined to the opinion, that, without proving an actual or legal presence by two witnesses, the overt act laid in this indictment cannot be proved.

But this opinion is controverted on two grounds.

The first is, that the indictment does not charge the prisoner to have been present.

The second, that although he was absent, yet, if he caused the assemblage, he may be indicted as being present, and convicted on evidence that he caused the treasonable act.

The first position is to be decided by the indictment itself. The court understands the allegation differently from the attorney for the United States. The court understands it to be directly charged, that the prisoner did assemble with the multitude, and did march with them. Nothing will more clearly test this construction than putting the case into a shape which it may possibly take. Suppose the law to be that the indictment would be defective unless it alleged the presence of the person indicted at the act of treason. If upon a special verdict facts should be found which amounted to a levying of war by the accused, and his counsel should insist that he could not be condemned because the indictment was defective in not charging that he was himself one of the assemblage which constituted the treason, or because it alleged the procurement defectively, would the attorney admit this construction of his indictment to be correct? I am persuaded that he would not, and that he ought not to make such a concession. If, after a verdict, the indictment ought to be construed to allege that the prisoner was one of the assemblage at Blennerhassett's island, it ought to be so construed now. But this is unimportant, for if the indictment alleges that the prisoner procured the assemblage, that procurement becomes part of the overt act, and must be proved as will be shown hereafter. . . .

While I declare that this doctrine contradicts every idea I had ever entertained on the subject of indictments, since it admits that one case may be stated, and a very different case may be proved, I will acknowledge that it is countenanced by the authorities adduced in its support. To counsel or advise a treasonable assemblage, and to be one of that assemblage, are certainly distinct acts, and, therefore, ought not to be charged as the same act. The great objection to this mode of proceeding is, that the proof essentially varies from the charge in the character and essence of the offense, and in the testimony by which the accused is to defend himself. These *dicta* of Lord Hale, therefore, taken in the extent in which they are understood by the counsel of the United States, seem to be repugnant to the declarations we find everywhere, that an overt act must be laid, and must be proved. . . .

But suppose the law to be as is contended by the counsel for the United States. Suppose an indictment, charging an individual with personally assembling among others, and thus levying war, may be satisfied with the proof that he caused the assemblage. What effect will this law have upon this case?

The guilt of the accused, if there be any guilt, does not consist in the assemblage, for he was not a member of it. The simple fact of assemblage no more affects one absent man than another. His guilt, then consists in procuring the assemblage, and upon this fact depends his criminality. The proof relative to the character of an assemblage must be the same whether a man be present or absent. In the general, to charge any individual with the guilt of an assemblage, the fact of his presence must be proved. It constitutes an essential part of the overt act. If, then, the procurement be substituted in the place of presence, does it not also constitute an essential part of the overt act? Must it not also be proved? Must it not be proved in the same manner that presence must be proved? If in one case the presence of the individual makes the guilt of the assemblage his guilt, and in the other case the procurement by the individual makes the guilt of the assemblage his guilt, then presence and procurement are equally component parts of the overt act, and equally require two witnesses.

Collateral points may, say the books, be proved according to the course of the common law; but is this a collateral point? Is the fact, without which the accused does not participate in the guilt of the assemblage, if it was guilty, a collateral point? This cannot be. The presence of the party, where presence is necessary, being a part of the overt act, must be positively proved by two witnesses. No presumptive evidence, no facts from which presence may be conjectured or inferred, will satisfy the constitution and the law. If procurement take the place of presence, and become part of the overt act, then no presumptive evidence, no facts from which the procurement may be conjectured or inferred, can satisfy the constitution and the law. The mind is not to be led to the conclusion that the individual was present, by a train of conjectures or inferences, or of reasoning; the fact must be proved by two witnesses. Neither where procurement supplies the want of presence, is the mind to be conducted to the conclusion that the accused procured the assembly, by a train of conjectures or inferences, or of reasoning; the fact itself must be proved by two witnesses, and must have been committed within the district.

If it be said that the advising or procurement of treason is a secret transaction which can scarcely ever be proved in the manner required by this opinion; the answer which will readily suggest itself is, that the difficulty of proving a fact will not justify conviction without proof. Certainly it will not justify conviction without a direct and positive witness in a case where the constitution requires two. The more correct inference from this circumstance would seem to be, that the advising of the fact is not within the constitutional definition of the crime. To advise or procure a treason is in the nature of conspiring or plotting treason, which is not treason in itself.

If, then, the doctrines of [British commentators on the law of treason] are to be understood in the sense in which they are pressed by the counsel for the prosecution, and are applicable in the United States, the fact that the accused procured the assemblage on Blennerhassett's island must be proved, not circumstantially, but positively by two witnesses, to charge him with that assemblage. But there are still other most important considerations, which must be well weighed before this doctrine can be applied to the United States.

The eighth amendment to the constitution has been pressed with great force, and it is impossible not to feel its application to this point. The accused cannot be truly said to be "informed of the nature and cause of the accusation," unless the indictment shall give him that notice which may reasonably suggest to him the point on which the accusation turns, so that he may know the course to be pursued in his defense.

It is also well worthy of consideration, that this doctrine, so far as it respects treason, is entirely supported by the operation of the common law, which is said to convert the accessory before the fact into the principal, and to make the act of the principal his act. The accessory before the fact is not said to have levied war. He is not said to be guilty under the statute. But the common law attaches to him the guilt of that fact which he has advised or procured, and, as contended, makes it his act. This is the operation of the common law, not the operation of the statute. It is an operation then, which can only be performed where the common law exists to perform it. It is the creature of the common law, and the creature presupposes its creator. To decide, then, that this doctrine is applicable to the United States, would seem to apply the decision that the United States, as a nation, have a common law which creates and defines the punishment of crimes accessorial in their nature. It would imply the further decisions that these accessorial crimes are not, in the case of treason, excluded by the definition of treason, given in the constitution. I will not pretend that I have not individually an opinion on these points, but it is one which I should give only in a case absolutely requiring it, unless I could confer respecting it with the judges of the Supreme Court.

I have said that this doctrine cannot apply to the United States, without implying those decisions respecting the common law which I have stated, because, should it be true, as is contended, that the constitutional definition of treason comprehends him who advises or procures an assemblage that levies war, it would not follow that such adviser or procurer might be charged as having been present at the assemblage. If the adviser or procurer is within the definition of levying war, and, independent of the agency of the common law, does actually levy war, then the advisement or procurement is an overt act of levying war. If it be the overt act on which he is to be convicted, then it must be charged in the indictment, for he can only be convicted on proof of the overt acts which are charged. . . . It may possibly be the opinion of the Supreme Court, that those who procure a treason, and do nothing further, are guilty under the constitution; I only say that opinion has not yet been given; still less has it been indicated, that he who advises shall be indicted as having performed the fact.

It is, then, the opinion of the court, that this indictment can be supported only by testimony which proves the accused to have been actually or constructively present when the assemblage took place on Blennerhassett's island, or by the admission of the doctrine that he who procures an act may be indicted as having performed that act.

It is further the opinion of the court, that there is no testimony whatever which tends to prove that the accused was actually or constructively present when that assemblage did take place. Indeed, the contrary is most apparent. With respect to admitting proof of procurement to establish a charge of actual presence, the court is of opinion, that if this be admissible in England on an indictment for levying war, which is far from being conceded, it is admissible only by virtue of the operation of the common law upon the statute, and, therefore, is not admissible in this country unless by virtue of a similar operation; a point far from being established, but on which, for the present, no opinion is given. If, however, this point be established, still the procurement must be proved in the same manner, and by the same kind of testimony, which would be required to prove actual presence.

The second point in this division of the subject is, the necessity of adducing the record of the previous conviction of some one person who committed the fact alleged to be treasonable.

This point presupposes the treason of the accused, if any has been committed, to be accessorial in its nature. Its being of this description, according to the British authorities, depends on the presence or absence of the accused at the time the fact was committed. The doctrine on this subject is well understood, has been most copiously explained, and need not be repeated. That there is no evidence of his actual or legal presence is a point already discussed and decided. It is, then, apparent that, but for the exception to the general principle which is made in cases of treason, those who assembled at Blennerhassett's island, if that assemblage was such as to constitute the crime, would be principals, and those who might really have caused that assemblage, although, in truth, the chief traitors would, in law, be accessories.

It is a settled principle in the law that the accessory cannot be guilty of a greater offense than his principal. The maxim is *accessorius sequitur naturam sui principalis;* the accessory follows the nature of his principal. Hence results the necessity of establishing the guilt of the principal before the accessory can be tried. For the degree of guilt which is incurred by counselling or commanding the commission of a crime depends upon the actual commission of that crime. No man is an accessory to murder unless the fact has been committed. . . .

If, then, this was a felony, the prisoner at the bar could not be tried until the crime was established by the conviction of the person by whom it was actually perpetrated.

Is the law otherwise in this case, because, in treason all are principals?

Let this question be answered by reason and by authority.

Why is it that in felonies, however, atrocious, the trial of the accessory can never precede the conviction of the principal? Not because the one is denominated the principal and the other the accessory, for that would be ground on which a great law principle could never stand. Not because there was, in fact, a difference in the degree of moral guilt, for in the case of murder committed by a hardy villain for a bribe, the person plotting the murder and giving the bribe, is, perhaps, of the two the blacker criminal; and, were it otherwise, this would furnish no argument for precedence in trial.

What, then, is the reason?

It has been already given. The legal guilt of the accessory

depends on the guilt of the principal; and the guilt of the principal can only be established in a prosecution against himself.

Does not this reason apply in full force to a case of treason?

The legal guilt of the person who planned the assemblage on Blennerhassett's island depends, not simply on the criminality of the previous conspiracy, but on the criminality of that assemblage. If those who perpetrated the fact be not traitors, he who advised the fact cannot be a traitor. His guilt, then, in contemplation of law, depends on theirs, and their guilt can only be established in a prosecution against themselves. Whether the adviser of this assemblage be punishable with death as a principal or as an accessory, his liability to punishment depends on the degree of guilt attached to an act which has been perpetrated by others, and which, if it be a criminal act, renders them guilty also. His guilt, therefore, depends on theirs, and their guilt cannot be legally established in a prosecution against him.

The whole reason of the law, then, relative to the principal and accessory, so far as respects the order of trial, seems to apply in full force to a case of treason committed by one body of men in conspiracy with others who are absent. . . .

The present indictment charges the prisoner with levying war against the United States, and alleges an overt act of levying war. That overt act must be proved, according to the mandates of the constitution and of the act of Congress, by two witnesses. It is not proved by a single witness. The presence of the accused has been stated to be an essential component part of the overt act in this indictment, unless the common law principle respecting accessories should render it unnecessary; and there is not only no witness who has proved his actual or legal presence; but the fact of his absence is not controverted. The counsel for the prosecution offer to give in evidence subsequent transactions, at a different place, and in a different state,

in order to prove what? The overt act laid in the indictment?
That the prisoner was one of those who assembled at Blennerhassett's island? No, that is not alleged. It is well known that
such testimony is not competent to establish such a fact. The
constitution and law require that the fact should be established
by two witnesses, not by the establishment of other facts from
which the jury might reason to this fact. The testimony, then,
is not relevant. If it can be introduced, it is only in the character of corroborative or confirmatory testimony, after the overt
act has been proved by two witnesses, in such manner that the
question of fact ought to be left with the jury. The conclusion
that in this state of things no testimony can be admissible, is
so inevitable, that the counsel for the United States could not
resist it. I do not understand them to deny, that if the overt act
be not proved by two witnesses so as to be submitted to the
jury, that all other testimony must be irrelevant, because no
other testimony can prove the act. Now an assemblage on
Blennerhassett's island is proved by the requisite number of
witnesses, and the court might submit it to the jury, whether
that assemblage amounted to a levying of war, but the presence
of the accused at that assemblage being nowhere alleged
except in the indictment, the overt act is not proved by a
single witness, and of consequence, all other testimony must
be irrelevant. . . .

Much has been said in the course of the argument on points,
on which the court feels no inclination to comment particularly,
but which may, perhaps, not improperly, receive some notice.

That this court dares not usurp power is most true.

That this court dares not shrink from its duty is not less true.

No man is desirous of placing himself in a disagreeable situation. No man is desirous of becoming the peculiar subject of
calumny. No man, might he let the bitter cup pass from him
without self-reproach, would drain it to the bottom. But if he
has no choice in the case; if there is no alternative presented to

him but a dereliction of duty, or the opprobrium of those who are denominated the world, he merits the contempt as well as the indignation of his country, who can hesitate which to embrace.

That, gentlemen, in a case the most interesting, in the zeal with which they advocate particular opinions, and under the conviction in some measure produced by that zeal, should on each side press their arguments too far, should be impatient at any deliberation in the court, and should suspect or fear the operation of motives to which alone they can ascribe that deliberation, is a perhaps, frailty incident to human nature; but if any conduct on the part of the court could warrant a sentiment that they would deviate to the one side or the other from the line prescribed by duty and by law, that conduct would be viewed by the judges themselves with an eye of extreme severity, and would long be recollected with deep and serious regret.

The arguments on both sides have been intently and deliberately considered. Those which could not be noticed, since to notice every argument and authority would swell this opinion to a volume, have not been disregarded. The result of the whole is a conviction as complete as the mind of the court is capable of receiving on a complex subject, that the motion must prevail.

No testimony relative to the conduct or declarations of the prisoner elsewhere, and subsequent to the transaction on Blennerhassett's island, can be admitted, because such testimony, being in its nature merely corroborative, and incompetent to prove the overt act in itself, is irrelevant, until there be proof of the overt act by two witnesses.

This opinion does not comprehend the proof by two witnesses that the meeting on Blennerhassett's island was procured by the prisoner. On that point the court, for the present, withholds its opinion for reasons which have been already assigned; and as it is understood from the statements made on the part of the prosecution, that no such testimony exists, if there be such, let it be offered and the court will decide upon it.

The jury have now heard the opinion of the court on the law of the case.

They will apply that law to the facts, and will find a verdict of guilty or not guilty, as their own consciences may direct.

30. *The Bill of Rights*

BARRON v. BALTIMORE (1833)

(7 Peters 243)

Although the Bill of Rights was added to the Constitution in 1791, in jurisprudential terms its enforcement is a recent innovation, largely arising from the modern court's incorporation of most of its provisions in the due process clause of the Fourteenth Amendment. Indeed, *Barron v. Baltimore* was the first decision in which the Fifth Amendment (and by implication seven others) was explicated by the Court.

In the course of paving some streets, the city of Baltimore diverted several streams from their natural courses. Sediment carried by these streams shortly settled in the once deep water by Barron's wharf and blocked access by ships. Barron brought action against the city for loss of his private property, "taken" without "just compensation," and his innovative counsel claimed federal jurisdiction on the basis of the Fifth Amendment's ambiguity; it merely states that "*No person* shall . . . be deprived of life, liberty, or property, without due process of law; nor shall private property be taken for public use, without just compensation." (Italics added.)

At issue then was the reach of those amendments in the Bill of Rights (the Second through the Eighth) which were not, like the

First, specifically aimed at congressional action. Were they designed to limit state as well as federal behavior?

Marshall listened to Barron's counsel argue the broad position, but when Baltimore's legal representative (the ubiquitous Roger B. Taney) arose to present the city's brief, the record states, he was "stopped by the Court." For a unanimous bench, Marshall dismissed the writ of error for lack of federal jurisdiction. The Bill of Rights, he stated tersely, conferred no authority over state action—it could be understood only as a check upon the national government.

Marshall realized from his personal knowledge that in Virginia most of the leading advocates of a Bill of Rights had, in 1787-88, unfurled the banner of liberty in hopes of blocking the adoption of the Constitution. In Virginia and elsewhere, men who in reality opposed ratification because they were opposed to the taxation and commerce power conferred upon Congress, denounced the new frame of government because it lacked a Bill of Rights. The Bill of Rights, in short, had to be understood as a states' rights objective, a proposition confirmed in the First Congress when Madison, fulfilling a constitutionalist pledge that amendments would be introduced to remedy the supposed defect, drafted a number which prohibited state as well as national infringements on individual freedom. But these broad prohibitions were flatly rejected by the Senate—whose members were chosen by state legislatures. Thus Marshall was historically on safe ground in declaring that—despite the ambiguity in wording—the whole Bill of Rights was intended as a circumscription only of national power.

MARSHALL, C. J., delivered the opinion of the court.

The judgment brought up by this writ of error having been rendered by the court of a State, this tribunal can exercise no jurisdiction over it, unless it be shown to come within the provisions of the 25th section of the Judicial Act.

The plaintiff in error contends that it comes within that clause in the 5th amendment to the constitution, which inhibits the taking of private property for public use, without just compensation. He insists that this amendment, being in favor of the liberty of the citizen, ought to be so construed as to restrain the legislative power of a State, as well as that of the United States. If this proposition be untrue, the court can take no jurisdiction of the cause.

The question thus presented is, we think, of great importance, but not of much difficulty.

The constitution was ordained and established by the people of the United States for themselves, for their own government and not for the government of the individual States. Each State established a constitution for itself, and, in that constitution, provided such limitations and restrictions on the powers of its particular government as its judgment dictated. The people of the United States framed such a government for the United States as they supposed best adapted to their situation, and best calculated to promote their interests. The powers they conferred on this government were to be exercised by itself; and the limitations on power, if expressed in general terms, are naturally, and, we think, necessarily applicable to the government created by the instrument. They are limitations of power granted in the instrument itself; not of distinct governments, framed by different persons and for different purposes.

If these propositions be correct, the 5th amendment must be understood as restraining the power of the general government, not as applicable to the States. In their several constitutions they have imposed such restrictions on their respective governments as their own wisdom suggested; such as they deemed most proper for themselves. It is a subject on which they judge exclusively, and with which others interfere no further than they are supposed to have a common interest.

The counsel for the plaintiff in error insists that the constitution was intended to secure the people of the several States against the undue exercise of power by their respective state governments; as well as against that which might be attempted by their general government. In support of this argument he relies on the inhibitions contained in the 10th section of the 1st article.

We think that section affords a strong if not a conclusive argument in support of the opinion already indicated by the court.

The preceding section contains restrictions which are obviously intended for the exclusive purpose of restraining the exercise of power, by the departments of the general government. Some of them use language applicable only to congress; others are expressed in general terms. The 3rd clause, for example, declares that "no bill of attainder or *ex post facto* law shall be passed." No language can be more general; yet the demonstration is complete that it applies solely to the government of the United States. In addition to the general arguments furnished by the instrument itself, some of which have been already suggested, the succeeding section, the avowed purpose of which is to restrain state legislation, contains in terms the very prohibition. It declares that "no State shall pass any bill of attainder or *ex post facto* law." This provision, then, of the 9th section, however comprehensive its language, contains no restrictions on state legislation.

The 9th section having enumerated, in the nature of a bill of rights, the limitations intended to be imposed on the powers of the general government, the 10th proceeds to enumerate those which were to operate on the state legislatures. These restrictions are brought together in the same section, and are by express words applied to the States. "No State shall enter into any treaty," &c. Perceiving that in a constitution framed by the people of the United States for the government of all, no limitation of the action of government on the people would apply to the state government, unless expressed in terms; the restrictions contained in the 10th section are in direct words so applied to the States.

It is worthy of remark, too, that these inhibitions generally restrain state legislation on subjects intrusted to the general government, or in which the people of all the States feel an interest.

A State is forbidden to enter into any treaty, alliance, or confederation. If these compacts are with foreign nations, they interfere with the treaty-making power, which is conferred entirely on the general government; if with each other, for political purposes, they can scarcely fail to interfere with the general purpose and intent of the constitution. To grant letters of marque and reprisal, would lead directly to war; the power of declaring which is expressly given to congress. To coin money is also the exercise of a power conferred on congress. It would be tedious to recapitulate the several limitations on the powers of the States which are contained in this section. They will be found, generally, to restrain state legislation on subjects intrusted to the government of the Union, in which the citizens of all the States are interested. In these alone were the whole people concerned. The question of their application to States is not left to construction. It is averred in positive words.

If the original constitution, in the 9th and 10th sections of the 1st article, draws this plain and marked line of discrimination between the limitations it imposes on the powers of the general government, and on those of the States; if in every inhibition intended to act on state power, words are employed which directly express that intent; some strong reason must be assigned for departing from this safe and judicious course in framing the amendments, before that departure can be assumed.

We search in vain for that reason.

Had the people of the several States, or any of them, required changes in their constitutions; had they required additional safeguards to liberty from the apprehended encroachments of their particular governments; the remedy was in their own hands, and would have been applied by themselves. A convention would have been assembled by the discontented State, and the required improvements would have been made by itself. The unwieldy and cumbrous machinery of procuring a recommendation from two thirds of congress, and the assent of three fourths of their sister States, could never have occurred to any human being as a mode of doing that which might be effected by the State itself. Had the framers of these amendments intended them to be limitations on the powers of the state governments, they would have imitated the framers of the original constitution, and have expressed that intention. Had congress engaged in the extraordinary occupation of improving the constitutions of the several States by affording the people additional protection from the exercise of power by their own governments in matters which concerned themselves alone, they would have declared this purpose in plain and intelligible language.

But it is universally understood, it is a part of the history of the day, that the great revolution which established the constitution of the United States, was not effected without immense opposition. Serious fears were extensively entertained that those powers which the patriot statesmen, who then watched over the interests of our country, deemed essential to union, and to the attainment of those invaluable objects for which union was sought, might be exercised in a manner dangerous to liberty. In almost every convention by which the constitution was adopted, amendments to guard against the abuse of power were recommended. These amendments demanded security against the apprehended encroachments of the general government, not against those of the local governments.

In compliance with a sentiment thus generally expressed to quiet fears thus extensively entertained, amendments were proposed by the required majority in congress, and adopted by the States. These amendments contain no expression indicating an intention to apply them to the state governments. This court cannot so apply them.

We are of opinion that the provision in the 5th amendment to the constitution, declaring that private property shall not be taken for public use without just compensation, is intended solely as a limitation on the exercise of power by the government of the United States, and is not applicable to the legislation of the States. We are therefore of opinion, that there is no repugnancy between the several acts of the general assembly of Maryland, given in evidence by the defendants at the trial of this cause, in the court of that State, and the constitution of the United States. This court, therefore, has no jurisdiction of the cause; and it is dismissed.

Index

THE AMERICAN HERITAGE SERIES

Negro Protest Thought in the Twentieth Century AHS 56
Francis Broderick, August Meier
New Deal Thought AHS 70 Howard Zinn
The Progressives AHS 54 Carl Resek
Roosevelt, Theodore *The Writings of Theodore Roosevelt* AHS 53 William H. Harbaugh
The Supreme Court: Law Versus Discretion AHS 72 Wallace Mendelson
Wilson, Woodrow, *The Political Thought of Woodrow Wilson* AHS 68 E. David Cronon

TOPICAL VOLUMES

The American Economic System: Representative Selections AHS 27 Massimo Salvadori
American Military Thought AHS 75 Walter Millis
The Church and the City AHS 61 Robert Cross
Freedom of the Press: 1800 – 1965 AHS 74 Harold L. Nelson
Nonviolence in America: A Documentary History AHS 60 Staughton Lynd